The Complete ASP.NET Core 3 API Tutorial

Hands-On Building, Testing, and Deploying

Les Jackson

Apress®

The Complete ASP.NET Core 3 API Tutorial: Hands-On Building, Testing, and Deploying

Les Jackson
Melbourne, VIC, Australia

ISBN-13 (pbk): 978-1-4842-6254-2   ISBN-13 (electronic): 978-1-4842-6255-9
https://doi.org/10.1007/978-1-4842-6255-9

Managing Director, Apress Media LLC: Welmoed Spahr
Acquisitions Editor: Joan Murray
Development Editor: Laura Berendson
Coordinating Editor: Jill Balzano

Cover image designed by Freepik (www.freepik.com)

Distributed to the book trade worldwide by Springer Science+Business Media New York, 233 Spring Street, 6th Floor, New York, NY 10013. Phone 1-800-SPRINGER, fax (201) 348-4505, e-mail orders-ny@springer-sbm.com, or visit www.springeronline.com. Apress Media, LLC is a California LLC and the sole member (owner) is Springer Science + Business Media Finance Inc (SSBM Finance Inc). SSBM Finance Inc is a **Delaware** corporation.

For information on translations, please e-mail booktranslations@springernature.com; for reprint, paperback, or audio rights, please e-mail bookpermissions@springernature.com.

Apress titles may be purchased in bulk for academic, corporate, or promotional use. eBook versions and licenses are also available for most titles. For more information, reference our Print and eBook Bulk Sales web page at http://www.apress.com/bulk-sales.

Any source code or other supplementary material referenced by the author in this book is available to readers on GitHub via the book's product page, located at www.apress.com/9781484262542. For more detailed information, please visit http://www.apress.com/source-code.

Printed on acid-free paper

For Quynh

Table of Contents

About the Author

Les Jackson is originally from Glasgow, Scotland, but has lived and worked in Melbourne, Australia, since 2009. Since completing his computer science degree in 1998, he has worked in IT, primarily in the telecommunications industry and with the incumbent national telecom providers. Les holds several industry accreditations and has reacquired a Microsoft Certified Solutions Developer certification, although he still believes there is no substitute for experience and passion and says, "beware of people touting certifications!" Aside from his day job, Les enjoys producing content for his YouTube channel and blog, where he hopes to grow his wonderful audience over the coming years. In his downtime he likes cycling, trying to grow vegetables, making (and drinking) beer, and traveling with his partner.

About the Technical Reviewer

 As a freelance Microsoft technologies expert, **Kris van der Mast** helps his clients to reach their goals. Actively involved in the global community, he is a Microsoft MVP since 2007. First for ASP.NET and since 2016 achieving in two disciplines: Azure and Visual Studio and Development Technologies. Kris is also a Microsoft ASP Insider, Microsoft Azure Advisor, aOS ambassador, and a Belgian Microsoft Extended Experts Team (MEET) member. In the Belgian community, Kris is active as a board member of the Belgian Azure User Group AZUG and is chairman of the Belgian User Group Initiative (BUG). Since he started with .NET back in 2002, he's also been active on the ASP.NET forums where he is also a moderator. His personal site can be found at `www.krisvandermast.com`. Kris is a public (inter)national speaker and is a co-organizer of the CloudBrew conference.

Personal note:

I enjoyed reviewing this book. It's easy to follow, and I liked the fact that unit tests were added to the story. The approach of using Docker, and how to set it up, gives this book that extra which the reader will find handy in her/his professional environment.

Acknowledgments

Writing this book (my first) has been a real eye-opener for me... I greatly underestimated the extent to which I would rely on other people (either directly or indirectly) to inspire, encourage, and just generally help me to finish it. So, in true "Oscars style," and in no particular order, I'd like to thank the following groups of people in helping to bring this book into the world. Without them, this book would not exist.

For their good humor, endless support, and indulgence of me, I'd like to thank my friends, family, and wonderful partner (to whom this book is dedicated).

For their patience, support, and belief in a first-time author, I'd like to express sincere thanks to the wonderful, professional editorial staff at Apress.

For their insights, time, and willingness to share their knowledge, I'd like to thank the fantastic community of C#/.NET professionals.

And finally, along with the countless others that have read my blog or watched my YouTube channel, I'd like to thank you – the reader of this book. You may never know just how significant supporting me in this way has been...

CHAPTER 1

Introduction

Why I Wrote This Book

Aside from the fact that everyone is supposed to have "at least one book in them," the main reason I wrote this book was for you – the reader. Yes, that's right; I wanted to write a no-nonsense, no-fluff/filler book that would enable the *general reader*[1] to follow along and build, test, and deploy an ASP.NET Core API to Azure. I wanted it to be a practical, straightforward text, producing a tangible, valuable outcome for the reader.

Of course, you will be the judge on whether I succeeded (or not)!

Apress Edition

Prior to publishing this book now with Apress, I had released two earlier editions of the book. Having taken a Lean Startup approach (releasing versions as is when they were ready), I received feedback on each of those to make each successive version better. With the release of .NET Core 3.1 in November 2019, it seemed like the perfect time to release the second edition which was updated for that version of the framework, as well as some other updates, primarily a move to PostgreSQL as the backend Database.

This Apress edition sees the introduction of the use of Data Transfer Objects (DTOs), as well as the use of the Repository Pattern, both of which speak to the idea of decoupling interfaces from implementation, which has a range of benefits as you will see. I've also added an endpoint to our example API that responds to the "PATCH" verb, which allows us to perform partial updates on resources. This was a sorely missing component from the previous versions of the book and was long overdue for inclusion.

---

[1]Fans of *Peep Show*, I took this term from one of my favorite episodes of Season 9: `www.imdb.com/title/tt2128665/?ref_=ttep_ep4`

1

L. Jackson, *The Complete ASP.NET Core 3 API Tutorial*, https://doi.org/10.1007/978-1-4842-6255-9_1

The Approach of This Book

I've taken a "thin and wide" approach with this book, meaning that I wanted to cover a lot of material from the different stages in the development of an API (wide), without delving into extraneous detail or theory for each (thin). We will, however, cover all the areas in enough practical detail, in order that you gain a decent understanding of each – that is, we won't skip anything important!

I like to think of it like a *tasting menu*. You'll get to try a little bit of everything, so that by the end of the meal you'll have an appreciation of what you'd like to eat more of at some other time, you should also feel suitably satisfied!

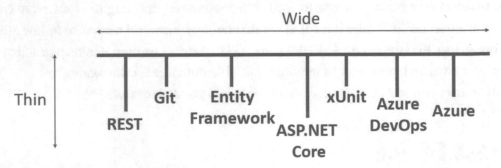

Figure 1-1. *Thin and wide approach*

Les' Personal Anecdote   The first time I tried (or even heard of) a tasting menu was in a Las Vegas casino (I think it was the MGM Grand) in the early 2000s. In addition to trying the eight items on the menu, we also went with the "wine pairing" option – which as the name suggests meant you got a different glass of wine with each course, specifically selected to compliment the dish.

I think this is the reason why I can't remember the name of the casino.

Where Can You Get the Code?

While I think you'll get more value by following along throughout the book and typing in the code yourself (the book has been written so you can follow along step by step), you may of course prefer to download the code and use that as a reference. Indeed, as there may be errata (heaven forbid!), it's prudent that I provide a repository for you, so you can just head over to GitHub and get the code there.

Main Solution Repository (API and Unit Tests)

`https://github.com/binarythistle/Complete-ASP-NET-3-API-Tutorial-Book`

Secure Daemon Client Repository

`https://github.com/binarythistle/Secure-Daemon-Client`

Conventions Used in This Book

The following style conventions are used in this book.

ℹ   General *additional* information for the reader on top of the main narrative, hint or tip.

⚠️arning!   Some point of notice, so the reader should proceed with caution.

☞ Learning Opportunity   Self-directed learning opportunity. Something the reader can do on their own to facilitate learning and understanding.

C🎂bration Checkpoint   Good job, milestone, worth calling out. Allows you to reflect and check learning.

 Les' Personal Anecdote   Personal story or viewpoint to add context to a point I'm making. I'll usually try to be humorous here – so be warned. Not required reading to complete working through the book!

Version of the .net Core Framework

At the time of writing (May 2020), I'm using version 3.1 of the .NET Core Framework.

Contacting the Author

You can contact me through the following channels:

- les@dotnetplaybook.com

- `https://dotnetplaybook.com/`

- `www.youtube.com/binarythistle`

    While I'll do my best to reply to you, I'm unlikely to be able to respond to detailed, lengthy technical questions.

Defects and Feature Improvements

Defects (errata) and suggestions for improvement should be sent to les@dotnetplaybook.com

    Any corrections, additions, or improvements to the code will be reflected in the GitHub Repository.

CHAPTER 2

Setting Up Your Development Environment

Chapter Summary

In this chapter, we detail the tools and setup you'll require to follow the examples in this book.

When Done, You Will

- Understand what tools you'll need to install

- Have installed those tools and configured your environment ready for development

The Three Amigos: Windows, Mac, and Linux

One of the benefits of the .NET Core Framework (when compared with the original .NET Framework) is that it's truly cross-platform,[1] meaning that you can develop and run the same apps on Windows, OSX (Mac), or Linux. For the vast majority of this book, the OS that you run on should make little difference in following along with the examples, so the choice of OS is almost irrelevant and of course entirely up to you.

---

[1]Yes, there were things like "Mono," but overall, I'd say the original .NET Framework was Microsoft Windows-centric.

© Les Jackson 2020

L. Jackson, *The Complete ASP.NET Core 3 API Tutorial*, https://doi.org/10.1007/978-1-4842-6255-9_2

I've moved to PostgreSQL as the database backend which is available natively on Windows, Linux, and OSX. I will, however, be running it as a Docker container, but more of that later.

ℹ️   I list the additional software that you need to follow along with the book below but have decided not to go into step-by-step detail about how to install them, for the following reasons:

- The book would become way too bloated if I provided instructions for all three OSs (remember – no filler content!).

- My instructions would go out of date quickly and would possibly confuse more than help.

- The various vendors typically provide perfectly decent install guides that they maintain and keep up to date (if not, I'll provide them!).

Note If there's any additional *nonstandard* config/setup required, I will of course cover that.

Your Ingredients

I'm going to assume you have the absolute basic things like a PC or Mac, a web browser, and an Internet connection (if not, you'll have to get all of those!), so the software I've listed below is the extra stuff you'll likely need to follow along.[2]

Ingredient	What is it?	Cost	Required for	Platform
VS Code	Cross-platform, fully featured text editor	Free	Writing code! **Note:** This is just my personal preference; you can of course choose an editor that you are more comfortable with	Cross-platform

(*continued*)

---

[2]Links to where you can locate the software have been provided separately in the section that follows.

Ingredient	What is it?	Cost	Required for	Platform
.NET Core SDK	.NET Core Runtime and SDK	Free	It's the framework we'll be building our API on. As mentioned in the opening, we'll use 3.1 in this book	Cross-platform
Git	Local source Code control	Free	Local source control and pushing our code to GitHub for eventual publishing to Azure	Cross-platform
PostgreSQL	Local database	Free	We'll use this as our local development/test database	Cross-platform or Docker image
DBeaver CE	Database-independent management tool	Free	Writing and executing SQL queries, setting up DB users, etc.	Cross-platform
Postman	API Testing Tool	Free	You can opt to use a web browser to test our API; Postman just gives us more options and is highly recommended	Cross-platform
Docker Desktop/ Docker CE	Containerization platform (run Docker containers)	Free	**[Optional]** I use Docker to quickly spin up and run a PostgreSQL database without the need to install it (PostgreSQL) locally on my desktop	Cross-platform: Docker Desktop – Windows and OSX Docker CE – Linux
GitHub.com	Cloud-based git repository used for team collaboration	Free	Used as the code repository component of our continuous integration/continuous delivery (CI/CD) pipeline	N/A – browser-based
Azure	The Microsoft cloud services offering	Free[3]	We'll use Azure to host our production API as well as our "production" PostgreSQL Database	N/A – browser-based

(continued)

---

[3]At the time of writing new, sign-ups get $280USD credit (to use within first 30 days), with an additional 12 months of "popular" services free. Other charges may be applicable though; please check the Azure website for the latest offer: https://azure.microsoft.com/

Ingredient	What is it?	Cost	Required for	Platform
Azure DevOps	Cloud-based build/ test/deployment platform	Free	We use Azure DevOps primarily as the vehicle to publish our API to Azure. We will also leverage its centralized build/ test features	N/A – browser-based

Links to the Software and Sites

- **VS Code:** https://code.visualstudio.com/download

- **.NET Core SDK:** https://dotnet.microsoft.com/download

- **Git:** https://git-scm.com/downloads

- **PostgreSQL (Native Install):** www.postgresql.org/download/

- **PostgreSQL (Docker Image):** https://hub.docker.com/_/postgres

- **DBeaver:** https://dbeaver.io/download/

- **Postman:** www.postman.com/

- **Docker Desktop (Windows and OSX):** www.docker.com/products/ docker-desktop

- **Docker CE (Linux):** https://docs.docker.com/get-docker/

- **GitHub:** https://github.com/

- **Azure:** https://portal.azure.com/

- **Azure DevOps:** https://dev.azure.com/

Install VS Code

I'm suggesting Visual Studio Code (referred to now on only as VS Code) as the text editor of choice for following this book as it has some nice features, for example, IntelliSense code completion, syntax highlighting, integrated command/terminal, git integration, debug support, etc.

It's also cross-platform, so no matter if you're using Windows, OSX, or Linux, the experience is pretty much the same (which is beneficial for someone writing a book!).

You do of course have other options, most notably Visual Studio,[4] which is a fully integrated development environment (IDE) available on Windows and now OSX. If you don't want to use a full IDE, then there are a range of other text editors, for example, Notepad ++ on Windows, TextMate on OSX, etc., that you can use.

Les' Personal Anecdote   I'm often asked why I choose to use VS Code over Visual Studio, and I always answer with the same analogy.

I compare it to learning to drive a manual transmission (aka "stick shift) vs. learning to drive a car with an automatic transmission. In my view, if you learn to drive a manual transmission, you can transfer to driving an automatic with relative ease. I don't think the reverse is as true.

Therefore, while VS Code can be a little more "involved" and may not do as much for you as Visual Studio, I think it just provides you with a better understanding of how things work. Once you get the hang of things though, Visual Studio is an incredible tool.

Anyway, to install VS Code, go to `https://code.visualstudio.com/download`, select your OS, (see Figure 2-1), and follow the provided instructions for your OS.

---

[4]The "free" version of Visual Studio is called the "Community Edition"; just Google it for the download site.

Figure 2-1. *VS Code download*

Once installed start it up and we'll install a few useful extensions.

C# for Visual Studio Code

Like a lot of other text editors, VS Code allows you to install Microsoft or third-party provided "extensions" (or plugins if you prefer) that extend the functionality of VS Code to meet your specific development requirements. For this project the most important extension is *C# For Visual Studio Code*. It gives us C# support for syntax highlighting and IntelliSense code completion among other things; to be honest I'd be quite lost without it.

Anyway, to install this extension (and any others if you wish)

1. Click the "Extensions" icon in the left-hand toolbar of VS Code.

2. Type all or part of the name of the extension you want, for example, C#.

3. Click the name of the extension you'd like.

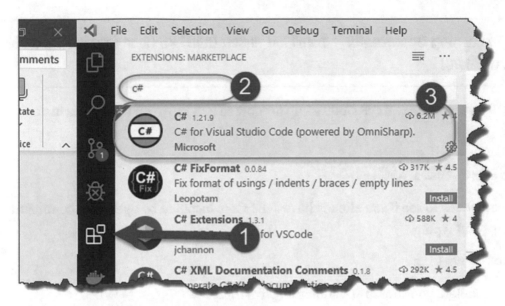

Figure 2-2. *Install C# extension for VS Code*

Upon clicking the desired extension, you'll get a detail page explaining a bit about the extension (along with the number of downloads and a review/rating). To install, simply click the "Install" button – that's it!

Insert GUID

We'll be using "GUIDs" later in the tutorial, so we may as well install the "Insert GUID" extension too; see the following extension details.

Figure 2-3. *Install Insert GUID extension for VS Code*

☞ **Learning Opportunity**   Install the "Insert GUID" VS Code extension yourself –
it's not hard!

OK, we're done with VS Code setup for now so let's move on to the next install.

Install .NET Core SDK

You can check to see if you already have .NET Core installed by opening a command
prompt and typing

```
dotnet --version
```

If installed, you should see something like this.

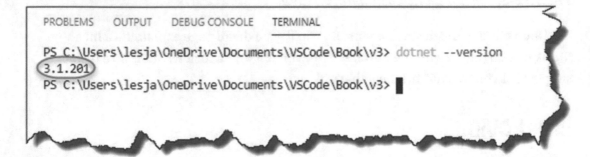

Figure 2-4. *Check .NET Core Version*

Even if it is installed, it's probably worth checking to see what the latest version is to
make sure that you're not too far behind. From the screenshot in Figure 2-4, you can see
I'm running 3.1 which at the time of writing is the latest version.

If it's not installed (or you want to update your version), pop over to `https://`
`dotnet.microsoft.com/download`, and select "Download .NET Core SDK," as shown in
the following figure.

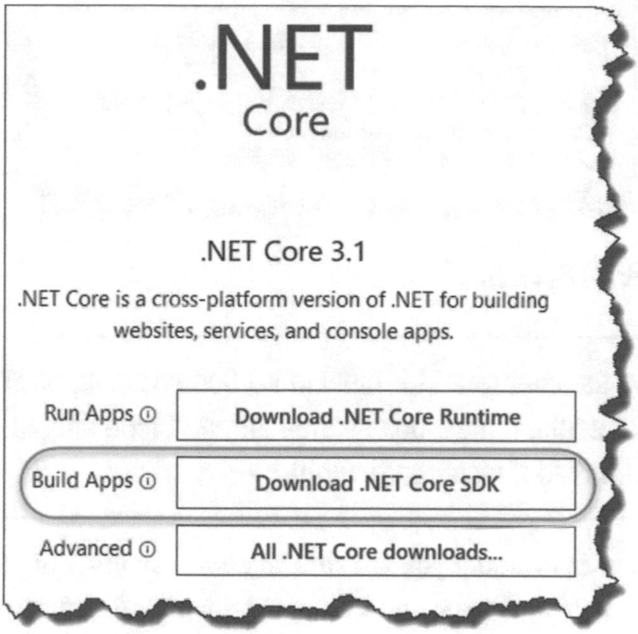

Figure 2-5. Download .NET Core SDK

It's important to select the "SDK" (software development toolkit) option as opposed to the "Runtime" option for what I think are quite obvious reasons. (The runtime version is just that it provides only the necessary resources to **run** .NET Core apps. The SDK Version allows us to **build and run** apps; it includes everything in the Runtime package.)

As usual follow the respective install procedures for your OS; once completed, you should now be able to run the same `dotnet --version` command as shown in Figure 2-5, resulting in the latest version being returned.

Install GIT

As with .NET Core, you may already have Git installed (indeed there's probably a much greater chance that it is given its ubiquity).

At a command prompt/terminal, type

```
git --version
```

If already installed, you'll see something similar to that shown in Figure 2-6.

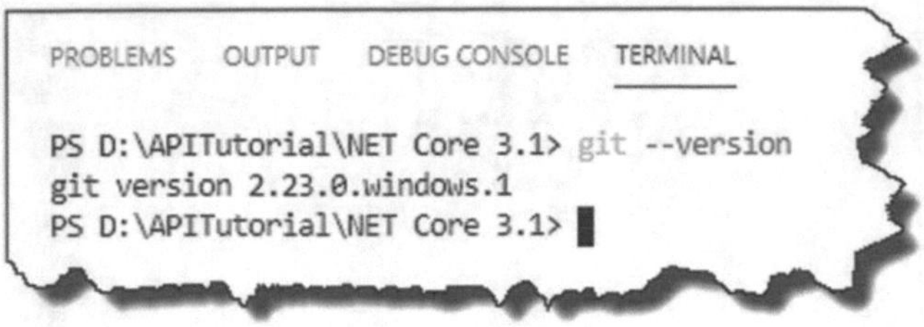

Figure 2-6. *Check GIT version*

ℹ FYI I'm using the integrated terminal in VS Code running on Windows; depending on your setup, it may look slightly different (you should still see a version number returned if installed though).

If not installed, or the version you are running is somewhat out of date, go over to https://git-scm.com/downloads, and follow the download and install options for your OS.

Name and Email

Just to complete the setup of Git, we need to tell it who we are by way of a name and email address, as this information is required by Git in order for it to know *who* is making changes to the code.

To do so enter the following commands in a terminal session, replacing "you@example.com" and "Your Name" with suitable values:

```
git config --global user.email "you@example.com"
git config --global user.name "Your Name"
```

For example see my configuration in Figure 2-7.

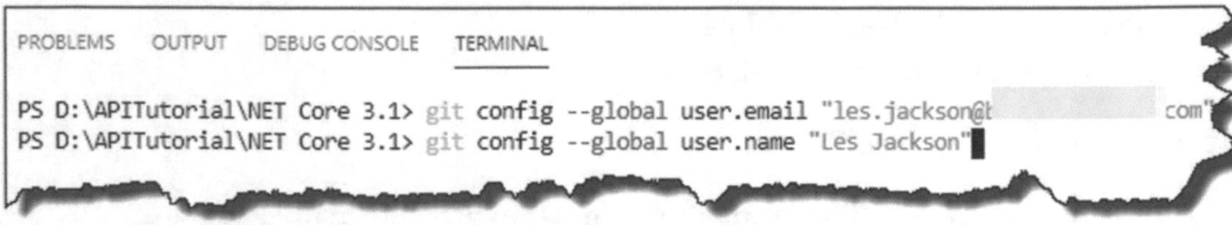

Figure 2-7. *Configure GIT name and email*

There are no additional setup instructions for Git at this stage. We'll cover setting up and using Git repositories later in the book. For now, though, we're done!

Install Docker [Optional]

If you're intending to install PostgreSQL directly on your development machine, or you already have a version running somewhere that you can use, then you can skip this section if you like. However, if like me you don't like "faffing" around installing large apps on your local machine, then Docker is a great option for you (although paradoxically, Docker is quite a large application as of itself!)

What Is Docker?

Docker is a containerization platform that enables you to

- Package *your* apps as images and allow others to download and run them as containers (on Docker).

- Obtain other developer or software vendor "images" (from a repository), and run them as containers on your machine (so long as you've installed Docker).

The core concept of a Docker image is that they are self-contained, meaning that the image has everything it needs for it to run, avoiding complex installations, locating and installing third-party support libraries, etc. It ultimately avoids the "it works on my machine" argument.

There is a little bit of a learning curve to it (not much though), and once you master the basics, it can save you so much time and effort, that as a developer, I can't recommend it highly enough.

Docker Desktop vs. Docker CE

Confusingly (for me at least), if you're running Windows or OSX, you need to install something called *Docker Desktop*. If, however, you're a Linux person, then you should install *Docker Community Edition* or CE. There are probably torturously pedantic reasons for this, which I'm not aware of, nor would I be interested in learning about, so all you really need to know is where to get them!

- **Docker Desktop Here:** www.docker.com/products/docker-desktop

- **Docker CE Here:** https://docs.docker.com/get-docker/

Before you can download and install Docker Desktop, you need to sign up for a Docker Hub account; this is a free sign-up so nothing really to worry about. It also comes in useful if you want to upload your own images to the Docker Hub for distribution.

⚠ **Warning!**   At the time of writing, Docker Desktop can only be installed "directly" on Windows 10 Professional. However, if you're running Windows 10 Home, you can work around this by using something called Windows Subsystem for Linux (WSL).

As I've said before, I'm not going to go into detail on how to do this as the Docker guys have provided great instructions for this here:

https://docs.docker.com/docker-for-windows/install-windows-home/.

Docker Desktop installation is super simple; for Docker CE you will need to refer to the install instructions for your specific distro – again, however, it's straightforward.

Post-installation Check

Irrespective of which flavor of Docker you install, post-installation, open a command line, and type

docker --version

You should get something like the following.

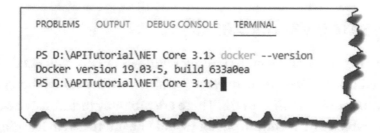

Figure 2-8.   *Check Docker version*

To further test that it is fully working, type

```
docker run hello-world
```

If this is the first time you've run this, Docker will go to the Docker Hub, pull down the hello-world image, and run it; you should see something like this.

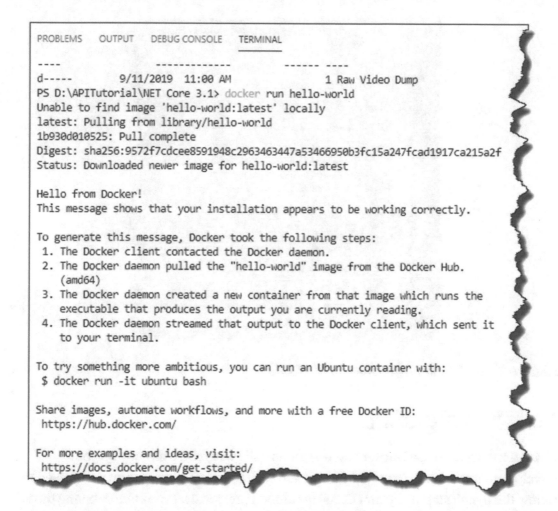

Figure 2-9. *Hello World Docker image download and run*

We don't need to go into too much more detail about what's happening here (although the output generated by hello-world does a pretty good job); suffice to say that Docker is set up and ready to go. I'll cover more on Docker as we move through the tutorial.

Docker Plugin for VS Code

If you're using VS Code as your development editor and you've decided to go with Docker, then I highly recommend you install the Docker extension from Microsoft. I've shown this below but will leave it to you to install.

Figure 2-10. *Docker extension for VS Code*

Install PostgreSQL

If you don't want to use Docker and want to install PostgreSQL directly on your development machine (or on another server, virtual machine, etc.), then you'll need to follow the install steps for your OS. As mentioned previously, I won't be detailing those steps in detail here as the PostgreSQL guys have done a great job of that already here: www.postgresql.org/download/.

> ⚠ **Warning!**   I've spent many hours getting PostgreSQL up and running on a Linux box and connecting in from another machine. Now this is due largely to the fact I'm not particularly great with Linux, and so those of you that are adept with Linux would undoubtedly have less trouble.
>
> For me though, struggling with the nuances of installing a DB detract from the act of coding, which is what I *really* want to be doing. Hence the reason why I *strongly* suggest the use of Docker.
>
> Native Windows and OSX installations of PostgreSQL are (as usual) much easier.

Install DBeaver CE

Whether you're going to use Docker or a native PostgreSQL install, either way we'll want to do some small bits of DB admin as well as write SQL queries to read and write data into our DB. You can of course use the command-line options that come with the PostgreSQL install, but I like to also have a graphical environment at my disposal as the "barrier to entry" is significantly reduced when compared to the command-line alternative.

Just remember: My focus in this book is *coding an API,* not being an expert PostgreSQL DB administrator.

DBeaver vs. pgAdmin

Probably the most popular admin tool for PostgreSQL is pgAdmin,[5] and in fact this would have been the tool I'd have recommended previously.

> **Les' Personal Anecdote**   The choice of admin tool here is a totally personal one. I have used pgAdmin in its prior iterations, and it was totally fine, but since they moved it to a "web version," running in its own little webserver, I've avoided it. Can't quite put my finger on why; I think mostly it just comes across as a bloated and counterintuitive piece of software. It's a web app that requires the install of a local webserver? Doesn't "smell" right to me.

---

[5]`www.pgadmin.org/`

Having looked at several graphical database management tools for PostgreSQL, I've landed on DBeaver Community Edition – which is free. This is a database agnostic management tool that you can use to connect to and manage most of the popular RDBMSs[6] out there. It's also cross-platform, which is even better – you can download your copy here: `https://dbeaver.io/download/`.

We'll go through connecting to and setting up PostgreSQL later in the book. For now, though, we're done.

Les' Personal Anecdote   Just before we move on, I just wanted to say that for me, the king of database management tools is still SQL Server Management Studio. In my *personal view*, nothing comes close to it in terms of usability, speed, features, etc.

The only reason I've not used it is simply because I've decided to use PostgeSQL as the RDBMS (you can only use SQL Server Management Studio to manage MS SQL Servers – it also only runs on Windows).

Install Postman

This is optional, and up to you if you want to install – but I *highly recommend* it. I'll be using it at various points throughout the book, and given that it's both free and excellent, I don't see why you wouldn't. If you're going to be doing API development going forward, then it's essentially mandatory. It's available as both a browser plugin or as a stand-alone client. For more details on how to install and download, go over to `www.getpostman.com/downloads/`, and take a look.

No further configuration is required at this point – I cover how to use it later.

---

[6]Relational Database Management Systems.

Trust Local Host Development Certs

Throughout the tutorial we'll be hitting localhost endpoints over http and https. For those connections using https, we may encounter some errors/exceptions along the lines that the certificate is not valid. We do not want to turn off SSL certificate validation; instead, we want to trust our local development certificate.

To do that, at a command prompt, type

```
dotnet dev-certs https --trust
```

You'll get a message box similar to the following.

Figure 2-11. *Trust local certificates*

Click "Yes" to install the certificate and you should be good to go.

Wrapping It Up

All the other required components are Web-based and only require

- Web browser

- Internet connection

- User account

I won't insult your intelligence by detailing how to create an account on those services – it's easy. When we come on to the later sections, I will cover the setup and configuration for each where required – so don't worry. For now, all you need is an account on each of the following:

- **GitHub:** `https://github.com/`

- **Azure:** `https://portal.azure.com/`

- **Azure DevOps:** `https://dev.azure.com/`

All of which (at least initially!) are free.

CHAPTER 3

Overview of Our API

Chapter Summary

In this (very short!) chapter, I'll take you through the API that you're going to build and the problem it's attempting to solve. We'll also cover the REST API pattern at a high level.

When Done, You Will

- Understand a bit more about the REST pattern.

- Understand what you are going to build throughout the rest of this book.

- Understand why you are going to be building this solution.

- Have an appreciation of JavaScript Object Notation (JSON).

What Is a REST API?

APIs will eventually cure world hunger, bring about lasting peace, and enable mankind to explore the universe together, forever, in harmony[1] – or so some people (usually salesmen types) would have you believe. I of course don't believe that and am being somewhat facetious.

REST (or representational state transfer if you prefer) is an architectural style defined by Roy Fielding in 2000, that is used for creating web services. OK yes, but *what does that* mean? In short REST, or *RESTful* APIs, are a lightweight way to transfer textual

---

[1]Credits to the late great Bill Hicks, whom I'm paraphrasing.

© Les Jackson 2020
L. Jackson, *The Complete ASP.NET Core 3 API Tutorial*, https://doi.org/10.1007/978-1-4842-6255-9_3

representations of "resources," for example, books, authors, cars, etc. They are usually (although don't need to be) built around the HTTP protocol and the standard set of HTTP verbs, for example, GET, POST, PUT, etc.

In recent years REST APIs have gained favor over other web services design patterns, for example, SOAP, as they are considered simpler and quicker to develop, as well as lending themselves to the concept of interoperability more than other approaches. ASP.NET Core APIs have a RESTful approach built in, which we see as we start to build out our example.

For me personally, actually building out the API is going to help you understand "REST" more fully than if I were to continue writing about it here, so we'll leave the theory there for now. Be assured though that I do cover the central REST concepts as we build out our API endpoints.

☞ **Learning Opportunity**   If you're not comfortable with my description of REST, there are loads of resources already produced on this topic, so if you'd like more info, I'd suggest you do some Googling!

Again though, I think you'll learn more about REST APIs when you come to building them.

Our API

The API we are going to develop is a simple but useful one (well useful for me anyway!). With my ever-advancing years and worsening state of decrepitude, I wanted to write an API that would store "command-line snippets," (e.g., `dotnet new web -n <project name>`), as I'm finding it harder and harder to recall them when needed. In essence it'll become a command-line repository that you can query should the need arise.

Each "resource" will have the following attributes:

- **Howto**: Description of what the prompt will do, for example, add a firewall exception, run unit tests, etc.

- **Platform**: Application or platform domain, for example, Ubuntu Linux, Dot Net Core, etc.

- **Commandline**: The actual command line snippet, for example, `dotnet build`.

Here's a list of some snippets (aka "resources") as an example.

HowTo	Platform	Commandline
How to genrate a migration in EF Core	.Net Core EF	dotnet ef migrations add <Name of Migration>
How to update the database (run migration)	.Net Core EF	dotnet ef database update
List Service Status - Linux	Ubuntu	service --status-all
Start a service ubuntu	Ubuntu	sudo service <service name> start
Stop a service Ubuntu	Ubuntu	sudo service <service name> stop
Restart a service Ubunti	Ubuntu	sudo service <service name> restart
How to List all active migrations	.Net Core EF	dotnet ef migrations list
Roll back a migration	.Net Core EF	dotnet ef migrations remove
Create a Solutuon File	.Net Core CLI	dotnet new sln --name <Name of Solution>
Add a Project Reference to another project	.Net Core CLI	dotnet add <path to "host" proejct> reference <path to referenced project>
Add Projects to Solution File	.Net Core CLI	dotnet sln <Solution File> add <project1 .csproj file> <projectn .csproj file>
Override run command	Docker CLI	docker run <image name> command!
List running containers	Docker CLI	docker ps
List all containers that have ever run	Docker CLI	docker ps --all
Create a container from an image	Docker CLI	docker create <image name>

Figure 3-1. *Example command-line snippets*

Our API will follow the standard set of create, read, update, and delete (CRUD) operations common to most REST APIs, as described in the following table below.

Verb	URI	Operation	Description
GET	/api/commands	Read	Read all command resources
GET	/api/commands/{Id}	Read	Read a single resource (by Id)
POST	/api/commands	Create	Create a new resource
PUT	/api/commands/{Id}	Update (Full)	Update all of a single resource (by Id)
PATCH	/api/commands/{Id}	Update (Partial)	Update part of a single resource (by Id)
DELETE	/api/commands/{Id}	Delete	Delete a single resource (by Id)

ℹ **Quick Note**   The Verb and URI *in combination* should be unique for a given API. We cover this in more detail later, but just make a mental note of that for now.

Payloads

As mentioned earlier, REST APIs are "a lightweight way to transfer *textual* representations of resources." What do we mean by this?

Well, when you make a call to retrieve data from a REST API, the data will be returned to you in some serialized, textual format, for example:

- JavaScript Object Notation (JSON)

- Extensible Markup Language (XML)

- Hypertext Markup Language (HTML)

- Yet Another Markup Language (YAML)

and so on.

Upon receiving that serialized string payload, you'll then do something with it, most likely some kind of deserialization operation so you can use the resource or object within the consuming application. With regard to REST APIs, there is no prescribed payload format, although most usually JSON will be used and returned. We will be using JSON as our payload format in this book given its lightweight nature and ubiquity in the industry.

Five Minutes On JSON

What is JSON?

- Stands for "JavaScript Object Notation."

- Open format used for the transmission of "object" data (primarily) over the Web.

- It consists of attribute–value pairs (see the following examples).

- A JSON object can contain other "nested" objects.

Anatomy of a Simple JSON Object

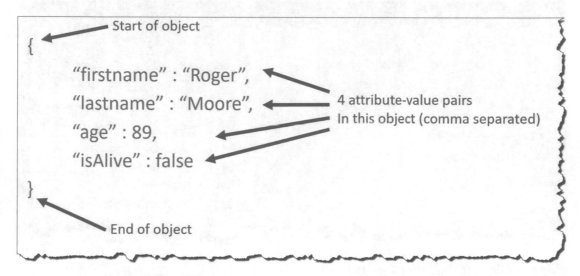

Figure 3-2. *A Simple JSON object*

In the example in Figure 3-2, we have a "Person" object with four attributes:

- firstname
- lastname
- age
- isAlive

With the following respective values

- Roger [This is a string data-type and is therefore delineated by double quotes ' " ']
- Moore [Again this is a string and needs double quotes]
- 89 [Number value that does not need quotes]
- false [Boolean value, again does not need the double quotes]

Paste this JSON into something like jsoneditoronline.org, and you can interrogate its structure some more.

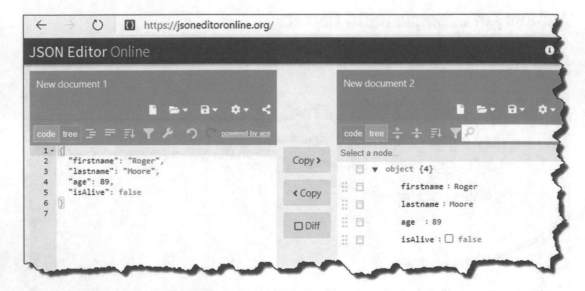

Figure 3-3. *JSON Editor Online*

A (Slightly) More Complex Example

As mentioned in the overview of JSON, an object can contain "nested" objects; observe our person example with a nested address object:

```
{
        "firstname" : "Roger",
        "lastname" : "Moore",
        "age" : 89,                    "Object" Attribute
        "isAlive" : false,
        "address" :                    Start of "nested" object value
        {
                "streetAddress" : "1 Main Street",
                "city": "London",                        3 Attribute-Value pairs
                "postcode" : "N1 3XX"
        }
}
```

Figure 3-4. *Nested JSON object*

Here, we can see that we have a fifth Person object attribute, `address`, which does not have a standard value like the others but in fact contains another object with three attributes:

- `streetAddress`

- `city`

- `postcode`

The values of all these attributes contain strings, so no need to labor that point further. This nesting can continue ad nauseum.

Again, posting this JSON into our online editor yields a slightly more interesting structure.

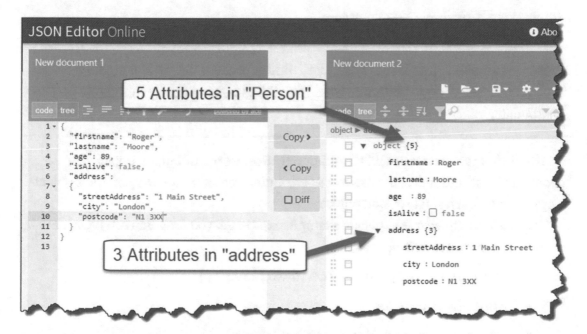

Figure 3-5. *Object navigation in JSON Editor Online*

A Final Example

On to our last example which this time includes an array of phone number objects.

```
{
        "firstname" : "Roger",
        "lastname" : "Moore",
        "address" :
        {
                "streetAddress" : "1 Main Street",
                "city": "London"              "Array" Attribute
        },
        "phoneNumbers" :              Square brackets denote the
        [                             beginning, (and end), of array
                { "type" : "home", "number" : "+61 03 1234 5678" },
                { "type" : "mobile", "number" : "+61 0405 111 222"}
        ]                                                         2 (object) array items
}
```

Figure 3-6. *Introducing JSON arrays*

Note   I removed "age" and "isAlive" attributes from the person object as well as the "postcode" attribute from the address object purely for brevity and readability.

You'll observe that we added an additional attribute to our Person object, "phoneNumbers", and unlike the "address" attribute, it contains an array of other objects as opposed to just a single nested object.

The reason I chose these specific examples was to get you familiar with JSON and some of its core constructs, specifically

- The start and end of an object, "curly brackets": { }

- Attribute–value pairs

- Nested objects (or objects as attribute values)

- Array of objects, "square brackets": []

Personally, on my JSON travels, these constructs are the main ones you'll come across and, as far as an introduction goes, should give you pretty good coverage of most scenarios – certainly with regard to the API we're building, which will both return and accept simple JSON objects.

CHAPTER 4

Scaffold Our API Solution

Chapter Summary

In this chapter we will "scaffold" our two projects and place them within a *solution*. We'll also talk about the "bare-bones" contents of a typical ASP.NET Core application and introduce you to two key classes: `Program` and `Startup`.

When Done, You Will

- Have created our main API Project
- Have created our Unit Test Project
- Place both projects within a solution
- Have a solid understanding of the anatomy of an ASP.NET Core project
- Get introduced to the `Program` and `Startup` classes in an ASP.NET Core project

Solution Overview

Before we start creating projects, I just wanted to give you an overview of what we'll end up with at the end of this chapter (I don't know about you, but it helps me if I know the end goal I'm working toward). First off, a bit about our "solution hierarchy."

© Les Jackson 2020
L. Jackson, *The Complete ASP.NET Core 3 API Tutorial*, https://doi.org/10.1007/978-1-4842-6255-9_4

Component	What is it?	Main Config. File	Relationships
Solution	Primary container, holds 1 or more related Projects	.sln	Projects are Children
Project	Self-contained "project" of related functionality	.csproj	Solution is Parent Projects are siblings

A "Solution" is really nothing more than a container for one or more related projects; projects in turn contain the code and other resources to do something useful. You would not put code directly into a Solution.

Projects can of course exist without a parent Solution; going further, Projects can reference one and other without the need for a Solution. So why bother with a solution? Great question; it boils down to

- Personal preference on how you want to "group" related projects

- If you're using Visual Studio (this always usually creates a solution for you)

- Whether you want to "build" all projects within a solution together

We will use a Solution as we are going to have two interrelated Projects:

- Source Code Project (Our API)

- Unit Test Project (Unit Tests for our API)

The overall layout for our solution is detailed in Figure 4-1.

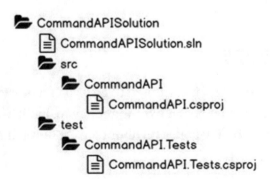

Figure 4-1. *Our Solution hierarchy*

You'll see that we have subfolders within the main solution folder to segregate source code (*src*) and unit test projects (*test*). OK, so let's start creating our solution and projects!

Scaffold Our Solution Components

Move to your working directory (basically where you like to store the solution and projects), and create the following folders:

- Create main "solution" folder called ***CommandAPISolution***.

- Create two subdirectories called in solution folder called ***src*** and ***test***.

You should have something like the following.

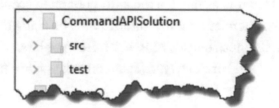

Figure 4-2. *Basic folder setup*

- Open a terminal window (if you haven't already), and navigate to the "inside" of the ***src*** folder you just created.

⋮ .NET Core provides a number of "templates" we can use when creating a new project; selecting a particular template will impact any additional "scaffold" code automatically generated.

To see a list of the templates available, type

```
dotnet new
```

You should see something like the following.

```
MVC ViewStart                                       viewstart       [C#]
Blazor Server App                                   blazorserver    [C#]
ASP.NET Core Empty                                  web             [C#], F#
ASP.NET Core Web App (Model-View-Controller)        mvc             [C#], F#
ASP.NET Core Web App                                webapp          [C#]
ASP.NET Core with Angular                           angular         [C#]
ASP.NET Core with React.js                          react           [C#]
ASP.NET Core with React.js and Redux                reactredux      [C#]
Razor Class Library                                 razorclasslib   [C#]
ASP.NET Core Web API                                webapi          [C#], F#
ASP.NET Core gRPC Service                           grpc            [C#]
dotne                                               gitignore
```

Figure 4-3. *.NET Core Project templates*

You'll notice that there's a template called "webapi" that we could use to generate this project. However, I felt that as most of the auto-generated scaffold code is important, we create this ourselves. Therefore, for this tutorial we'll be using the "web" template, which effectively is the simplest, empty, ASP.NET Core template.

To generate our new "API" project, type (again ensure you are "inside" the *src* directory)

```
dotnet new web -n CommandAPI
```

Where

- web is our template type.

- -n CommandAPI names our project and creates our project and folder.

You should see something like the following.

```
PS D:\APITutorial\NET Core 3.1\CommandAPISolution\src> dotnet new web -n CommandAPI
The template "ASP.NET Core Empty" was created successfully.

Processing post-creation actions...
Running 'dotnet restore' on CommandAPI\CommandAPI.csproj...
  Restore completed in 92.05 ms for D:\APITutorial\NET Core 3.1\CommandAPISolution\src

Restore succeeded.

PS D:\APITutorial\NET Core 3.1\CommandAPISolution\src>
```

Figure 4-4. *API Project generation*

As per our given layout, a folder called ***CommandAPI*** should have been created in *src*; change into this folder and listing the contents you should see.

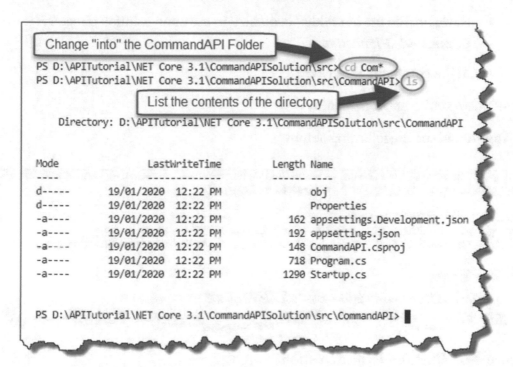

Figure 4-5. *Listing the contents of our API Project*

ℹ️   If you're not familiar with navigating folders using a command-line interface, it may be worth Googling some basic commands. As I'm using a "PowerShell" terminal, the commands I used are similar to those you'd find on a Unix/Linux system. If you're using a Windows Command Prompt, you'd type `cd <name of directory>` followed by `dir`; the `dir` command is similar to `ls` here in that it lists the content of the current directory.

OK, we're done scaffolding our *API project*; now we need to repeat for our Unit Test project.

- Navigate into the ***test*** folder[1] contained in the main solution directory ***CommandAPISolution***.

- At the command line, type

```
dotnet new xunit -n CommandAPI.Tests
```

You should see the following output.

```
PS D:\APITutorial\NET Core 3.1\CommandAPISolution\test> dotnet new xunit -n CommandAPI.Tests
The template "xUnit Test Project" was created successfully.

Processing post-creation actions...
Running 'dotnet restore' on CommandAPI.Tests\CommandAPI.Tests.csproj...
  Restore completed in 1.37 sec for D:\APITutorial\NET Core 3.1\CommandAPISolution\test\Comman

Restore succeeded.

PS D:\APITutorial\NET Core 3.1\CommandAPISolution\test>
```

Figure 4-6. *Unit Test Project creation*

☞ **Learning Opportunity**   What is xUnit? Remember the command we typed to get a list of all available templates? Try that again to see what the xUnit template is. Can you see any templates that look similar, maybe with a similar name component? Perhaps do some research into what they are too.

Creating Solution and Project Associations

OK, so we've created our two projects, but now we need to

- Create a Solution File that links both projects to the overall solution.

- Reference Our API Project in our Unit Test Project.

---

[1]Hint: cd .. moves you up a directory.

Back at our terminal/command line, change back into the main Solution folder: **CommandAPISolution**; to check if you're in the right place, perform a directory listing, and you should see something like this.

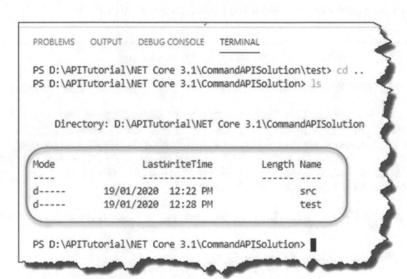

Figure 4-7. *Check our directory listing*

You should see the two directories: ***src*** and ***test***.

Now, issue the following command to create our solution (.sln) file:

```
dotnet new sln --name CommandAPISolution
```

This should create our *empty solution* file, as shown here.

```
PROBLEMS   OUTPUT   DEBUG CONSOLE   TERMINAL

PS D:\APITutorial\NET Core 3.1\CommandAPISolution> dotnet new sln --name CommandAPISolution
The template "Solution File" was created successfully.
PS D:\APITutorial\NET Core 3.1\CommandAPISolution>
```

Figure 4-8. *Create the solution file*

We now want to associate both our "child" projects to our solution; to do so, issue the following command:

```
dotnet sln CommandAPISolution.sln add src/CommandAPI/CommandAPI.csproj test/
CommandAPI.Tests/CommandAPI.Tests.csproj
```

> **Note**   The preceding command is all one line.

You should see that both projects are added to the solution file.

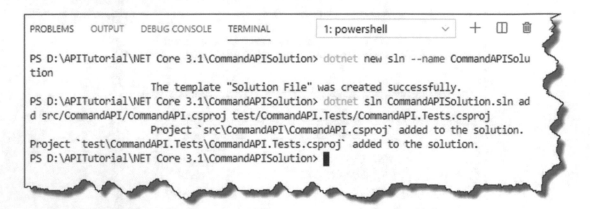

Figure 4-9.   *Projects added to our solution*

> ⚠   If you get an error, double-check that you have typed the full path correctly. It's quite long, so the opportunity to make a mistake is there. Believe me – I have spent many a time rectifying typos of this sort.

All this really does is tell our solution that it has two projects. The projects themselves are unaware of each other. This is similar to a parent knowing that they have two children, but the children being *unaware* of each other – we're going to rectify that now, well for one of the siblings anyway.

We need to place a "reference" to our ***CommandAPI*** project *in* our ***CommandAPI. Tests*** project; this will enable us to reference the ***CommandAPI*** project and "test" it from our ***CommandAPI.Tests*** project. You can either manually edit the ***CommandAPI.Tests. csproj*** file or type the following command:

```
dotnet add test/CommandAPI.Tests/CommandAPI.Tests.csproj reference src/
CommandAPI/CommandAPI.csproj
```

You should get something like the following.

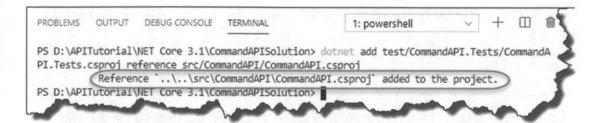

Figure 4-10. *API Project added as a reference*

Open VS Code (or whatever editor you chose), and open the ***CommandAPISolution*** folder[2]; find the ***CommandAPI.Tests.csproj*** file, and open it – you should see a reference (as well as other things) to the CommandAPI project:

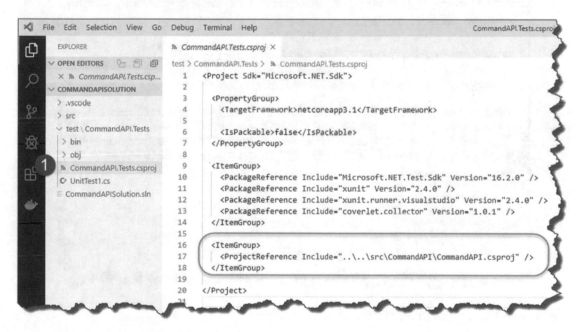

Figure 4-11. *Check reference has been added*

☞ **Learning Opportunity**   Why do we only place a reference this way? Why don't we place a reference to our unit test project in our API projects .csproj file?

---

[2]In VS Code got to File ➤ Open Folder and select your solution or project folder.

You can now build both projects (ensure you are still in the root *solution* folder) by issuing

```
dotnet build
```

Note   This is one of the advantages of using a solution file (you can build both projects from here).

Assuming all is well, the *solution build* should succeed, which comprises our two projects.

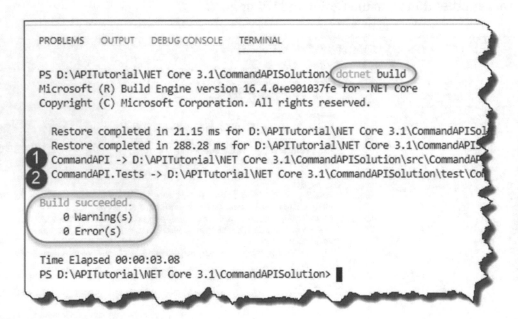

Figure 4-12.   *Perform our first build*

♨ **Celebration Checkpoint**   Good Job! You've reached your first milestone; our app is scaffolded up and ready to rock and roll (that means coding).

But (there's always a but isn't there?), before we move on to the next chapter, I think a little bit about the anatomy of a ASP.NET Core app is probably appropriate. The more familiar you are with this, the easier you'll find the rest of the tutorial.

Anatomy of An ASP.NET Core App

The following table describes the *core*[3] files and folders that you will typically encounter when you create an ASP.NET Core project. Just be aware that depending on the project (or scaffold template) type you select, you may have additional files and folders – however, the ones described here are common to most project types.

File/folder	What is it?
.VS Code	This folder stores your VS Code workspace settings, so it's not really anything to do with the actual project. In fact, if you've chosen to dev this in something other than VS Code, you won't have this file (you may have something else)
bin (folder)	Location where final output binaries along with any dependencies and or other deployable files will be written to
obj (folder)	Used to house intermediate object files and other transient data files that are generated by the compiler during a build
Properties (folder) *launchSettings.json*	Contains the ***launchSettings.json*** file. This file can be used to configure application environment variables, for example, Development. It is also used to configure how the webserver running your app will operate, for example, which port it will listen on, etc.
appsettings.json appsettings. Development.json	File used to hold, surprise surprise, "application settings." In the sections that follow, we'll store the connection string to our database here Also, environment-specific settings can be contained in additional settings files (e.g., Development) as shown by the ***appsettings.Development.json*** file
<ProjectName>. csproj	The configuration for the project principally tells us the .NET Core Framework version we're using along with other Nuget packages (see info box) that the application will reference and use Also, as you've previously seen, this is where we can place references to other projects that we need to be aware of
Program.cs	It all starts here This class configures the "hosting" platform, along with the "Main()" entry point method for the entire app

(continued)

---

[3]Core in this sense is pertaining to "part of something that is central to its existence or character," not .NET Core.

File/folder	What is it?
Startup.cs	This class is used to configure the application services and the request pipeline. More on those later. In my opinion, if you learn the workings of the Startup class, you'll be in a *really* good position to understand how ASP.NET Core applications work generally – so it's worth investing some effort here

ⓘ   Nuget is a package management platform that allows developers to reference and consume external, prepackaged code that they can use in their apps. We'll add different packages to our project files as we move through the book and require extra functionality.

In short

- ***launchSettings.json***

- ***appsettings.json*** (and other environment-specific settings files)

- ***<ProjectName>.csproj***

- ***Program.cs***

- ***Startup.cs***

All work in symbiotic bliss with each other to get the application up and running and working according to the runtime environment. As we go through the book, we'll cover off more and more of the functions and features of each of the given items when they become relevant.

However, as they are so foundational to every ASP.NET Core solution, we're going to talk briefly about both the Program and Startup classes here.

The Program and Startup Classes

The Program Class

As previously mentioned, this is the main entry point for the entire app and is used to configure the "hosting" environment. It then goes on to use the Startup class to finalize the configuration of the app.

Let's take a quick look at the templated code (which we're *not* going to change) and see what it does.

ⓘ Unless otherwise stated, when we're working with a project, it's going to be our main "API Project" (and not the unit test project). So, for the examples coming up, and elsewhere in the book, reference this project first.

I'll explicitly state when we need to use the unit test project.

```
namespace CommandAPI
{
    public class Program
    {
        public static void Main(string[] args)
        {
            CreateHostBuilder(args).Build().Run();
        }

        public static IHostBuilder CreateHostBuilder(string[] args) =>
            Host.CreateDefaultBuilder(args)
                .ConfigureWebHostDefaults(webBuilder =>
                {
                    webBuilder.UseStartup<Startup>();
                });
    }
}
```

Figure 4-13. *Standard contents of Program class*

The execution sequence is as follows.

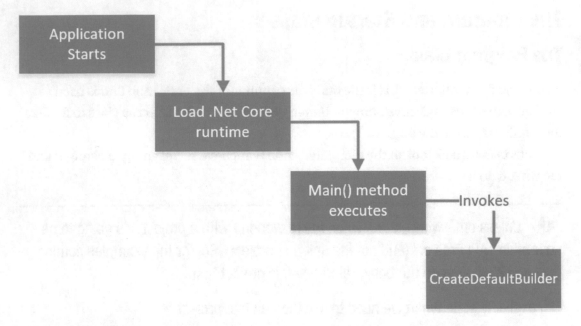

Figure 4-14. *Program Class execution sequence*

The CreateDefaultBuilder method uses the default builder pattern to create a web host, which can specify things like the webserver to use and config sources as well as selecting the class we use to complete the configuration of the app services. In this case we use the default Startup class for this; indeed, since the default contents are sufficient for our needs, we'll move on.

Note   We do cover .NET Core Configuration in more detail later in the book.

The Startup Class

The Program class is the entry point for the app, but most of the interesting startup stuff is done in the Startup class. The Startup class contains two methods that we should look further at:

- ConfigureServices
- Configure

The execution sequence is as follows.

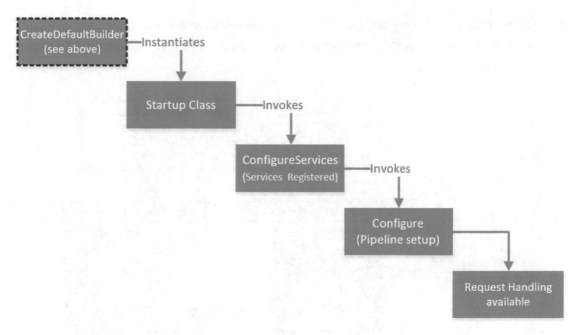

Figure 4-15. *Startup class execution sequence*

ConfigureServices

In ASP.NET Core we have the concept of "services," which are just objects that provide functionality to other parts of the application. For those of you familiar with the concept of *dependency injection,*[4] this is where dependencies are registered inside the default Inversion of Control (IoC) container provided by .NET Core. We'll cover dependency injection in much more detail when we come to working with our "repository" in Chapter 6.

Configure

Once services have been registered, `Configure` is then called to set up the *request pipeline.* The request pipeline can be built up of multiple *middleware components* that take (in this case http) requests and perform some operation on them.

Depending on how the multiple middleware components are created, it will affect at what stage they get involved with the request and what (if anything) they do to impact it.

In the following diagram, you can see how a request would traverse the middleware components added in the `Configure` method. The nature of the request (e.g., is it an

---

[4]This can be a tricky subject; I cover this in some detail in Chapter 6 and throughout the tutorial.

attempt to open a Web Socket?) and the logic in the middleware will determine what will happen to that request, with the ability to "short-circuit" traversing further middleware if required (not shown).

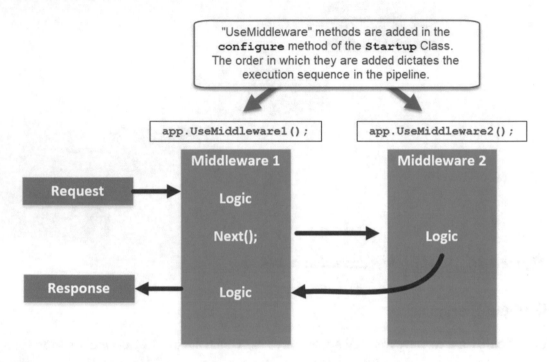

Figure 4-16. *Very simple example of .NET Core Middleware*

🎓 **Learning Opportunity**   In the preceding diagram, I've use a generic construct to describe the middleware components – app.UseMiddleware1(), etc. Take a look at the Configure method in our Startup class, and have a look at the *actual* middleware components that are being added.

Hint   They'll start with "app."

The *Request Pipeline* and middleware, in general, are an expansive area which could occupy a whole chapter of the book on its own. In keeping with the "thin and wide" approach, I feel we've covered enough to move on and start coding (we cover the Request Pipeline in more detail in Chapter 14 when we discuss Authentication and Authorization).

CHAPTER 5

The "C" in MVC

Chapter Summary

In this chapter we'll go over some high-level theory on the Model–View–Controller (MVC) pattern, detail out our API application architecture, and start to code up our API controller class.

When Done, You Will

- Understand what the MVC pattern is
- Understand our API application architecture, including concepts such as
  - Repositories
  - Data transfer objects (DTOs)
  - Database contexts
- Add a controller class to our API project.
- Create a Controller Action (or API Endpoint if you prefer) that returns "hard-coded" JSON.
- Place our solution under source control.

© Les Jackson 2020
L. Jackson, *The Complete ASP.NET Core 3 API Tutorial*, https://doi.org/10.1007/978-1-4842-6255-9_5

Quick Word on My Dev Setup

I just want to level set here on the current state of my development setup I'm going to use moving forward:

- I have VS Code open and running.

- In VS Code I have opened the **CommandAPISolution** solution *folder*.

- This displays my folder and file tree down the left-hand side (containing both our *projects*).

- I'm also using the integrated terminal within VS Code to run my commands.

- The integrated terminal I'm using is "PowerShell" – you can change this; see info box in the following.

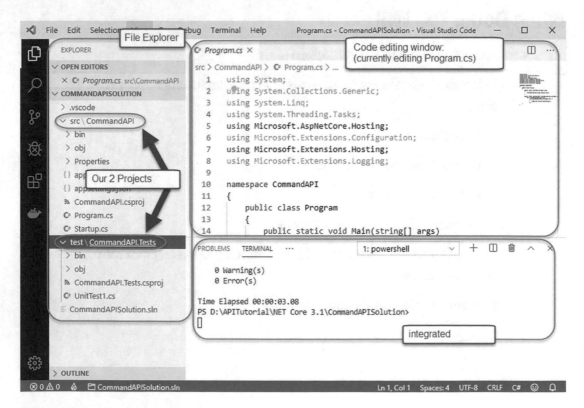

Figure 5-1. *My VS Code setup*

ⓘ You can change the terminal/shell/command-line type within VS Code quite easily.

1. In VS Code hit "F1" (this opens the "command palette" in VS Code).

2. Type *shell* at the resulting prompt, and select "*Terminal: Select Default Shell.*"

3. You can then select from the Terminals that you have installed.

Start Coding!

First, let's just check that everything is set up and working OK from a very basic startup perspective. To do this from a command-line type (ensure that you're "in" the API project directory – ***CommandAPI***)

```
dotnet run
```

You should see the webserver start with output similar to the following.

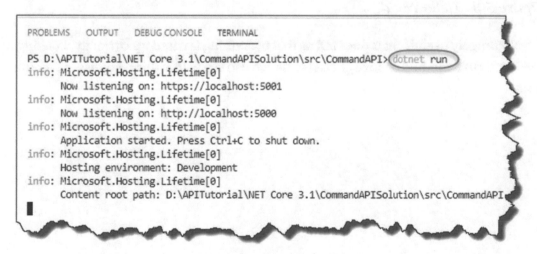

Figure 5-2. *Running our API for the first time*

You can see that the webserver host has started and is listening on ports 5000 and 5001 for http and https, respectively.

ℹ️   To change that port allocation, you can edit the ***launchSettings.json*** file in the ***Properties*** folder; for now though there would be no benefit to that. We'll talk more about this file when we come to our discussion on setting the runtime environment in Chapter 8.

If you go to a web browser and navigate to
http://localhost:5000
You'll see the following.

Figure 5-3.   *Hello World!*

Not hugely useful, but it does tell us that everything is wired up correctly. Looking in the Configure method of our Startup class, we can see where this response is coming from.

```
public void Configure(IApplicationBuilder app, IWebHostEnvironment env)
{
    if (env.IsDevelopment())
    {
        app.UseDeveloperExceptionPage();
    }

    app.UseRouting();

    app.UseEndpoints(endpoints =>
    {
        endpoints.MapGet("/", async context =>
        {
            await context.Response.WriteAsync("Hello World!");
        });
    });
}
```

Figure 5-4. *Where our greeting comes from*

ⓘ For those of you that have worked with any of the 2.x versions of the .NET Core Framework (for those of you ***that haven't***, you can ignore this), this will look slightly different to what you may have seen before. As opposed to

- `app.UseEndPoints`

You would have seen

- `app.Run(async)`

The previous version of the framework would also make use of

- `services.AddMvc()`: In our `ConfigurerServices` method

- `app.UseMVC()`: In our `Configure` method

Further discussion on the differences between versions 2.x and 3.x of the .NET Core Framework can be found here: `https://docs.microsoft.com/en-us/aspnet/core/migration/22-to-30`.

Stop our host from listening (Ctrl+C on Windows – should be the same for Linux/ OSX), and *remove* the highlighted section of code (shown previously) from our Configure method. Add the highlighted code shown next to our Startup class, making sure to update both the ConfigureServices and Configure methods:

```
using Microsoft.AspNetCore.Builder;
using Microsoft.AspNetCore.Hosting;
using Microsoft.Extensions.DependencyInjection;
using Microsoft.Extensions.Hosting;

namespace CommandAPI
{
    public class Startup
    {
        public void ConfigureServices(IServiceCollection services)
        {
            //SECTION 1. Add code below
            services.AddControllers();
        }

        public void Configure(IApplicationBuilder app,
        IWebHostEnvironment env)
        {
            if (env.IsDevelopment())
            {
                app.UseDeveloperExceptionPage();
            }

            app.UseRouting();

            app.UseEndpoints(endpoints =>
            {
                //SECTION 2. Add code below
                endpoints.MapControllers();
            });
        }
    }
}
```

What does this code do?

1. Registers services to enable the use of "Controllers" throughout our application. As mentioned in the info box, in previous versions of .NET Core Framework, you would have specified `services.AddMVC`. Don't worry; we cover what the **M**odel–**V**iew–**C**ontroller (MVC) pattern is below.

2. We "MapControllers" to our endpoints. This means we make use of the Controller services (registered in the `ConfigureServices` method) as endpoints in the *Request Pipeline*.

ℹ **Reminder**   The code for the entire solution can be found here on GitHub:

`https://github.com/binarythistle/Complete-ASP-NET-3-API-Tutorial-Book`

As we have done before, run the project (ensure you *save the file* before doing this[1])

```
dotnet run
```

Now, navigate to the same URL in a web browser (http://localhost:5000), and we should get "nothing."

Call the Postman

Now is probably a good time to get Postman up and running as it's a useful tool that allows you to have a more detailed look at what's going on.

So, if you've not done so already, go to the Postman website (`www.getpostman.com`), and download the version most suitable for your environment, (I use the Windows desktop client, but there's a Chrome plugin along with desktop versions for other operating systems).

We want to make a request to our API using Postman, so click "New."

---

[1]Plenty of times I've run code after making changes, and the changes were not reflected. Yes, that's right – hadn't saved the file.

Figure 5-5. *Start a New Request in Postman*

The select "request."

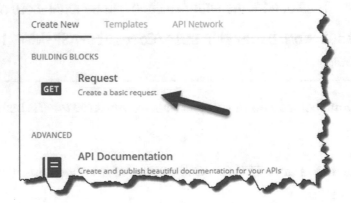

Figure 5-6. *Create a basic request*

Give the request a simple name, for example, "Test Request."

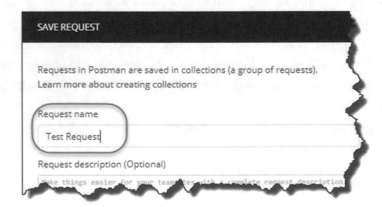

Figure 5-7. *Name your request*

You'll also need to create a "Collection" to house the various API requests you want to create (e.g., GET, POST, etc.):

1.   Click "+ Create Collection."

2.   Give it a name, for example, "CommandAPI."

3.   Select OK (the tick), and ensure you select your newly created collection (not shown).

4.   Click Save to Command API.

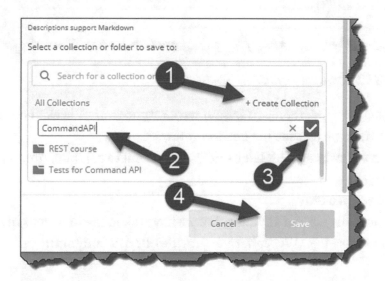

Figure 5-8. *Request Collection*

You should then have a new tab available to populate with the details of your request. Simply type

`http://localhost:5000`

or

`https://localhost:5001`

into the "Enter request URL" text box, ensure "GET" is selected from the drop-down next to it, and hit SEND; it should look something like the following.

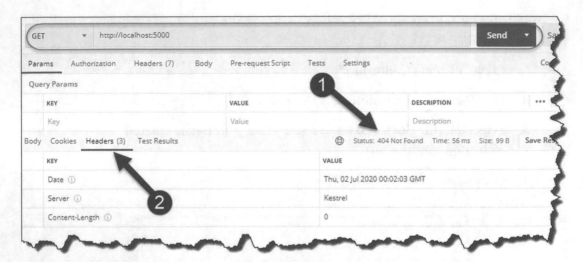

Figure 5-9. *GET Request results in Postman*

If you've clicked Send, then you should see a response of "404 Not Found"; clicking on the headers tab, you can see the headers returned.

We'll return to Postman a bit later, but it's just useful to get it up, running, and tested now.

What have we broken?

We've not actually broken anything, but we have taken the first steps in setting up our application to use the MVC pattern to provide our API endpoint.

What Is MVC?

I'm guessing if you're here, you probably have some idea of what the MVC (Model–View–Controller) pattern is. If not, I provide a brief explanation here, but as

1.   There are already 1000s of articles on MVC.

2.   MVC theory is not the primary focus of this tutorial.

I won't go into *too* much detail. Again, I feel you'll learn more about MVC by building a solution, rather than reading long textual explanations. I think when we cover off the Application Architecture below, things will make much more sense though.

Model–View–Controller

Put simply, the MVC pattern allows us to *separate the concerns* of different parts of our application:

- **M**odel (our Domain Data)
- **V**iew (User Interface)
- **C**ontroller (Requests and Actions)

In fact, to make things even simpler, as we're developing an API, we won't even have any **V**iew artefacts.[2] A high-level representation of this architecture for our API is shown here.

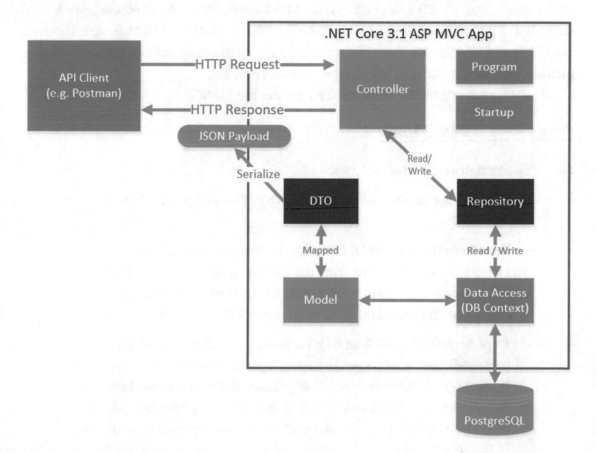

Figure 5-10. *Our API Application Architecture*

---

[2]You could argue that the serialized JSON payload is a "view" from a conceptual perspective.

It's also worth noting, in case it wasn't clear, that the MVC pattern is just that – an application architecture *pattern* – it is agnostic from technical implementation. As this happens to be a book about a particular technology (.NET Core), we cover how .NET Core implements MVC; however, there are other implementations of the MVC pattern using different frameworks and languages.

Models, Data Transfer Objects, Repositories, and Data Access

You're probably happy enough with the concept of a Model – it's just data, right? Yes, that's simple enough. So, looking at the architecture diagram in Figure 5-10, you're then wondering what's a DTO, a Repository, and a DB Context. And I don't blame you – I struggled with the distinction between these concepts too at first. In fact, we could leave out DTOs and Repositories from our solution and it would work without them. So why include them at all? Great question; let me try and explain.

First, let me answer the "what" before I answer the "why."

What's the Distinction?

Let's step through each of those classes:

- **Model**: Represents the *internal domain* data of our application (the "M" in MVC).

- **Data Transfer Objects** (**DTOs**): Are the *representations* of our Domain Models to our *external consumers,* meaning that we don't expose internal implementation detail (our Models) to external concerns. This has multiple benefits as we'll discuss later.

- **Data Access** (aka **DB Context**): Takes our Models and represents (or "mediates") them down to a *specific persistence layer* (e.g., PostgreSQL, SQL Server, etc.). Going forward, I'll refer to our Data Access class as a "DB Context" which is a technology-specific term taken from "Entity Framework Core" – don't worry; more on that later in Chapter 7.

- **Repository**: Provides a *technology agnostic* (or persistence ignorant) view of our permanently stored data to our application.

So, what do you take from this? The main concept (which is repeated throughout the book) is that we should be *decoupling implementational detail* from the *interface* or *contract* we want to provide to consumers. But *why* is that a good thing?

Why Decoupling Is Good?

I've kind of alluded to that earlier, and we'll cover it in more detail when we come to implementing these concepts, but in short decoupling our interfaces (or contracts) from our implementations provides the following benefits:

- **Security**: We may not want to expose potentially sensitive data contained in our implementation (think our Model) to our external consumers. Providing an external representation (e.g., a DTO) with sensitive information removed addresses this.

- **Change Agility**: Separating out our interface – which should remain consistent so as not to break our "contract" with our consumers – means we can then change our implementation detail without impacting that interface. We then have the confidence to react quickly to market demands without fear of breaking existing agreements. We'll demonstrate this concept more when we come onto using *dependency injection* and our *repository*.

Bringing It Together

In the chapters that follow, we'll leverage MVC as well as the other concepts discussed earlier to

- **Chapter 5**: Create a *Controller* to manage all our API requests (see our CRUD actions in Chapter 3).

- **Chapter 6**: Create a *Model* to internally represent our resources (in this case our library of command-line prompts)

- **Chapter 6**: Create a **Repository** to provide a technology agnostic view of our persisted data.

- **Chapter 7**: Leverage Entity Framework Core to create a **DB Context** that will allow us to persist our Model down to PostgreSQL.

- **Chapter 9**: Create **DTO** representations of our Model for external use.

Let's wrap our architectural overview there (again, don't worry – we'll deep dive these concepts later) and move on to creating our Controller.

Our Controller

Making sure that you are in the main API project directory (*CommandAPI*), create a folder named "*Controllers*" underneath *CommandAPI* as a subfolder.

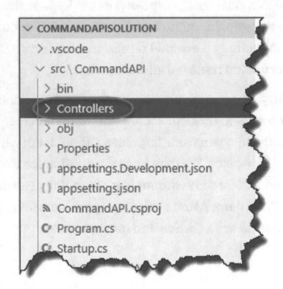

Figure 5-11. *Controllers Folder in our API Project*

Inside the *Controllers* folder you just created, create a file called *CommandsController.cs*.

ⓘ Quick Tip   If you're using VS Code, you can create both folders and files from within the VS Code directory explorer. Just make sure when you're creating either that you have the correct "parent" folder selected.

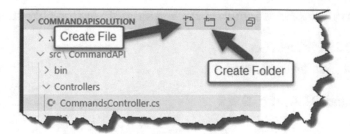

Figure 5-12. *File and folder creation in VS Code*

Your directory structure should now look like this.

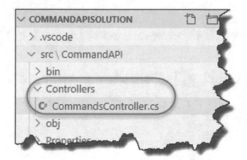

Figure 5-13. *Our directory structure*

Ensure that you postfix the ***CommandsController*** file with a ".cs" extension to denote it's a C# file.

Both the folder and naming convention of our controller file follow a standard, conventional approach; this makes our applications more readable to other developers; it also allows us to leverage from the principles of "Convention over Configuration."

Now, to begin with we're just going to create a simple "action" in our Controller that will return some hard-coded JSON (as opposed to serializing data that will ultimately come from our DB). Again, this just makes sure we have everything wired up correctly.

ⓘ   A controller "Action" (I may also refer to it as an *endpoint*) maps to our API CRUD operations as listed in Chapter 3; our first action though will just return a simple hard-coded string.

The code in your *CommandsController* class should now look like this:

```
using System.Collections.Generic;
using Microsoft.AspNetCore.Mvc;

namespace CommandAPI.Controllers
{
    [Route("api/[controller]")]
    [ApiController]
    public class CommandsController : ControllerBase
    {
        [HttpGet]
        public ActionResult<IEnumerable<string>> Get()
        {
            return new string[] {"this", "is", "hard", "coded"};
        }
    }
}
```

Again, if you don't fancy typing this in, the code is available here on GitHub: https://github.com/binarythistle/Complete-ASP-NET-3-API-Tutorial-Book

We'll come onto what all this means next, but first lets' build it.

Ensure that you don't have the server running from our recent example (Ctrl + C to terminate), save the file, then type

```
dotnet build
```

This command just compiles (or builds) the code. If you have any errors, it'll call them out here; assuming all's well (which is should be), you should see the following.

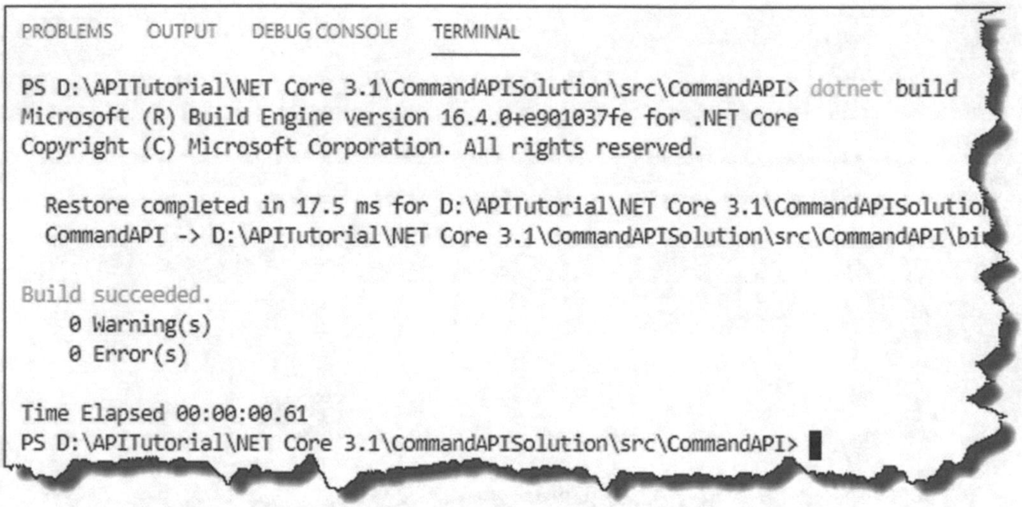

Figure 5-14. *Successful API run*

Now, **run** the app.

☛ **Learning Opportunity**   I'm deliberately not going to detail *that* command going forward now; you should be picking this stuff up as we move on. If in doubt, refer to earlier in the chapter on how to *run* your code (as opposed to *building* it as we've just done).

Go to Postman (or a web browser if you like), and in the URL box, type
`http://localhost:5000/api/commands`

Ensure that "Get" is selected in the drop-down (in Postman), then click "Send"; you should see something like this.

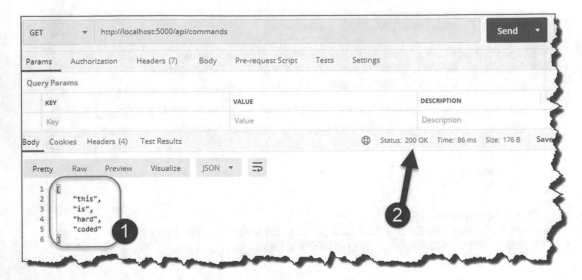

Figure 5-15. *Our first API endpoint response*

1. This is the hard-coded json string returned.

2. We have a 200 OK HTTP response (basically everything is good).

I guess technically you could say that we have implemented an API that services a simple "GET" request! Excellent, but I'm sure most of you want to take the example a little further.

Back to Our Code

OK so that's great, but what did we actually do? Let's go back to our code and pick it apart.

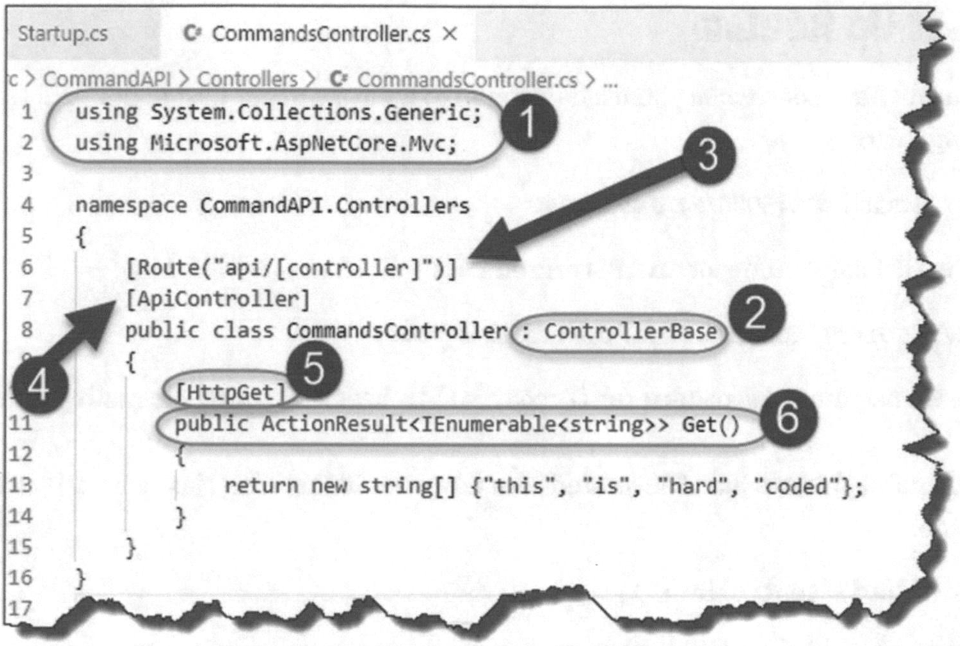

Figure 5-16. *Deep dive on our first controller action*

1. Using Directives

We included two using directives here:

- `System.Collections.Generic` (supports IEnumerable)
- `Microsoft.AspNetCore.Mvc` (supports pretty much everything else detailed below)

2. Inherit from Controller Base

Our Controller class inherits from `ControllerBase` (it does not provide View support which we don't need). You can inherit from `Controller` also if you like, but as you can probably guess, this provides additional support for Views that we just don't need.

`ControllerBase is further detailed on Microsoft Build.`[3]

---

[3]https://docs.microsoft.com/en-us/dotnet/api/microsoft.aspnetcore.mvc.
controllerbase?view=aspnetcore-3.1

3. Set Up Routing

As you will have seen when you used Postman to issue a GET request to our API, you had to navigate to

http://localhost:5000/**api/commands**

The URI convention for an API controllers is

http://<server_address>/**api/<controller_name>**

where we use the route pattern /api/<controller_name> following the main part of the URI.

To enable this, we have "decorated" our CommandsController class with a [Route] attribute:

[Route("api/[controller]")]

ℹ️   You'll notice that when we talk about the name of our controller from a *route perspective*, we use "Commands" as opposed to the fuller "Commands**Controller**".

Indeed, the name of our controller really is "Commands"; the use of the "Controller" postfix in our class definition is an example of configuration over convention. Basically, it makes the code easier to read if we use this convention, that is, we know it's a controller class.

⚠️   **Warning!**   We have specified our route using the [controller] "wildcard," which dynamically derives that segment of the route from the name of our controller (minus the "Controller" portion) as we've explained before. So, in our case, this gives us the route:

api/commands

What this means is that if you *change the name of your Controller* for whatever reason, the *route will change also*. This may have quite unexpected consequences for our consumers, in effect breaking our contract - so be careful!

You can "rectify" this behavior by hardcoding the name of your route as so it would become

```
[Route("api/commands")]
```

I'll leave the semi-dynamically declared route for now as I think that is what you'll most likely see out there in the field, but feel free to change to the hard-coded approach if you're more comfortable with that.

4. APIController Attribute

Decorating our class with this attribute provides the following out-of-the-box behaviors for our controller:

- Attribute Routing

- Automatic HTTP 400 Error responses (e.g., 400 Bad Request, 405 Not Allowed, etc.)

- Default Binding Sources (more on these later)

- Problem details for error status codes

It's not mandatory to use it but highly recommended, as the default behaviors it provides are *really* useful; for a further deep dive on this, refer to the Microsoft documentation.[4]

5. HttpGet Attribute

Cast your mind back to the start of the tutorial, and you'll remember that we specified our standard CRUD actions for our API and that each of those actions aligns to a particular http verb, for example, GET, POST, PUT, etc.

Decorating our first simple action with [HttpGet] is really just specifying which verb our action responds to.

---

[4]https://docs.microsoft.com/en-us/aspnet/core/web-api/
index?view=aspnetcore-2.2#annotation-with-apicontroller-attribute

You can test this by changing the verb type in Postman to "POST" and calling our API again. As we have no defined action in our API Controller that responds to POST, we'll receive a 4xx HTTP error response.

ℹ   As mentioned before, the Verb Attribute (e.g., GET) in combination with the route (e.g., `api/commands`) *should be unique* for each action (endpoint) within our API.

If you take a look back to our full list of the API endpoints in Chapter 3, you'll notice that this is indeed the case.

---

6. Our Controller Action

This is quite an expansive area,[5] and there are multiple ways you can write your controller actions. I've just opted for the "`ActionResult`" return type which was introduced as part of .NET Core 2.1.

In short, you'll have an `ActionResult` return type for each API CRUD action, so we'll end up with six by the time we're finished.

Synchronous vs. Asynchronous?

In the recent example, our controller actions are *synchronous*, meaning that when they get called by a client (e.g., Postman), they will wait until a result is returned and in doing so *occupy a thread* (think of a thread as a small slice of a CPU's time). Once a result is returned, that thread is then released (back to a thread pool) where it can be reused by some other operation.

The problem with synchronous operations is that if there is enough of them (think a high traffic API), eventually all the available threads will be used from the thread pool, *blocking* further operations from running. That is where asynchronous Controller Actions would come in.

An *asynchronous* controller action will not wait for a long-running operation (e.g., complex Database query or call over the network) to complete and will hand the thread

---

[5]https://docs.microsoft.com/en-us/aspnet/core/web-api/action-return-types?view=
 aspnetcore-3.1

back to the pool while it waits. When the long-running operation does eventually have a result for us, a thread is reacquired by the controller action to complete the operation.

In short, asynchronous operations are really about *scalability* and not (as is sometimes claimed) speed. Just using an asynchronous controller action does nothing to improve the time the I/O operation (e.g., database query) takes to complete. It does, however, improve the situation where we may run out of threads (due to blocking) which has positive implications for scaling. There is also some nice usability implications when applied to User Interface design (have you ever used an application that "freezes" when performing a long-running operation?).

I did debate whether to use asynchronous controller actions in our example; however, in keeping with the "Thin and Wide" approach of the book, I thought it would introduce unnecessary complexity that would detract from the core thrust of the book, so I have omitted for now.

This section has already taken up enough space, so let's move on!

Source Control

OK this has been quite a long chapter, and we've covered a lot of ground. Before we wrap it up, I want to introduce the concept of *source control*.

What is source control?

Source control is really about the following two concepts:

1. Tracking (and rolling back) changes in code

2. Coordinating those changes when there are multiple developers/
   contributors to the code (referred to as *Continuous Integration*;
   we'll deep dive into this in Chapter 12)

The general idea is that throughout a code project's life cycle, many changes will be made to the source code, and we really need a way to track those changes, for reasons including but not limited to

- **Requirements Traceability**: Ensuring that the changes relate back to
  a requested feature/bug fix.

- **Release Notes**: Wrapping up our changes so we can publish new
  release notes for our app.

- **Rolling Back**: If we know what changed (and we broke something), we can either (a) fix it or (b) roll back the change – a source control system allows us to do that.

On top of tracking changes, the other primary reason for using a source control solution is to coordinate the changes to the codebase when multiple developers are working on it. If you're the only person working on your code, you're not going to really conflict with yourself (well not usually anyway). What about when you have more than one person making changes to the same codebase? How can that happen without things like overwriting each other's changes? Again, this is where a source control solution comes in to play – it coordinates those changes and identifies conflicts should they arise.

Now, we're not going to delve too deep into the workings of source control, but we are going to put our project "under source control" for two reasons:

1. To introduce you to the concept

2. So we can automatically deploy our app to production via a CI/CD[6] pipeline – more in Chapter 12

Git and GitHub

Now, there are various source control solutions out there, but by far the most common is Git (and those based around Git), to such an extent that "source control" and Git are almost synonyms. Think about "vacuum cleaners" and "Hoover" (or perhaps now Dyson), and you'll get the picture.

What's the difference?

Git is the source control system that

- You can have running on your local machine to track local code changes

- You can have running on a server to manage parallel, distributed team changes

---

[6]Continuous Integration/Continuous Delivery (or Deployment).

While you can use Git in a distributed team environment, there are a number of companies that have taken it further placing "Git in the Cloud," with such examples as

- GitHub (probably the most well-recognized – and now acquired by Microsoft)

- Bitbucket (from Atlassian – the makers of Jira and Confluence)

- Gitlabs

We're going to use both Git (locally on our machine) and GitHub as part of this tutorial (as mentioned in Chapter 2).

Setting Up Your Local Git Repo

If you followed along in Chapter 2, you should already have Git up and running locally; if not, or you're unsure, pop back to Chapter 2, and take a look.

At a terminal/command line *in* the main **solution** directory, (***CommandAPISolution***), type (if your API app is still running you may want to stop it by hitting Ctrl + c)

```
git init
```

This should initialize a local Git repository in the *solution directory* that will track the code changes in a hidden folder called ***.git*** (note the period "." prefixing "git").

Now type

```
git status
```

This will show you all the "untracked" files in your directory (basically files that are not under source control); at this stage, that is everything.

```
PROBLEMS    OUTPUT    DEBUG CONSOLE    TERMINAL

PS D:\APITutorial\NET Core 3.1\CommandAPISolution> git init
Initialized empty Git repository in D:/APITutorial/NET Core 3.1/CommandAPISolution/.git/
PS D:\APITutorial\NET Core 3.1\CommandAPISolution> git status
On branch master

No commits yet

Untracked files:
  (use "git add <file>..." to include in what will be committed)
        CommandAPISolution.sln
        src/
        test/

nothing added to commit but untracked files present (use "git add" to track)
PS D:\APITutorial\NET Core 3.1\CommandAPISolution> █
```

Figure 5-17. *Untracked files in our new Git Repo*

.gitignore file

Before we start to track our solution files (and bring them under source control), there are certain files that you shouldn't bring under source control, in particular, files that are "generated" as the result of a build, primarily as they are surplus to requirements (they're not "source" files'!).

In order to "ignore" these file types, you create a file in your "root" solution directory called **.gitignore**, (again note the period "." at the beginning). Now this can become quite a personal choice on what you want to include or not, but I have provided an example that you can use (or ignore altogether – excuse the pun!):

```
*.swp
*.*~
project.lock.json
.DS_Store
*.pyc

# Visual Studio Code
.VS Code
```

```
# User-specific files
*.suo
*.user
*.userosscache
*.sln.docstates

# Build results
[Dd]ebug/
[Dd]ebugPublic/
[Rr]elease/
[Rr]eleases/
x64/
x86/
build/
bld/
[Bb]in/
[Oo]bj/
msbuild.log
msbuild.err
msbuild.wrn

# Visual Studio
.vs/

# Compiled Source
*.com
*.class
*.dll
*.exe
*.o
*.so
```

So if you want to use a *.gitignore* file (I recommend it – you don't want to put compiled assets in a *source repository*), create one, and pop it in the root of your solution directory, as I've done here (this shows the file in VS Code).

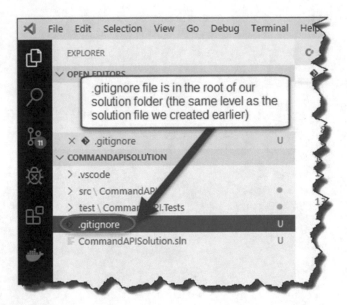

Figure 5-18. *Our .gitignore file*

Type git status again, and you should see this file now as one of the "untracked" files also.

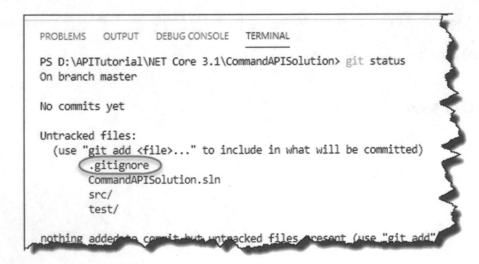

Figure 5-19. *Untracked .gitignore file*

Track and Commit Your Files

OK, we want to track "everything" (except those files ignored!); to do so, type (ensure you put the trailing period ".")

git add .

Followed by

git status

You should see the following.

```
PS D:\APITutorial\NET Core 3.1\CommandAPISolution> git add .
warning: LF will be replaced by CRLF in src/CommandAPI/appsettings.Development.json.
The file will have its original line endings in your working directory
PS D:\APITutorial\NET Core 3.1\CommandAPISolution> git status
On branch master

No commits yet

Changes to be committed:
  (use "git rm --cached <file>..." to unstage)
        new file:    .gitignore
        new file:    CommandAPISolution.sln
        new file:    src/CommandAPI/CommandAPI.csproj
        new file:    src/CommandAPI/Controllers/CommandsController.cs
        new file:    src/CommandAPI/Program.cs
        new file:    src/CommandAPI/Properties/launchSettings.json
        new file:    src/CommandAPI/Startup.cs
        new file:    src/CommandAPI/appsettings.Development.json
        new file:    src/CommandAPI/appsettings.json
        new file:    test/CommandAPI.Tests/CommandAPI.Tests.csproj
        new file:    test/CommandAPI.Tests/UnitTest1.cs
```

Figure 5-20.   *Tracked Files ready for Commit*

These files are being tracked and are "staged" for commit.

Finally, we want to "commit" the changes (essentially lock them in) by typing

git commit -m "Initial Commit"

This commits the code with a note (or "message"; hence the -m switch) about that particular commit. You typically use this to describe the changes or additions you have made to the code (more about this later); you should see the following.

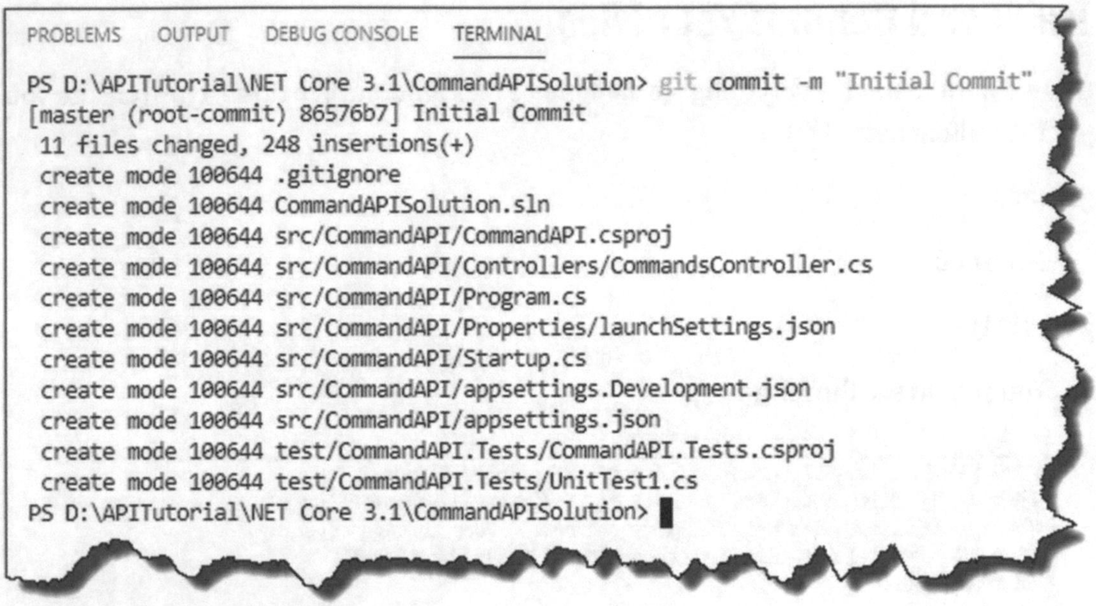

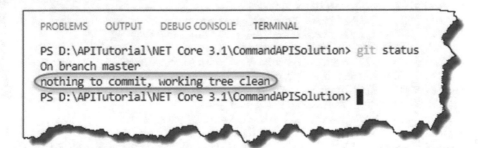

Figure 5-21. *Committed Files*

A quick additional git status and you should see the following.

```
PROBLEMS    OUTPUT    DEBUG CONSOLE    TERMINAL
PS D:\APITutorial\NET Core 3.1\CommandAPISolution> git status
On branch master
nothing to commit, working tree clean
PS D:\APITutorial\NET Core 3.1\CommandAPISolution>
```

Figure 5-22. *No further changes have occurred*

🎂 **Celebration Checkpoint**   Good job! We have basically placed our solution under *local* source control and have committed all our "changes" to our master branch in our first commit.

⚠ If this is the first time you've seen or used Git, I'd suggest you pause reading here and do a bit of Googling to find some additional resources. It's a fairly big subject on its own, and I don't want to cover it in depth here, mainly because I'd be repeating noncore content.

I will of course cover the necessary amount of Git to get the job done in this tutorial; further reading is purely optional!

The Git website also allows you to download the full *Pro Git* ebook; you can find that here: `https://git-scm.com/book/en/v2`

Set Up Your GitHub Repo

OK so the last section took you through the creation of a local Git repository, and that's fine for tracking code changes on your local machine. However, if you're working as part of a larger team, or even as an individual programmer, and want to make use of Azure DevOps (as we will in Chapters 12, 13, and 14), we need to configure a "remote Git repository" that we will

- Push to from our local machine.

- Link to an Azure DevOps Build Pipeline to kick off the build process.

Jump over to `https://github.com` (and if you haven't already – sign up for an account); you should see your own landing page once you've created an account/logged in; here's mine.

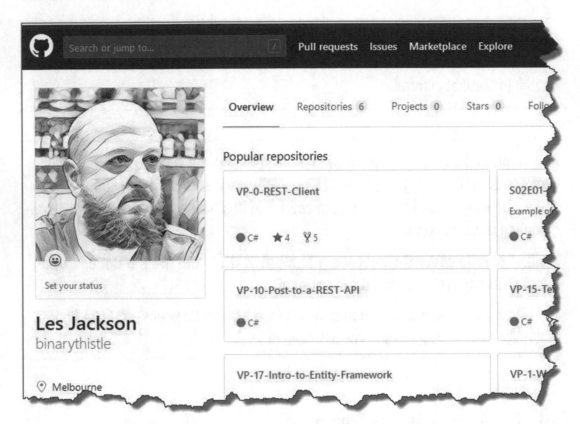

Figure 5-23. *GitHub Landing Page*

Create a GitHub Repository

In the top right-hand corner of the site, click on your face (or whatever the default image is if you're not a narcissist like me), and select "Your repositories."

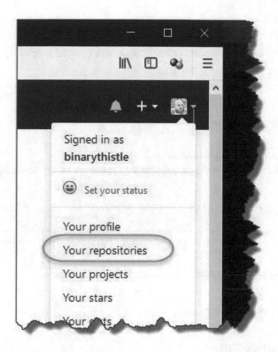

Figure 5-24. *Select your repositories*

Then click "New" and you should see the "Create a new repository" screen.

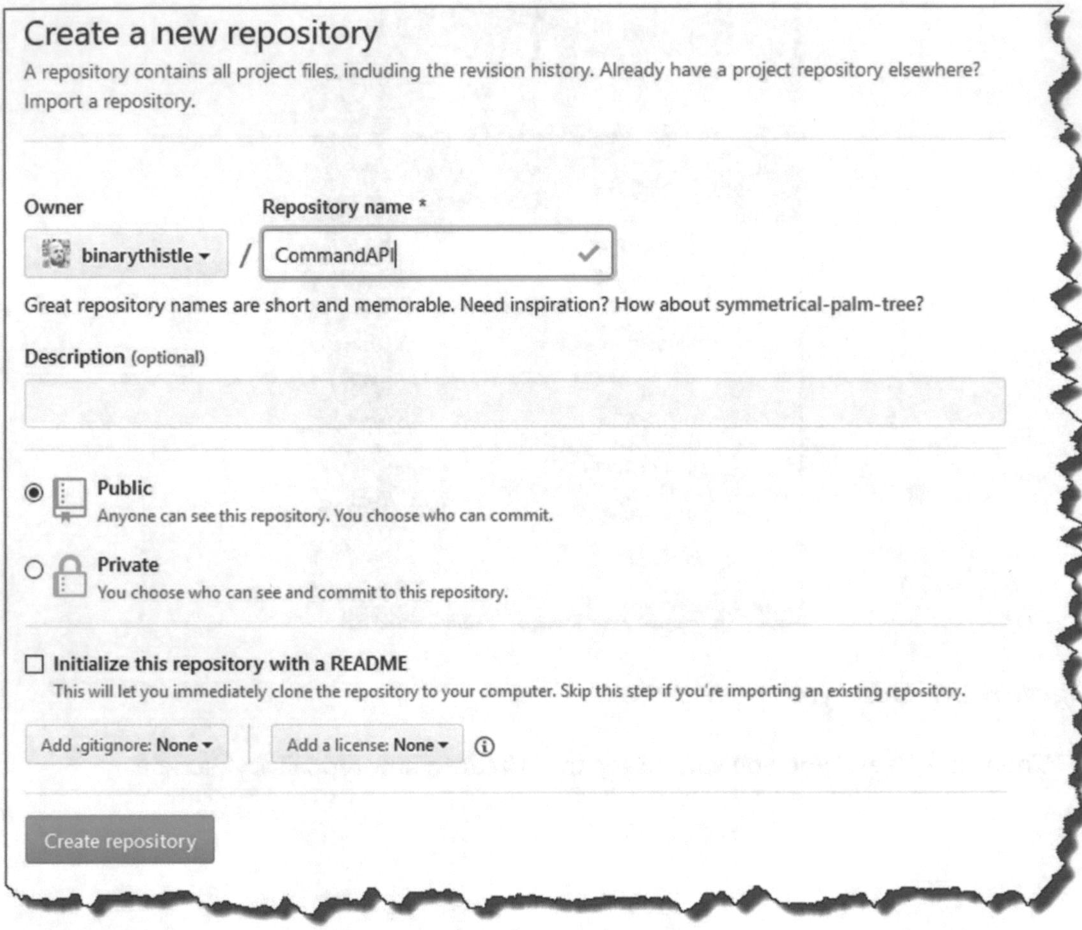

Figure 5-25. *Create your repository*

Give the repository a name (I just called mine ***CommandAPI***, but you can call it anything you like), and select either Public or Private. For this tutorial, I strongly recommend selecting *Public*, primarily as that's the option I've developed this tutorial with – and I know it works with the later sections of the book. Indeed, the option you select here is important as it has impacts when we come to set up our CI/CD pipeline in Chapter 12.

Then click "Create Repository"; you should see the following.

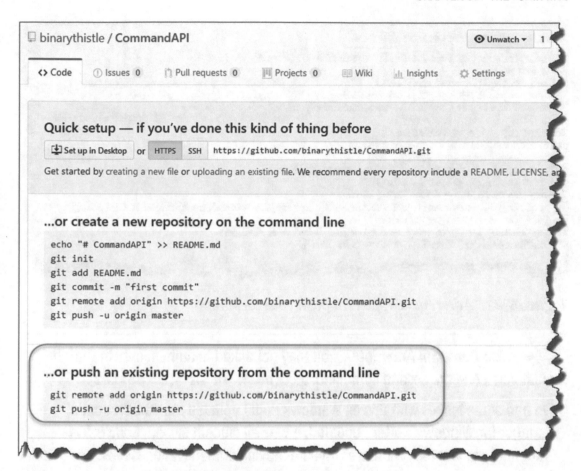

Figure 5-26. *GitHub repository created*

This page details how you can now link and push your local repository to this remote one (the section I've circled). So copy that text, and paste it into your terminal window (you need to make sure you're still in the root solution folder we were working in previously).

```
PROBLEMS   OUTPUT   DEBUG CONSOLE   TERMINAL

PS D:\APITutorial\NET Core 3.1\CommandAPISolution> git status
On branch master
nothing to commit, working tree clean
PS D:\APITutorial\NET Core 3.1\CommandAPISolution> git remote add origin https://github.com/binarythistl
PS D:\APITutorial\NET Core 3.1\CommandAPISolution> git push -u origin master
Enumerating objects: 19, done.
Counting objects: 100% (19/19), done.
Delta compression using up to 8 threads
Compressing objects: 100% (15/15), done.
Writing objects: 100% (19/19), 3.42 KiB | 876.00 KiB/s, done.
Total 19 (delta 2), reused 0 (delta 0)
remote: Resolving deltas: 100% (2/2), done.
To https://github.com/binarythistle/Complete-ASP.NET-Core-API-Tutorial-2nd-Edition-Net-Core-3.1.git
 * [new branch]      master -> master
Branch 'master' set up to track remote branch 'master' from 'origin'.
PS D:\APITutorial\NET Core 3.1\CommandAPISolution> █
```

Figure 5-27. *Add remote repo and push your local repo*

> **Les' Personal Anecdote**   You may get asked to authenticate to GitHub when you issue the second command: `git push -u origin master`.
>
> I've had some issues with this on Windows until I updated the "Git Credential Manager for Windows"; after I updated, it was all smooth sailing. Google "Git Credential Manager for Windows" if you're having authentication issues, and install the latest version!

So What Just Happened?

Well, in short

- We "registered" our remote GitHub repo with our local repo (first command).

- We then pushed our local repo up to GitHub (second command).

> **Note**   The first command line only needs to be issued once; the second one we'll be using more throughout the rest of the tutorial.

If you refresh your GitHub repository page, instead of seeing the instructions you just issued, you should see our solution!

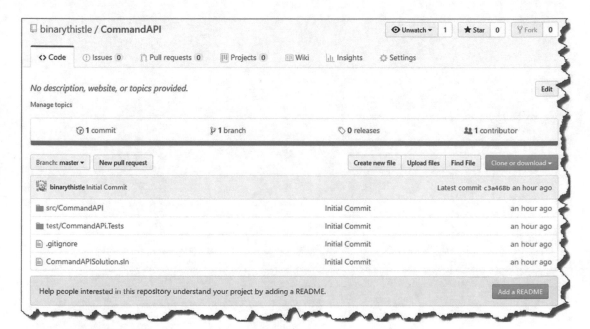

Figure 5-28.   *Our code is now on GitHub*

You'll notice "Initial Commit" as a comment against every file and folder – seem familiar?

Well that's it for this chapter – great job!

CHAPTER 6

Our Model and Repository

Chapter Summary

In this chapter we're going to introduce "data" to our API, so we'll begin our journey with our Model and Repository classes.

When Done, You Will

- Understand what a "Model" class is and code one up.

- Define our Repository Interface, and implement a "mock" instance of it.

- Understand how we use *Dependency Injection* to decouple interfaces from implementation.

Our Model

OK so we've done the "Controller" part of the MVC pattern (well a bit of it; it's still not fully complete – but the groundwork is in), so let's turn our attention to the Model part of the equation.

Just like our Controller, the first thing we want to do is create a *Models* folder in our main project directory.

Once you've done that, create a file in that folder, and name it *Command.cs*; your directory and file structure should look like this.

© Les Jackson 2020
L. Jackson, *The Complete ASP.NET Core 3 API Tutorial*, https://doi.org/10.1007/978-1-4842-6255-9_6

Figure 6-1. *Model Folder and Command Class*

Once created, lets code up our "Command" model – it's super simple and when done should look like this:

```
namespace CommandAPI.Models
{
    public class Command
    {
        public int Id {get; set;}
        public string HowTo {get; set;}
        public string Platform {get; set;}
        public string CommandLine {get; set;}
    }
}
```

As promised, very simple; just be sure that you've specified the correct namespace at the top of the code:

```
CommandAPI.Models
```

The rest of the class is a simplistic model that we'll use to "model" our command-line snippets. Possibly the only thing really of note is the Id attribute.

This will form the Primary Key when we eventually create a table in our PostgreSQL DB (noting this is required by Entity Framework Core.)

Additionally, it conforms to the concept of "Convention over Configuration." That is, we could have named this attribute differently, but it would potentially require further configuration so that Entity Framework could work with it as a primary key attribute. Naming it this way, however, means that we don't *need* to do this.

Data Annotations

We could leave our model class like that, but when we come to working with it, especially for creation and update actions, we want to ensure that we specify the properties of our Model that are mandatory and those that are not. For example, would there be any value in adding a command-line snippet to our solution without specifying some data for our CommandLine property? Probably not. We solve this by adding some *Data Annotations* to our class.

We can decorate our class properties with Data Annotations to specify things like

- Is it required or not?

- Maximum length of our strings

- Whether the property should be defined as Primary Key

- And so on.

In order to use them in the Command class, make the following updates to our code, making sure to include the using directive as shown:

```
using System.ComponentModel.DataAnnotations;

namespace CommandAPI.Models
{
    public class Command
    {
        [Key]
        [Required]
        public int Id {get; set;}

        [Required]
        [MaxLength(250)]
        public string HowTo {get; set;}
```

```csharp
        [Required]
        public string Platform {get; set;}

        [Required]
        public string CommandLine {get; set;}
    }
}
```

The Data Annotations added should be self-explanatory:

- All Properties are required (they cannot be null).

- Our Id property is a primary key.

- In addition, the HowTo property can only have a maximum of 250 characters.

With our annotations in place, when we come to creating an instance of our Model later, a validation error (or errors) will be thrown if any of them are not adhered to. They also provide a means by which to generate our database schema, which we'll come onto in Chapter 7.

As we have made a simple, yet significant, change to our code, let's add the file to source control, commit it, then push up to GitHub; to do so, issue the following commands in order (make sure you're in the Solution folder ***CommandAPISolution***):

```
git add .
git commit -m "Added Command Model to API Project"
git push origin master
```

You have used these all before, but to reiterate

- First command adds all files to our local Git repo (this means our new ***Command.cs*** file).

- Second command commits the code with a message.

- Third command pushes the commit up to GitHub.

If all worked correctly, you should see the commit has been pushed up to GitHub; see the following.

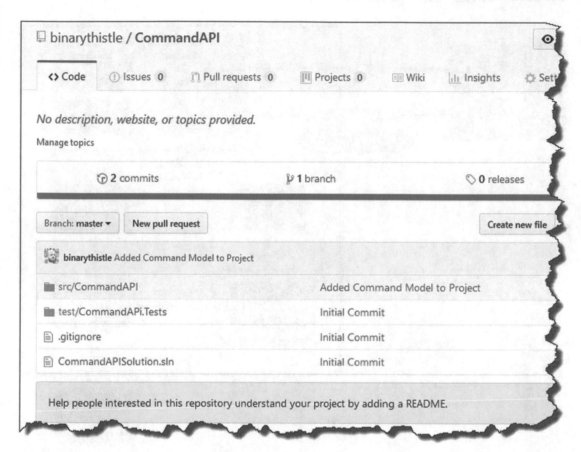

Figure 6-2. Our Committed Model Class

☞ **Learning Opportunity**   Looking at the GitHub page presented earlier, how can you tell which parts of our solution we included in the last commit and which were only included in the *initial commit*?

Our Repository

Taking a quick look back at our application architecture, I've outlined the components we've either started or, in the case of our Model, completed.

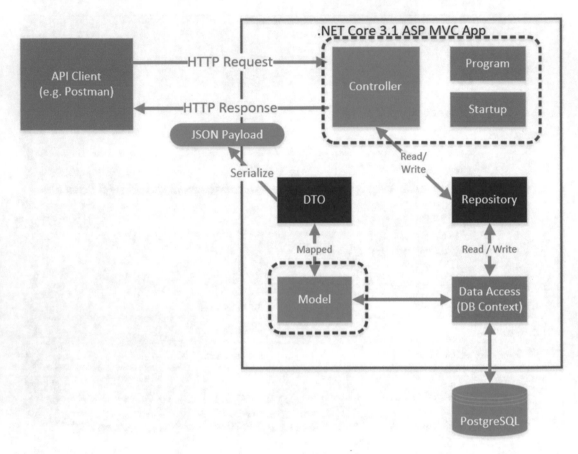

Figure 6-3. *Progress through our architecture*

It's all still a bit disjointed; to review we have

- Started our Controller that currently returns hard coded data

- Created our Model

The next step in our journey is to define our *Repository Interface,* which will provide our controller with a technology-agnostic way to obtain data.

What Is an Interface?

An interface is just as it sounds; it's a *specification* for *what* functionality we want it to provide (in this case to our Controller), but we don't detail *how* it will be provided – that comes later. It's essentially an agreement, or *contract*, with the consumer of that Interface.

When we think about what methods our Repository Interface *should* provide to our Controller (don't think about how yet), we can look back at out CRUD actions from Chapter 3 for some guidance.

Verb	URI	Operation	Description
GET	/api/commands	Read	Read all command resources
GET	/api/commands/{Id}	Read	Read a single resource (by Id)
POST	/api/commands	Create	Create a new resource
PUT	/api/commands/{Id}	Update (full)	Update all of a single resource (by Id)
PATCH	/api/commands/{Id}	Update (partial)	Update part of a single resource (by Id)
DELETE	/api/commands/{Id}	Delete	Delete a single resource (by Id)

In this case, they almost directly drive what out Repository should provide:

- Return a collection of all Commands.

- Return a single Command (based on its Id).

- Create a new Command Resource.

- Update an existing Command Resource (this covers PUT and PATCH).

- Delete an existing Command Resource.

To start implementing our Repository, back in the root our API Project (in the **CommandAPI** folder), create another folder and call it **Data** as shown here.

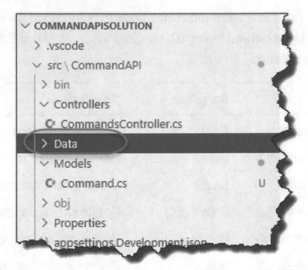

Figure 6-4. *Data Folder will hold our Repository Interface*

Inside this folder, create a file and name it ***ICommandAPIRepo.cs***.

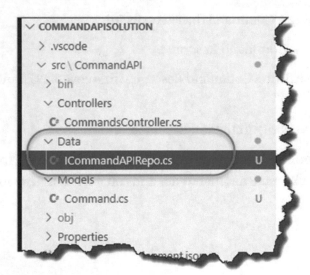

Figure 6-5. *Our ICommanderRepo.cs File*

Inside the file, add the following code:

```
using System.Collections.Generic;
using CommandAPI.Models;

namespace CommandAPI.Data
{
    public interface ICommandAPIRepo
    {
        bool SaveChanges();

        IEnumerable<Command> GetAllCommands();
        Command GetCommandById(int id);
        void CreateCommand(Command cmd);
        void UpdateCommand(Command cmd);
        void DeleteCommand(Command cmd);
    }
}
```

Your file should look like this; make sure you **save the file**, and let's take a look at what we have done.

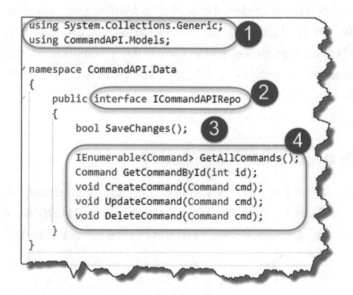

Figure 6-6. *ICommandAPIRepo Interface*

1. Using directives, noting that we have brought in the namespace for our Models.

2. We specify a public `interface` and give it a name starting with capital "I" to denote it's an interface.

3. We specify that our Repository should provide a "Save Changes" method; stick a pin in that for now, we'll revisit when we come to talking about Entity Framework Core in Chapter 7.

4. Section 4 defines all the other method signatures that consumers of this interface can use to obtain and manipulate data. They also serve another purpose, which I detail in the section below.

What About Implementation?

That's our Repository Interface complete. Yes, that's right; it's done, fully complete. So, your next question (well it was my next question when I was learning about interfaces), will be: OK, but where does stuff "get done"?

Great question!

Again, to labor the point, our interface is just a specification (or a contract) for our consumers. We still need to *implement* that contract with a *concrete class*. And this is the power and the beauty of using interfaces: we can create multiple *implementations* (concrete classes) to provide the same interface, but the consumer doesn't know, or care, about the implementation being used. All they care about is the interface and what it ultimately provides to them.

Still confused? Let's move to an example.

Our Mock Repository Implementation

We are going to create a concrete class that implements our interface using our model; however, we'll just be using "mock" data at this stage (we'll create another implementation of our interface to use "real" data in the next chapter).

So, in the same **Data** folder where we placed our repository interface definition, create a new file called **MockCommandAPIRepo.cs**, and add the following code:

```
using System.Collections.Generic;
using CommandAPI.Models;

namespace CommandAPI.Data
{
    public class MockCommandAPIRepo : ICommandAPIRepo
    {

    }
}
```

You should see something like this in your editor.

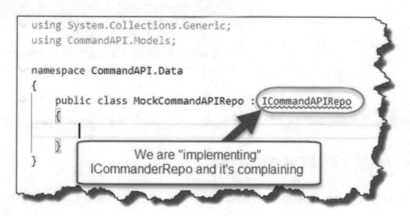

Figure 6-7. *Our Concrete Class Definition is complaining*

We have created a public class definition and specified that we want it to implement ICommanderRepo, as denoted by

: ICommanderRepo

And we can see that it's complaining; this is because we haven't "implemented" anything yet. If you're using VS Code or Visual Studio, place your cursor in the complaining section and press

CTRL + .

This will bring up some helpful suggestions on resolution; we want to select the first option "Implement Interface," as shown in the next figure.

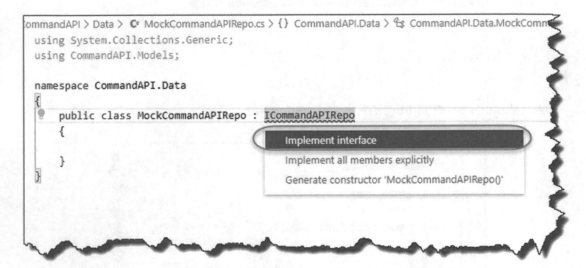

Figure 6-8. *Help is always appreciated!*

This should then generate some placeholder implementation code for our class.

```csharp
using System.Collections.Generic;
using CommandAPI.Models;

namespace CommandAPI.Data
{
    public class MockCommandAPIRepo : ICommandAPIRepo
    {
        public void CreateCommand(Command cmd)
        {
            throw new System.NotImplementedException();
        }

        public void DeleteCommand(Command cmd)
        {
            throw new System.NotImplementedException();
        }

        public IEnumerable<Command> GetAllCommands()
        {
            throw new System.NotImplementedException();
        }

        public Command GetCommandById(int id)
        {
            throw new System.NotImplementedException();
        }

        public bool SaveChanges()
        {
            throw new System.NotImplementedException();
        }

        public void UpdateCommand(Command cmd)
        {
            throw new System.NotImplementedException();
        }
    }
}
```

We're only going to write code for these

Figure 6-9. *Auto-generated Implementation code*

As you can see, it has provided all the method signatures for the members of our interface and populated them with a `throw new System.NotImpementedException();`

In our example we're only going to update our two "read" methods:

- `GetAllCommands`

- `GetCommandById`

This is enough to demonstrate the core concepts of using interfaces and by extension *Dependency Injection*. So, in those two methods, add the following code as shown below, remembering to save your work when done:

```
.
.
.
public IEnumerable<Command> GetAllCommands(){
  var commands = new List<Command>
  {
    new Command{
      Id=0, HowTo="How to generate a migration",
      CommandLine="dotnet ef migrations add <Name of Migration>",
      Platform=".Net Core EF"},
    new Command{
      Id=1, HowTo="Run Migrations",
      CommandLine="dotnet ef database update",
      Platform=".Net Core EF"},
    new Command{
      Id=2, HowTo="List active migrations",
      CommandLine="dotnet ef migrations list",
      Platform=".Net Core EF"}
  };
  return commands;
}

public Command GetCommandById(int id){
  return new Command{
    Id=0, HowTo="How to generate a migration",
    CommandLine="dotnet ef migrations add <Name of Migration>",
```

```
        Platform=".Net Core EF"};
}
    .
    .
    .
```

What this does is take our Model class and use it to create some simple mock data (again just hard-coded) and return it when these two methods are called. Not earth-shattering, but it is an implementation (of sorts) of our repository interface.

We now need to move on to making use of the ICommandAPIRepo interface (and by extension the MockCommandAPIRepo concrete class) from within our controller.

To do this we use Dependency Injection.

Dependency Injection

Dependency Injection (DI) has struck fear into many a developer getting to grips with it (myself included), but once you grasp the concept, not only is it pretty straightforward, it's also really powerful and you'll *want* to use it.

What makes it even easier in this instance is that DI is baked right into the heart of ASP.NET Core, so we can get up and running with it quickly without much fuss at all. Next, I'll take you through a quick theoretical overview; then we'll employ DI practically in our project (indeed, we'll continue to use it throughout the tutorial).

Again, as with many of the concepts and technologies in this tutorial, you could fill an entire book on DI, which I'm not going to attempt to do here. If you want a deep dive on this subject beyond what I outline below, the MSDN docs are decent[1].

Back to the Start (Up)

To talk about DI in .NET Core, we need to move back to our Startup class and in particular the ConfigureServices method.

---

[1]https://docs.microsoft.com/en-us/aspnet/core/fundamentals/dependency-injection?view=aspnetcore-3.1

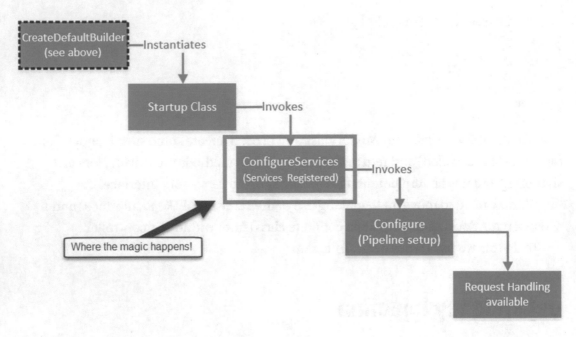

Figure 6-10. *Startup Class Sequence*

Casting your mind back, it is in the ConfigureServices method where our "services" are registered (in this case think of a service as *both* an interface and an implementation of it). But what exactly do we mean by *register*?

When we talk about registering services, what we are really talking about is something called a Service Container; this is where we "register" our services. Or to put it another way, this is where we tell the DI system to associate an interface to a given concrete class. See the following diagram.

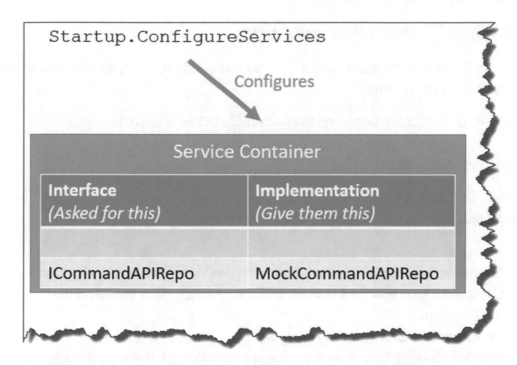

Figure 6-11. *Service Container with our Repository Service Registered*

Once we have registered our service in the Service Container, whenever we request to make use of a given interface from somewhere else in our app, the DI system will serve up, or "inject," the concrete class we've associated with the interface (aka the "dependency") in its place.

This means that if we ever need to swap out our concrete class for some other implementation, we only need to make the change in one place (the ConfigureServices method); the rest of our code does not need to change.

We will follow this practice in this tutorial by first registering our mock repository implementation against the ICommandAPIRepo interface; then we'll swap it out for something more useful in the next chapter without the need to change any other code (except the registration).

This decoupling of interface (contract) from implementation means that our code is infinitely more maintainable as it grows larger.

Enough theory; let's code.

Applying Dependency Injection

Back over in our API Project, open the Startup class, and add the following code to our ConfigureServices method:

```
public void ConfigureServices(IServiceCollection services)
{
  services.AddControllers();

  //Add the code below
  services.AddScoped<ICommandAPIRepo, MockCommandAPIRepo>();
}
```

The code is quite straightforward; it uses the service collection: services, to register our ICommandAPIRepo with MockCommandAPIRepo. The only other novelty is the use of the AddScoped method.

This has to do with something called "Service Lifetimes," which in essence tells the DI system how it should provision a service requested via DI; there are three methods available:

- **AddTransient**: A service is created each time it is requested from the Service Container.

- **AddScoped**: A service is created once per client request (connection).

- **AddSingleton**: A service is created once and reused.

Beyond what I've just outlined, I feel we may get ourselves off track from our core subject matter: building an API! So, we'll leave it there for now; again refer to Microsoft Docs as mentioned earlier if you want more info.

OK, so now that we have registered our service, the next step is to make use of it from within our Controller – how do we do that?

Constructor Dependency Injection

If I'm being honest, it was this next bit that tripped me up when I was learning DI, so I'll try and be a as clear as I can when describing how it works.

We can't just "new-up" an interface in the same way that we can with regular classes; see Figure 6-12.

```
using System.Collections.Generic;
using CommandAPI.Data;
using Microsoft.AspNetCore.Mvc;

namespace CommandAPI.Controllers
{
    [Route("api/[controller]")]                    We can't "new-up" an Interface.
    [ApiController]
    public class CommandsController : ControllerBase
    {
        private readonly ICommandAPIRepo _repository = new ICommandAPIRepo();

        [HttpGet]
        public ActionResult<IEnumerable<string>> Get()
        {
            return new string[] {"this", "is", "hard", "coded"};
        }
    }
}
```

Figure 6-12. *You can't write this code!*

You will get an error along the lines of "Can't create an instance of an abstract class or interface." You could revert to "newing-up" a concrete instance of our MockCommandAPIRepo class, but that would defeat the entire purpose of what we have just been talking about. So how do we do it?

The answer is that we have to give the DI system an *entry point* where it can perform the "injection of the dependency," which in this case, it means creating a class constructor for our Controller and providing ICommandAPIRepo as a required input parameter. We call this *Constructor Dependency Injection*.

ℹ   Pay very careful attention to the *Constructor Dependency Injection* code pattern that follows; as you'll see, this pattern is used time and time again throughout our code as well as in other projects.

Let's implement this. Move back over to our API project, and open our CommandsController class, and add the following constructor code (make sure you add the new using statement too):

```
// Remember this using statement
using CommandAPI.Data;
.
.
.
namespace CommandAPI.Controllers
{
  [Route("api/[controller]")]
  [ApiController]
  public class CommandsController : ControllerBase
  {
    //Add the following code to our class

    private readonly ICommandAPIRepo _repository;

    public CommandsController(ICommandAPIRepo repository)
    {
      _repository = repository;
    }
.
.
.
```

Let's go through what's happening.

```
using System.Collections.Generic;
using CommandAPI.Data;      1
using Microsoft.AspNetCore.Mvc;

namespace CommandAPI.Controllers
{
    [Route("api/[controller]")        ICommandAPIRepo -> MockCommandAPIRepo
    [ApiController]
    public class CommandsController : ControllerBase
    {                                                          4
      2  private readonly ICommandAPIRepo _repository;

   3   public CommandsController(ICommandAPIRepo repository)
       {
           _repository = repository;  5
       }
    }
       [HttpGet]
```

Figure 6-13. *Constructor Dependency Injection Pattern*

1. Add the new using statement to reference ICommandAPIRepo.

2. We create a private read-only field _repository that will be assigned the injected MockCommandAPIRepo object in our constructor and used throughout the rest of our code.

3. The Class constructor will be called when we want to make use of our Controller.

4. At the point when the constructor is called, the DI system will spring into action and inject the required dependency when we ask for an instance of ICommandAPIRepo. This is *Constructor Dependency Injection.*

5. We assign the injected dependency (in this case MockCommandAPIRepo) to our private field (see point 1).

And that's pretty much it! We can then use _repository to make use of our concrete implementation class, in this case MockCommandAPIRepo.

As I've stated earlier, we'll reuse this pattern multiple times through the rest of the tutorial; you'll also see it everywhere in code in other projects – take note.

Update Our Controller

We'll wrap up this chapter by implementing our two "Read" API controller actions using the mock repository implementation we have. So just to be clear we'll be implementing the following endpoints.

Verb	URI	Operation	Description
GET	/api/commands	Read	Read all command resources
GET	/api/commands/{Id}	Read	Read a single resource (by Id)

We'll start with implementing the endpoint that returns a collection of all our command resources, so move back into our Controller, and first **remove** our existing controller action.

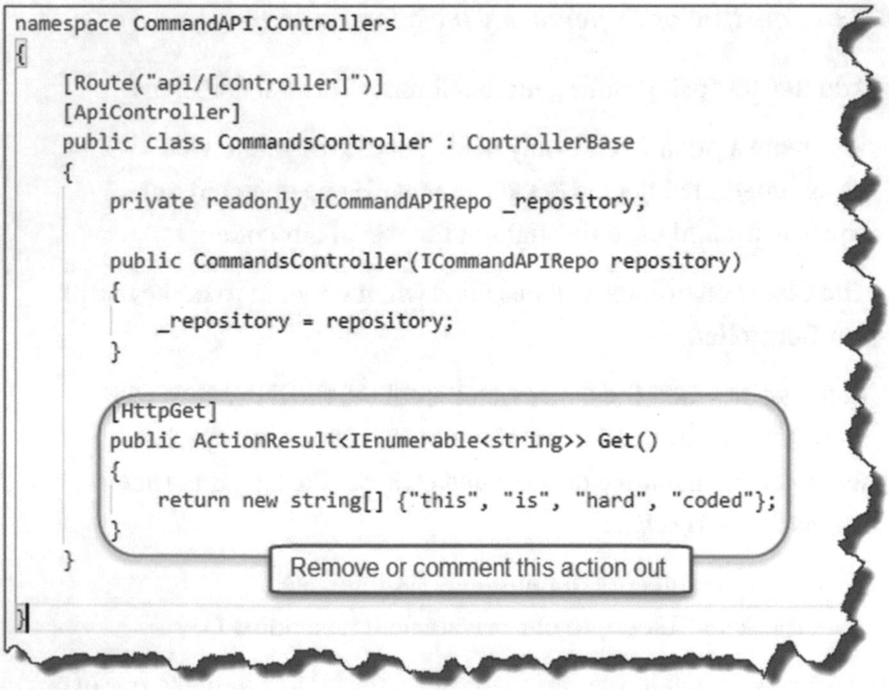

```
namespace CommandAPI.Controllers
{
    [Route("api/[controller]")]
    [ApiController]
    public class CommandsController : ControllerBase
    {
        private readonly ICommandAPIRepo _repository;

        public CommandsController(ICommandAPIRepo repository)
        {
            _repository = repository;
        }

        [HttpGet]
        public ActionResult<IEnumerable<string>> Get()
        {
            return new string[] {"this", "is", "hard", "coded"};
        }
    }
}
```

Remove or comment this action out

Figure 6-14. *Removal of our old Controller Action*

In its place, add the following code, remembering to add the required using statement at the top of the class too:

```
// Remember this using statement
using CommandAPI.Models;
.
.
.
namespace CommandAPI.Controllers
{
  [Route("api/[controller]")]
  [ApiController]
  public class CommandsController : ControllerBase
  {
    private readonly ICommandAPIRepo _repository;

    public CommandsController(ICommandAPIRepo repository)
    {
      _repository = repository;
    }

    //Add the following code
    [HttpGet]
    public ActionResult<IEnumerable<Command>> GetAllCommands()
    {
      var commandItems = _repository.GetAllCommands();

      return Ok(commandItems);
    }
.
.
.
```

I think the code is relatively straightforward but let's just step through it.

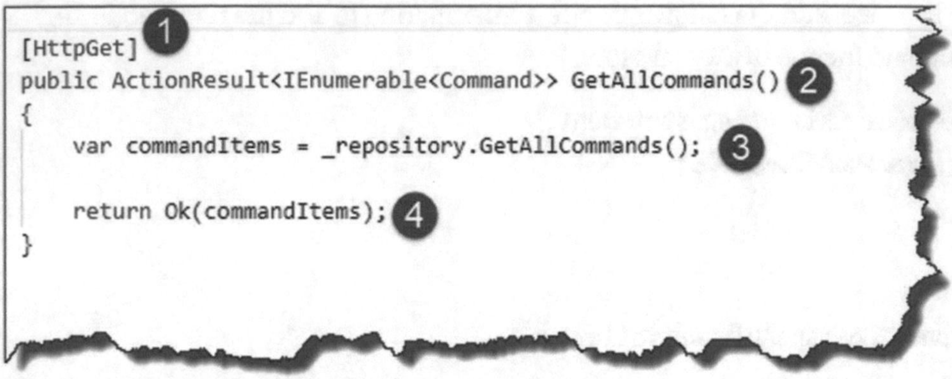

```
[HttpGet]                    1
public ActionResult<IEnumerable<Command>> GetAllCommands()  2
{
    var commandItems = _repository.GetAllCommands();  3

    return Ok(commandItems);  4
}
```

Figure 6-15. *New Controller Action using our Repository*

1. The controller action responds to the GET verb.

2. The controller action should return an enumeration
    (IEnumerable) of Command objects.

3. We call GetAllCommands on our repository and populate a local
    variable with the result.

4. We return a HTTP 200 Result (OK) and pass back our result set.

Make sure you save everything, run your code, and call the endpoint from Postman.

Figure 6-16. Successful API Endpoint Result

1. Verb set to GET.

2. Our URI is exactly the same as the one we have used before.

3. We get a 200 OK status result.

4. We have the hardcoded data returned from our mock repository!

🎂 **Celebration Checkpoint**   This is actually a really important checkpoint! We have implemented our repository interface, created and used a concrete (mock) implementation of it, and used it in our Controller via Dependency Injection!

Give yourself five gold stars and a pat on the back.

We have one more controller action to implement in this section: returning a single resource by supplying its Id. Back over in the Controller, add the following code to implement:

.
.
.

```
[HttpGet]
public ActionResult<IEnumerable<Command>> GetAllCommands()
{
  var commandItems = _repository.GetAllCommands();
  return Ok(commandItems);
}

//Add the following code for our second ActionResult
[HttpGet("{id}")]
public ActionResult<Command> GetCommandById(int id)
{
  var commandItem = _repository.GetCommandById(id);
  if (commandItem == null)
  {
    return NotFound();
  }
  return Ok(commandItem);
}
```

.
.
.

There's a bit more going on here; let's review.

```
[HttpGet("{id}")]  ①                                    ②
public ActionResult<Command> GetCommandById(int id)
{
    var commandItem = _repository.GetCommandById(id); ③
    if (commandItem == null)
    {
        return NotFound(); ④
    }
    return Ok(commandItem); ⑤
}
```

Figure 6-17. *GetCommandByID endpoint*

1. The route to this controller action includes an additional route parameter, in this case the Id of the resource we want to retrieve; we can specify this in the HttpGet attribute as shown.

2. The controller action requires an id to be passed in as a parameter (this comes from our route; see point 1) and returns an ActionResult of type Command.

3. We call GetCommandByID on our repository passing in the Id from our route, storing the result in a local variable.

4. We check to see if our result is null and, if so, return a 404 Not Found result.

5. Otherwise if we have a Command object, we return a 200 OK and the result.

Note   Our mock repository will always return a result irrespective of what Id we pass in, so the null check will never return false in this case. That will change when we come to our "real" repository implementation in Chapter 7.

Let's check our code by testing it in Postman; note that the route we'll require is

/api/commands/**n**

where **n** is an integer value.

Figure 6-18. *Single Command Resource Returned*

1. We're still using a GET request.

2. Our URI has changed to reflect the route we need to use to hit our endpoint.

3. 200 OK Status Retrieved.

4. Single Resource returned.

We'll wrap this chapter up here for now as we've covered a lot of ground, but we will revisit these two controller actions later when we come on to discussing Entity Framework Core, Data Transfer Objects, and Unit Testing.

Before we finish here though, remember to save everything and (ensuring you're in the main *solution* folder **CommandAPISolution**):

- `git add .`

- `git commit -m "Added Model and Mock Repository"`

- `git push origin master`

to update our Git repository (local and remote) with our changes.

In the next chapter, we move on to using "real" data that's persisted in a database backend rather than relying on hard-coded mock data.

CHAPTER 7

Persisting Our Data

Chapter Summary

In this chapter we'll move away from mock data and implement our data access and persistence layers to store and retrieve data in a PostgreSQL database.

When Done, You Will

- Have configured a PostgreSQL instance (including setting up a new instance in Docker if required)

- Have created a Database Context (DB Context) class using Entity Framework Core

- Have used "migrations" to create the necessary schema in our database

- Have created a new implementation of our repository interface to use our DB Context

- Have used Dependency Injection to swap out our mock repository for our DB Context version

We have a lot to cover so let's get cracking!

Architecture Progress Check

Before we move on with all of the given learning points, let's just check where we are in terms of progressing our application architecture. In the following diagram, I've outlined the components we've either started work on or in some cases completed altogether.

© Les Jackson 2020
L. Jackson, *The Complete ASP.NET Core 3 API Tutorial*, https://doi.org/10.1007/978-1-4842-6255-9_7

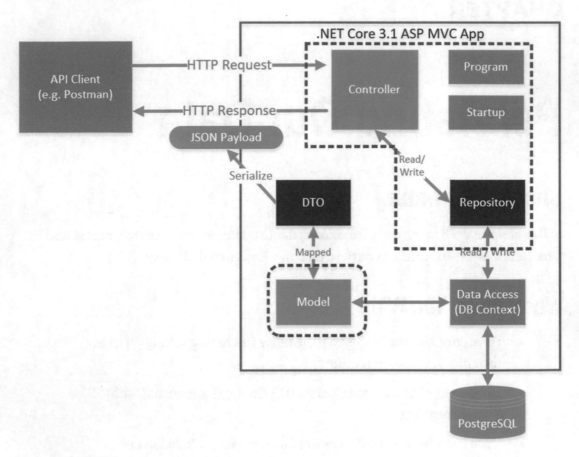

Figure 7-1. *Application Architecture Progress*

To review

- Our Model is completed.

- Our repository interface definition is complete.

- We've implemented a mock instance of our repository interface to return mock *Model* data.

- We've used constructor dependency injection in our controller to use our repository to implement our 2 GET controller actions. These both return mocked *Model* data.

We want to tie this altogether with a Database, DB Context, and an updated instance of our repository so we can work with real dynamic data that persists over time. So, what are we waiting for?

PostgreSQL Database

Before moving on to writing our DB Context, I first want to make sure we have an instance of PostgreSQL up and running and configured correctly.

Using Docker

Now, I'm going to use Docker to run my instance of PostgreSQL on my development machine, so if you've chosen that approach too (or you want to see how easy it is to spin up an instance), read on. If you've already got a PostgreSQL instance running, you can skip to the Connecting with DBeaver section.

Ensuring you have Docker installed and running (see Chapter 2) at a command prompt; simply type

```
docker run --name some-postgres -e POSTGRES_PASSWORD=mysecretpassword -p
5432:5432 -d postgres
```

Note   This is all on one line.

Assuming you have Docker installed and it's running (I don't like having Docker Desktop run automatically at startup, so I manually start it when needed), you should see the following.

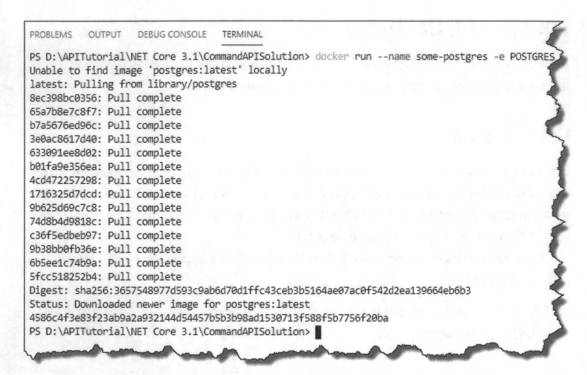

Figure 7-2. *PostgreSQL Image Downloaded and Running*

If this is the first time you've run this command, you'll see that Docker is "Unable to find image" locally, so it pulls one down from Docker Hub. Typing

```
docker ps
```

should show you the number of running containers.

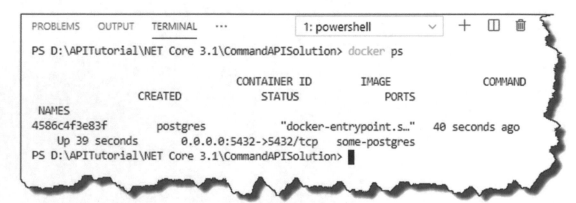

Figure 7-3. *The Docker PS Command*

Here, you can see that we have one, which should be our PostgreSQL instance.

Just before I take you through the command, we just issued in a bit more detail; if you installed the Docker plugin for VS Code, you should see something like this.

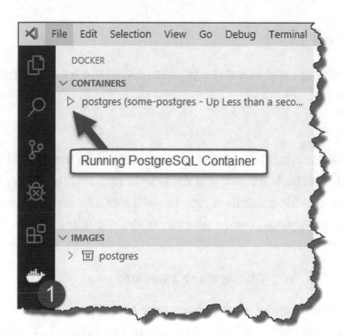

Figure 7-4. *Container Status in VS Code*

From here, you can stop the running container (right-click any entry in the containers box), and start it again, etc. You will also see that it lists the available images you have on your machine.

ℹ️   When you execute the "`docker run`" command again, assuming there isn't a later version of the PostgreSQL image on Docker Hub, Docker will not attempt to download a new image; it will simply use the cached copy locally available to you.

Docker Command Prompt

Just so you understand what's happening, let's just set through each of the command line arguments:

```
docker run
```

- Simple enough, this is just the primary command we use to run a container.

```
--name
```

- By default, a running Docker container will just be identified by an ID; this is OK, but when you come to issuing start and stop commands at the command line, these IDs can be cumbersome and prone to mistyping. The `-- name` argument just allows you to "name" your container.

```
-e POSTGRES_PASSWORD=mysecretpassword
```

- The `-e` argument just means that we are supplying one or more "environment variables" into the container at startup. In this case, we are setting the password for the default user: postgres.

```
-p [internal port] : [external port]
```

- The `-p` argument is REALLY important – this is our port mapping. Without going into too much detail, a container will usually have an "internal" port, and we need to map an "external" port through to it in order for us to connect. Here, the internal port our PostgreSQL is listening on is the standard 5432 PostgreSQL port, and we're just mapping externally to that same port number.

```
-d
```

- This argument just tells docker to run "detached," meaning that the command prompt is returned to us for subsequent use.

```
postgres
```

- This last argument is just the name of the image we want from Docker Hub.

If we go to `https://hub.docker.com/` and click "Explore" near the top of the screen, you'll get a list of the most popular Docker images available. These are most usually images provided by the vendor of the product in question.

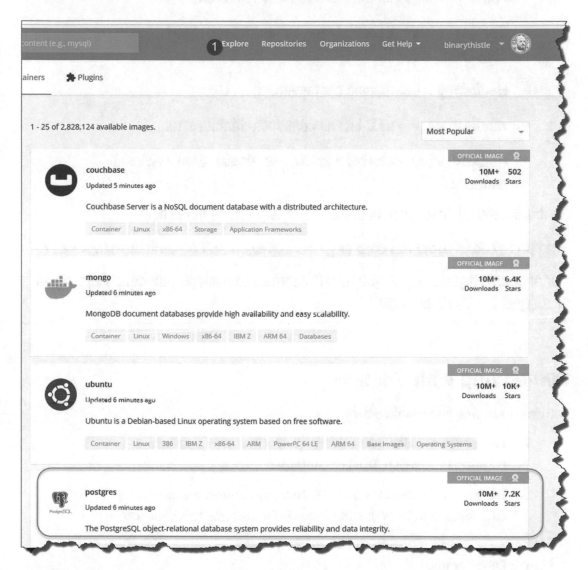

Figure 7-5. *Postgres Image on Docker Hub*

Here, you can see that Postgres is among the most popular image downloads.

ℹ   The other Docker commands you're likely to use are

- **docker start <container Id or Name>**: Start an existing container.

- **docker ps**: List running containers.

- **docker ps - -all**: List all containers that *have* run.

- **docker stop <container Id or Name>**: Stop a running container.

A more detailed description of these and others can be found here:

`https://docs.docker.com/engine/reference/commandline/docker/`

Or of course if you prefer a "graphical" interface to manage your containers, again I suggest the VS Code plugin.

Connecting with DBeaver

Before continuing you should either

1.   Have followed along with the given Docker steps and have a running PostgreSQL Docker container

2.   Have an instance of PostgreSQL running somewhere else that you can connect to from the machine you're running the API code on

Now, we want to connect in and see what we have.
Open DBeaver and

1.   Click the New Connection icon.

2.   Select PostgreSQL.

3.   Click Next.

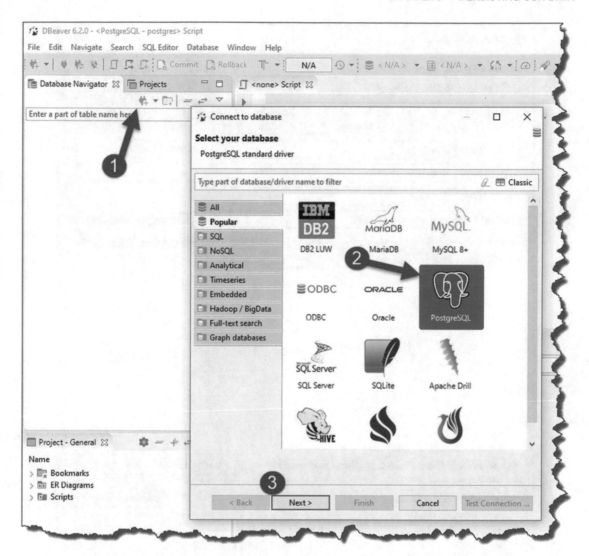

Figure 7-6. *PostgreSQL Connection in DBeaver*

You'll then be presented with the Connection Configuration settings for PostgreSQL. On the Main tab, enter the details as appropriate for you; note that the details I have here are good for the PostgreSQL instance I have running in Docker (localhost is fine for the host).

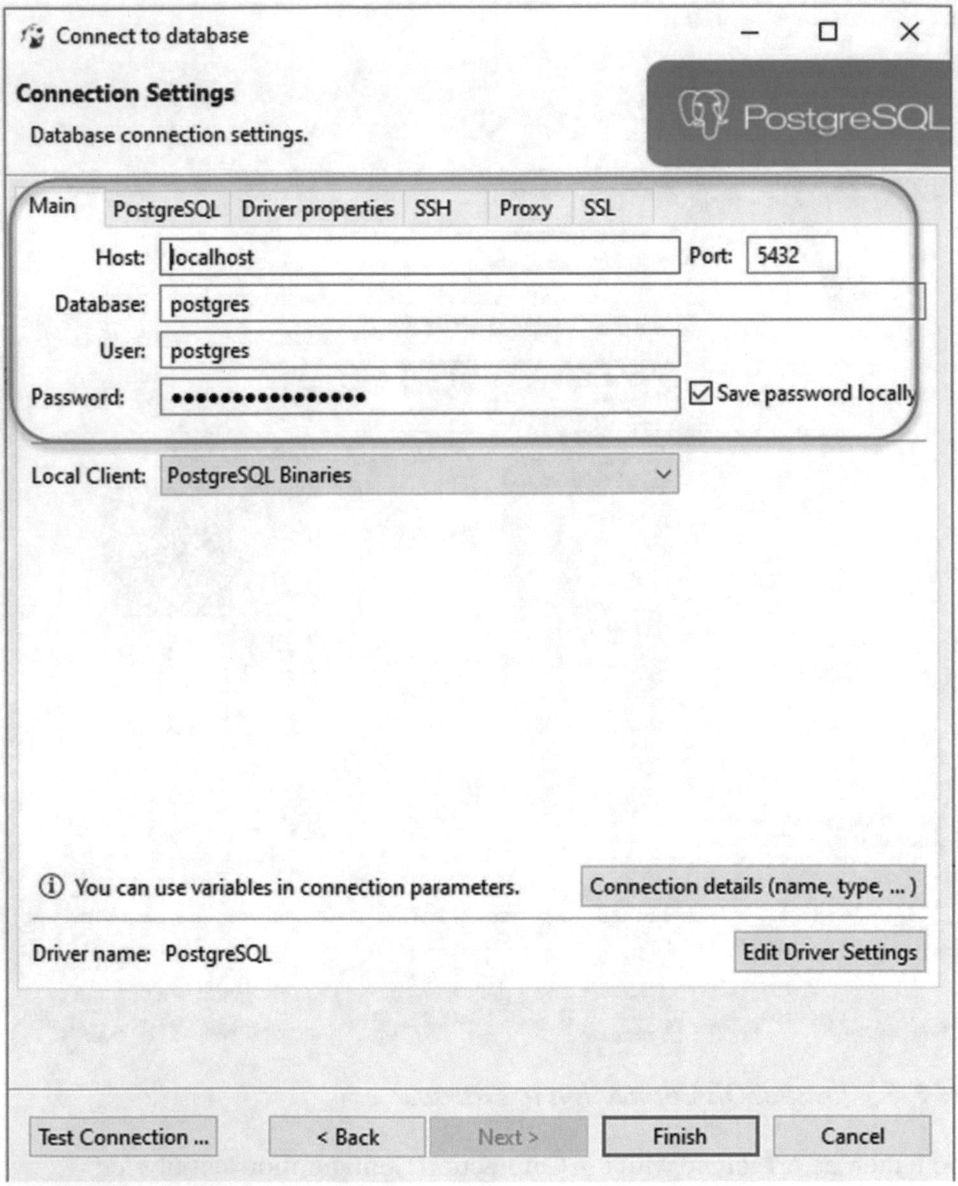

Figure 7-7. Connecting to PostgreSQL

Then move over to the PostgreSQL tab and tick "Show all databases."

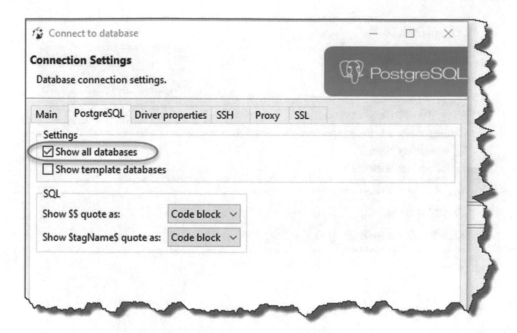

Figure 7-8. *Tick Show All Databases*

I'd then suggest you test the connection by clicking the "Test Connection..." button.

Figure 7-9. *Test Connection before moving on*

Assuming the connection is successful, you should see something like this.

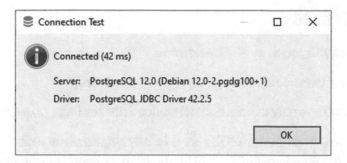

Figure 7-10. *Test Connection Successful*

You should be OK to click "Finish"; this will add your connection to the main DBeaver environment.

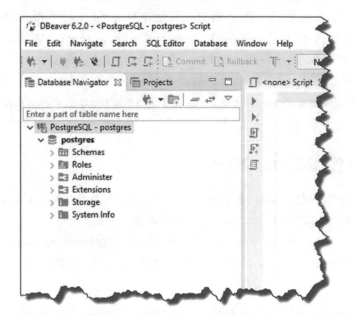

Figure 7-11. *PostgreSQL Connection in DB Beaver*

Here, you can see we have connected to the default database **postgres**; don't worry, we'll be creating our own database for our API later.

Connection Issues

Connection issues will most usually be down to

- Incorrect user credentials (username or password)

- Incorrect/wrongly configured network attributes (e.g., firewalls, etc.)

If you're running your PostgreSQL server locally on the same machine as your code environment, you can usually avoid all the pain of a "remote" database. If you are running your database on a separate machine or even in a virtual machine, issues here are almost always due to firewall or other network settings. I'm afraid I don't have the space to troubleshoot that here; in fact, it's one of the reasons I recommend Docker as I've spent many an unhappy hour troubleshooting exactly this!

The default "super user" for PostgreSQL is (not surprisingly) called **postgres**. Again, depending on how you installed, the server will depend on whether you set the password value for this. There are articles on how to reset this password (assuming you have administrator/root privileges on the machine you've installed on) if you get stuck.

Assuming you have successfully connected though, we can move on.

Entity Framework Core

Entity Framework Core (EF Core) is what's termed generically as an Object Relational Mapper (ORM), so what's that, and why should we use it?

To best answer that, I think you would look at the approach you'd need to take to reading and writing data to a database *without* the use of an ORM. In that case, you'd typically

- Need a (relatively low-level) working knowledge of the database schema.

- Have to write (vendor specific) SQL queries to manipulate the data set you wanted.

- Place your results into some kind of semi-proprietary result set object, ensure everything was mapped correctly (DB columns to your object attributes), and iterate through your results.

This all works, but it's a fairly manual process distracting developers from their core focus; surely there is a better way. Enter the ORM.

The What and Why of ORMs

An ORM acts as an "object wrapper" around specific database implementations, meaning

- Developers can use an object-oriented software development approach to data access.

- Developers don't need to know the nuances of vendor SQL.

- Developers don't need to perform proprietary mappings from database tables to code-based result sets.

This really equates to the following primary benefits:

- Speed of Development

- Code portability

- Code maintainability

We'll be using Entity Framework Core as our ORM of choice, but there are alternatives available, so again please remember to distinguish between our *technology implementation* of choice (Entity Framework Core) and the *generic concept* of ORMs.

If that's all still a bit abstract, as I've said before, I think the best way to understand and learn something new is to get our hands dirty and start coding.

Entity Framework Command-Line Tools

We're going to make use of the Entity Framework Core Command-Line tools (they basically allow you to create migrations, update the database, etc.; don't worry if you don't know what that means yet!). Just trust me; we need the tools!

First, check if you already have them installed; to do so, type

```
dotnet ef
```

You should see output similar to the following if you do.

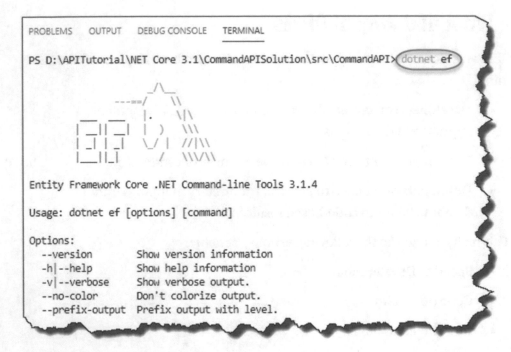

Figure 7-12. *Entity Framework Command Line Tools*

If you don't see that, simply run the following at the command line:

```
dotnet tool install --global dotnet-ef
```

and this will make the tools available to you globally.

Create Our DB Context

The next step in producing the data access layer via Entity Framework Core (EF Core) is to create a Database Context Class. The DB Context class acts as a *representation of the Database* and mediates between our data Models and their existence in the DB, as shown in Figure 7-13.

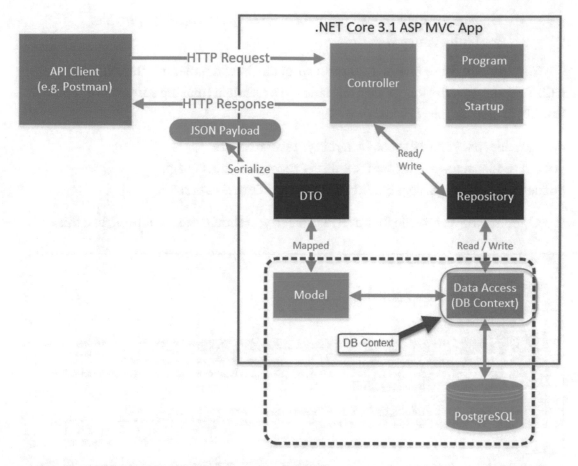

Figure 7-13. *The importance of the DB Context*

As mentioned in Chapter 5, we could use the DB Context direct from the Controller without using a repository. As you are aware though, we will be using both a repository and DB Context in this tutorial.

Reference Packages

In order to use the features of EF Core, we're going to have to add reference three packages in our API Project .csproj file:

- **Microsoft.EntityFrameworkCore**: Primary Entity Framework Core Package

- **Microsoft.EntityFrameworkCore.Design**: Design time components (required for migrations)

- **Npgsql.EntityFrameworkCore.PostgreSQL**: PosrgreSQL provider for Entity Framework Core

You can add these manually to the .csproj file, but I'd rather use the .NET Core CLI. To do so, run the following commands in a terminal (making sure you're "inside" the API Project folder: *CommandAPI*):

```
dotnet add package Microsoft.EntityFrameworkCore
dotnet add package Microsoft.EntityFrameworkCore.Design
dotnet add package Npgsql.EntityFrameworkCore.PostgreSQL
```

Opening the .csproj file for our API project, you should see something like this.

```
<Project Sdk="Microsoft.NET.Sdk.Web">

  <PropertyGroup>
    <TargetFramework>netcoreapp3.1</TargetFramework>
  </PropertyGroup>

  <ItemGroup>
    <PackageReference Include="Microsoft.EntityFrameworkCore" Version="3.1.1" />
    <PackageReference Include="Microsoft.EntityFrameworkCore.Design" Version="3.1.1">
      <IncludeAssets>runtime; build; native; contentfiles; analyzers; buildtransitive</IncludeAssets>
      <PrivateAssets>all</PrivateAssets>
    </PackageReference>
    <PackageReference Include="Npgsql.EntityFrameworkCore.PostgreSQL" Version="3.1.0" />
  </ItemGroup>
                                              Newly added package references
</Project>
```

Figure 7-14. *Package references added for persistence*

With the necessary packages added, we can move on.

ℹ️ As mentioned, the third package we added

(Npgsql.EntityFrameworkCore.PostgreSQL)

is the EF Core provider for PostgreSQL. If you want to use another database, then you'd add the relevant package here. For example, if you want to use SQL Server, you'd add the following package instead:

Microsoft.EntityFrameworkCore.SqlServer

We'll create the DB Context class in the "Data" folder along with our repository interface and classes, so create a new file called ***CommandContext.cs***, and place it in the ***Data*** folder; it should look like this.

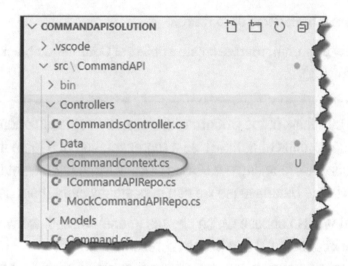

Figure 7-15. *Added DB Context*

Now, update the code in the ***CommandContext.cs*** file to mirror the following; be sure to include the "using" directives also:

```
using Microsoft.EntityFrameworkCore;
using CommandAPI.Models;

namespace CommandAPI.Data
{
    public class CommandContext : DbContext
    {
        public CommandContext(DbContextOptions<CommandContext> options)
          : base(options)
        {

        }

        public DbSet<Command> CommandItems {get; set;}
    }
}
```

Some points of note

- Ensure you have the EntityFrameworkCore and CommandAPI.Models using statements.

- Our class inherits from DbContext.

- It's really important that we create a DbSet of Command objects (see the following).

ℹ While you can think of the DbContext class as a representation of the Database, you could think of a DbSet as a representation of a table in the Database. That is, we are telling our DbContext class that we want to "model" our Commands in the Database (so we can persistently store them as a table).

This means that we can choose which classes (model classes) we want to put under DbContext "control" and hence represent in the DB.

Save the file and perform a dotnet build to ensure there are no compilation errors. As we've added a new class, it's probably worth performing the "trifecta" of Git commands to

- Place the new untracked file under source control.

- Commit the class to the repository (with a message).

- Push the code up to GitHub.

🎓 Learning Opportunity   Try to remember the git commands that you need to issue in order to achieve the items previously discussed – I'm not going to detail them again.

If you can't remember, refer to Chapter 5.

Update appsettings.json

OK, so that's all well and good, but there is still a "disconnect" between the PostgreSQL Server DB and our application (specifically our CommandContext class).

For those of you that have done a bit of programming before, you won't be surprised to hear that we have to provide a "Connection String" to our application that tells it how to connect to our database server.

We'll place our DB connection string in our *appsettings.json* file to begin with.

Before we do this though, we need to create a PostgreSQL Login that we can use as the "application user" of our (as yet to be created) database. This is the account that the API will use to authenticate to the PostgreSQL server with and derive its permissions to run our Entity Framework Core "migrations" that will

- Create a new database.

- Create or alter any tables.

- Read, write, and delete data.

☞ **Learning Opportunity**   Why should we not use the **postgres** user account that we previously used from within DBeaver to connect to our PostgreSQL server?

Creating a user can be done in one of two ways using DBeaver:

- SQL Command

- Using the Graphical Interface

I'll show you how to do this Via SQL; once you learn that, using the Graphical UI to perform the same action should be a piece of cake.

Create User – SQL

Open DBeaver (make sure you're connected to your PostgreSQL instance), and select SQL Editor ➤ New SQL Editor from the menu.

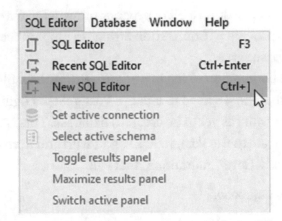

Figure 7-16. *Opening a New SQL Editor*

This should open up a new query widow; then simply enter the following SQL:

```
create user cmddbuser with encrypted password 'pa55w0rd!' createdb;
```

I've called our user cmddbuser and given it a password of pa55w0rd!; you can of course alter these values to your own needs.

You can the hold Ctrl + Enter to execute the SQL statement or select "Execute SQL Statement" from the SQL Editor menu.

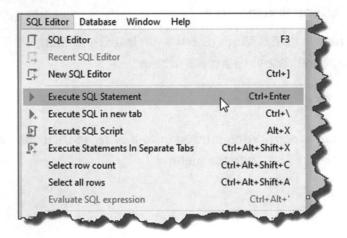

Figure 7-17. *Create our user by executing the SQL*

The command should execute successfully, and if you then expand: postgres ➤ Roles, you should see your newly created user. If you don't, right-click the "Roles" folder, and select "Refresh."

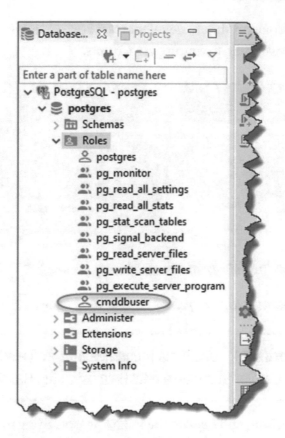

Figure 7-18. *Newly created DB User for our API*

Right-click the newly created role and select "View Role" (or you can just press F4).

Figure 7-19. *View Role Details*

The resulting information should detail that our user can log-in and create databases which is critical when we come to running migrations.

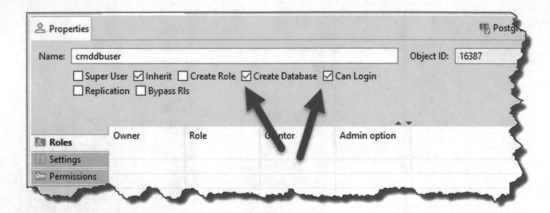

Figure 7-20. *Role permissions required for our new user*

📌 **Learning Opportunity**   Using the properties that we've set earlier as a guide, see if you can use DBeaver to create a new Role using the Graphical UI and menus.

Open ***appsettings.json***, and *append* the following json string to the correct point in the file (again make sure you replace the User ID and password to match the user *you* just created):

```
"ConnectionStrings":
{
    "PostgreSqlConnection":"User ID=cmddbuser;
    Password=pa55w0rd!;
    Host=localhost;
    Port=5432;
    Database=CmdAPI;
    Pooling=true;"
}
```

So, your file should look something like this.[1]

---

[1]If you get errors copying and pasting, check the double-quote characters and ensure the connection string value is on one line.

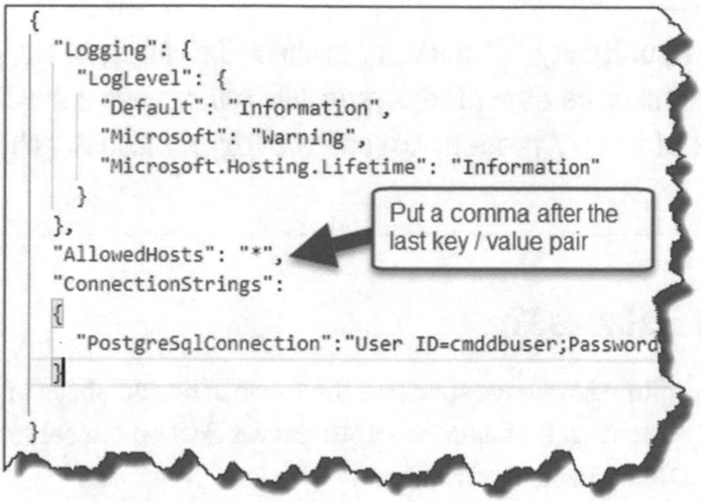

```
{
  "Logging": {
    "LogLevel": {
      "Default": "Information",
      "Microsoft": "Warning",
      "Microsoft.Hosting.Lifetime": "Information"
    }
  },
  "AllowedHosts": "*",
  "ConnectionStrings":
  {
      "PostgreSqlConnection":"User ID=cmddbuser;Password
  }
}
```

Put a comma after the last key / value pair

Figure 7-21. Connection string in appsettings.json

Some points to note about the connection string

- The "name" of the connection string is `PosrgreSqlConnection`.

- The connection string is made up of the following components, separated by a semicolon:

  - **User ID**: The login for our Postgres Server (we created this in the last section).

  - **Password**: The password for our login – stored in pain text – not very secure![2]

  - **Host**: The host name of our PostgreSQL server.

  - **Port**: The port our PostgreSQL server is listening on.

  - **Database**: This is our database (or will be our database – it does not exist yet).

  - **Pooling**: Connection pooling (essentially sharing) is being used.

---

[2]We will remedy this in the next chapter.

☞ **Learning Opportunity**   If you want to check the validity of any json (including the contents of the entire *appsettings.json* file), you can paste the JSON into something like `https://jsoneditoronline.org/` which will check the syntax for you.

Where's Our Database?

As previously mentioned, we have specified the name of our database in our connection string (**CmdAPI**), but the actual database does not yet exist on our server; a quick look at the databases in DBeaver will confirm that.

Figure 7-22. *Where's our database?*

We only have the default **postgres** database, but as yet, **CmdAPI** is not there. That is because our database will be created when we perform our first Entity Framework "migration." I explain what this is later in this section.

Revisit the Startup Class

To recap we have

- A Database Server (but actually no **CmdAPI** "database" as yet!)

- A Model (Command)

- DBContext (CommandContext)

- DBSet (CommandItems)

- Connection String to our database server

The last few things we have to do are

- Point our DBContext class to the connection string (currently it's not aware of it).

- "Register" our DBContext class in Startup ➤ ConfigureServices so that it can be used throughout our application as a "service" – seem familiar?

In order to supply our connection string (currently in ***appsettings.json***) to our DbContext class, we have to update our Startup class to provide a "Configuration" object for use (we use this configuration object to access the connection string).

Side note: Casting your mind back to the start of the tutorial, when we had a choice of project templates.

```
MVC ViewStart                                    viewstart        [C#]
Blazor Server App                                blazorserver     [C#]
ASP.NET Core Empty                               web              [C#], F
ASP.NET Core Web App (Model-View-Controller)     mvc              [C#], F
ASP.NET Core Web App                             webapp           [C#]
ASP.NET Core with Angular                        angular          [C#]
ASP.NET Core with React.js                       react            [C#]
ASP.NET Core with React.js and Redux             reactredux       [C#]
Razor Class Library                              razorclasslib    [C#]
ASP.NET Core Web API                             webapi           [C#], F#
ASP.NET Core gRPC Service                        grpc             [C#]
dotne                                            gitignore
```

Figure 7-23. *.NET Core Project Templates*

We chose "web" to provide us with an empty shell project. Well if you had chosen "webapi," the "Configuration" code we're about to introduce would have been provided as part of that project template. I deliberately choose not to do that so we have to manually add the following code – as I think it will help you learn the core concepts more fully.

OK, so add the following code (shown in **bold**) to our startup class:

```
using Microsoft.AspNetCore.Builder;
using Microsoft.AspNetCore.Hosting;
using Microsoft.Extensions.DependencyInjection;
using Microsoft.Extensions.Hosting;
using Microsoft.Extensions.Configuration;

namespace CommandAPI
{
    public class Startup
    {
        public IConfiguration Configuration {get;}
        public Startup(IConfiguration configuration)
        {
          Configuration = configuration;
        }

        public void ConfigureServices(IServiceCollection services)...
    .
    .
    .
```

I've shown the new sections in context of the whole file here.

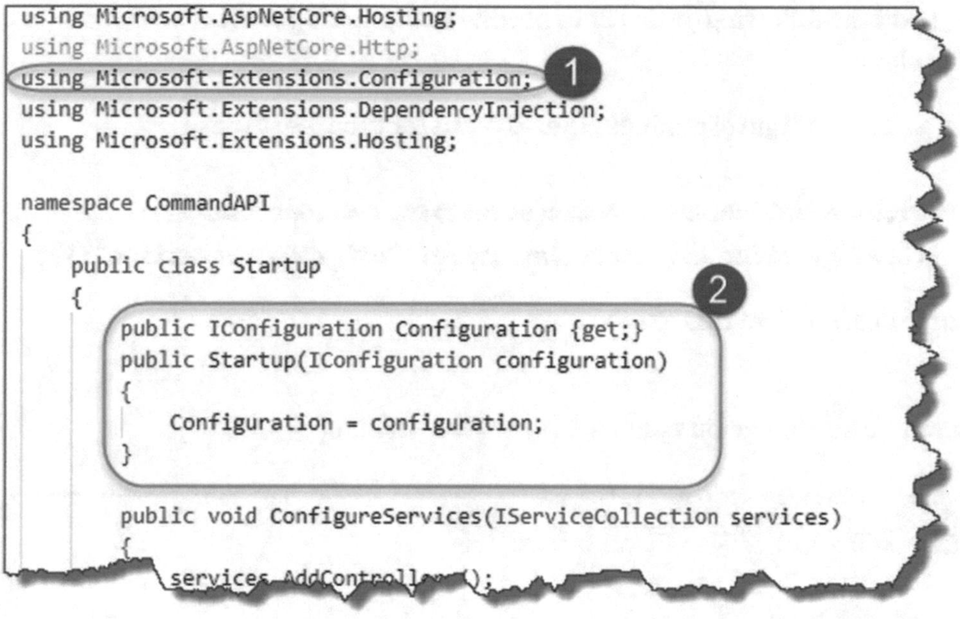

```
using Microsoft.AspNetCore.Hosting;
using Microsoft.AspNetCore.Http;
using Microsoft.Extensions.Configuration;          1
using Microsoft.Extensions.DependencyInjection;
using Microsoft.Extensions.Hosting;

namespace CommandAPI
{
    public class Startup
    {                                                   2
        public IConfiguration Configuration {get;}
        public Startup(IConfiguration configuration)
        {
            Configuration = configuration;
        }

        public void ConfigureServices(IServiceCollection services)
        {
            services.AddControllers();
```

Figure 7-24. *Using Dependency Injection to Add the Configuration API*

1. Add a new using directive: `Microsoft.Extensions.Configuration`.

2. Create an `IConfiguration` interface and set up in the class constructor.

Does this pattern seem familiar? If not, maybe return to Chapter 6 and review. What this code provides for us is access to the "Configuration API" (via an implementation of the `IConfiguration` interface), which means that we can now access the configuration stored in (among other places) the ***appsettings.json*** file. In particular, it means we can read in our connection string and pass it to the DB Context.

For more information on the `IConfiguration` interface, refer to the Microsoft Build Docs.[3]

The last thing we have to do is register our `DbContext` in the `ConfigureServices` method and pass it the connection string (via the configuration API). Add the following using directive to your `Startup` class:

- `using Microsoft.EntityFrameworkCore;`

---

[3]https://docs.microsoft.com/en-us/dotnet/api/microsoft.extensions.configuration.
iconfiguration?view=dotnet-plat-ext-3.1

And add the following (**bold**) lines of code to the ConfigureServices method in your Startup class:

```
public void ConfigureServices(IServiceCollection services)
{
    services.AddDbContext<CommandContext>(opt => opt.UseNpgsql
        (Configuration.GetConnectionString("PostgreSqlConnection")));

    services.AddControllers();
}
```

To put those changes in context, they are shown here.

```
using Microsoft.Extensions.Hosting;
using Microsoft.EntityFrameworkCore;    1

namespace CommandAPI
{
    public class Startup
    {
        public IConfiguration Configuration {get;}
        public Startup(IConfiguration configuration)
        {
            Configuration = configuration;
        }

        public void ConfigureServices(IServiceCollection services)
        {                                                         2
            services.AddDbContext<CommandContext>(opt => opt.UseNpgsql
            (Configuration.GetConnectionString("PostgreSqlConnection")));

            services.AddControllers();

            services.AddScoped<ICommandAPIRepo, MockCommandAPIRepo>();
```

Figure 7-25. *Registering our DB Context with our Services Container*

You'll observe the following:

1.   We include a new using directive.

2. We register our `CommandContext` class as a solution-wide DBContext
    (in the Service Container), and we point it to the connection string
    (`PostgreSqlConnection`) that is contained in our ***appsesstings.json***
    file. This is accessed via our `Configuration` object.

ℹ️   If you're using a different database to PostgreSQL, you'd need to change the
code in point 2; specifically, you'd swap out the

`opt.UseNpgsql`

For something else, for example, in the case of SQL Server, you'd use

`opt.UseSqlServer`

Phew! Quite a bit of coding there to wire up everything; we're almost done, but now
we need to move on to "migrating" our model from the app to the DB.

Create and Apply Migrations

We should have everything in place to create our database and the table containing our
Command Objects.

Code First vs. Database First

Just another side note, you may hear about "Code First" and "Database First" approaches
when it comes to Entity Framework – it speaks to whether

- We write "code first" then "push" or "migrate" that code to create our
  database and tables, or

- We create out Database and tables first and "import" or "generate"
  code (models) from the DB.

Here we are using "code first" (we've already created our command model), so we
now have to "migrate" that to our database; we do this via something called, drum roll,
Migrations!

Go to your command line, and ensure that you are "in" the API project folder (**CommandAPI**), and type the following (hitting Enter when you're done):

```
dotnet ef migrations add AddCommandsToDB
```

Now all being well, a number of things should have happened here.

First off, your command line should report something along the lines of the following.

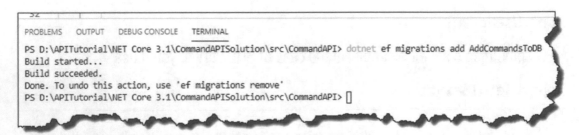

Figure 7-26. *Create our migration files ready to run*

Next you should see a new folder appear in our project structure, called "Migrations."

Figure 7-27. *Newly created migrations*

Specifically, you should make note of a new file called ***date time stamp + migration name_.cs***, for example:

20200524224711_AddCommandsToDB.cs

It is the contents of this file that when applied to the database will create our new table (and as it's the first time we've run a migration, our actual database will be created too). A quick look in the file and you'll see the following.

```
public partial class AddCommandsToDB : Migration
{
    protected override void Up(MigrationBuilder migrationBuilder)  ❶
    {
        migrationBuilder.CreateTable(
            name: "CommandItems",  ❷
            columns: table => new
            {
                Id = table.Column<int>(nullable: false)                                                                                 ❸
                    .Annotation("Npgsql:ValueGenerationStrategy", NpgsqlValueGenerationStrategy.IdentityByDefaultColumn),
                HowTo = table.Column<string>(maxLength: 250, nullable: false),
                Platform = table.Column<string>(nullable: false),      ❹
                CommandLine = table.Column<string>(nullable: false)
            },
            constraints: table =>
            {
                table.PrimaryKey("PK_CommandItems", x => x.Id);
            });                                              The data annotations we added to our
    }                                                       Command Model have been replicated.

    protected override void Down(MigrationBuilder migrationBuilder)  ❺
    {
        migrationBuilder.DropTable(
            name: "CommandItems");
    }
}
```

Figure 7-28. *Contexts of our Migrations File*

1. An "Up" method. This method is called to create new items.

2. The creation of a table "CommandItems" (where does this name come from?).

3. Database provider specific annotations/instructions.

4. Our table columns; note the data annotations we added to our model have been replicated.

5. A "Down" method. Used to roll back the changes made in the Up method.

⚠ **Warning!**   Point 3 is of note here. I previously thought the migrations file (not sure why I thought this) was agnostic of the database that you're using. That is incorrect.

The migrations file will look slightly different depending on which type of database you choose to use (e.g., SQL Server Vs. PostgreSQL etc.). I learned this when I

1. Used SQL Server as my database

2. Registered my DB Context in `ConfigureServices` with `opt.UseSqlServer`... (and not `opt.UseNpgsql`)

3. Ran and generated my Migrations File

4. Switched my provider to PostgreSQL (`opt.UseNpgsql`) then attempted to use that migrations file to generate my DB (we'll do this in a bit)

It failed.

You can examine an "SQL Server" migrations file and look for the differences in the Source Code for an older project here on GitHub.[4]

Long story short, you'll need to regenerate your migrations if you switch database providers.

Note   At this stage, we *still do not* have the **CmdAPI** database created; that comes next.

Finally, all that's left to is "update the database" to apply our changes – to do this, type

```
dotnet ef database update
```

Our migration is run, as reflected in the following output.

---

[4]https://github.com/binarythistle/Complete-ASP.NET-Core-API-Tutorial

```
PS D:\APITutorial\NET Core 3.1\CommandAPISolution\src\CommandAPI> dotnet ef database update
Build started...
Build succeeded.
Done.
PS D:\APITutorial\NET Core 3.1\CommandAPISolution\src\CommandAPI>
```

Figure 7-29. *Successfully run our migration*

ℹ **Tip**   If you get an error at this stage, in my experience, it usually always has to do with database "connection" issues. So, I'd check:

1. Can you still connect to the PostgreSQL server using DBeaver?

2. Double-check the formatting of the connection string. For example, copy and paste it into something like jsoneditoronline. org to check for syntactical JSON errors.

3. Double-check the values you've put into the connection string. For example, passwords are case-sensitive.

4. Double-check if you're using the correct connection string "name" when you're setting up the DBContext on the ConfigureServices method.

5. Perform a dotnet build to check that there are no syntax errors in the code (this is actually run when you do a dotnet ef database update – but it's worth checking separately).

6. Check that (a) the database user you created exists on the server and (b) check that it has the necessary permissions.

All going well, a number of things happen here:

1. Our database (**CmdAPI**) is created as it did not yet exist on the target server.

2. A table called **_EFMigrationsHistory** is created; this just stores
   the IDs of the migrations that have been run and allows Entity
   Framework to both roll back migrations to a certain point or
   correctly run migrations on a new endpoint server.

3. Our **CommandItems** table is created which is the persistent
   equivalent of our Command model.

If we also take a look at our PostgreSQL instance, this is reflected by the fact that we
have both our **CmdAPI** database and our **CommandItems** table.

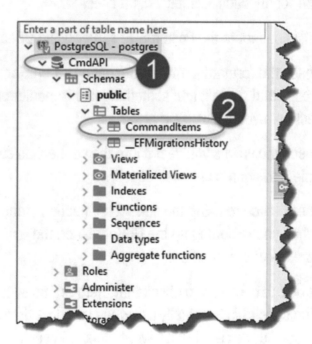

Figure 7-30. *Our Database and Table have been created*

1. **CmdAPI** database

2. **CommandItems** table

Adding Some Data

Up until now, we've been using hard-coded mock data in our API code. With the
establishment of our Database and DB context, we can now start to add some "real" data
for use in by our API.

You can add data a number of ways (including fully scripting this to import a lot of test data – we're not covering that today), but by far the simplest and most ubiquitous way to do that is via a SQL INSERT command that we can run from inside the DBeaver query window.

In terms of the data we should put in, I'd like to circle back to the creation and updating of the database and table; we used the following two commands:

- dotnet ef migrations add

- dotnet ef database update

Therefore, if we wanted to store this data in our table, we'd add the following data.

ID[5]	HowTo	Platform	CommandLine
1	Create an EF Migration	EF Core CLI	dotnet ef migrations add
2	Apply Migrations to DB	EF Core CLI	dotnet ef database update

To add this data via a SQL INSERT command in DBeaver

- Open DBeaver and connect to the server.

- From the SQL Editor Menu, select "New SQL Editor."

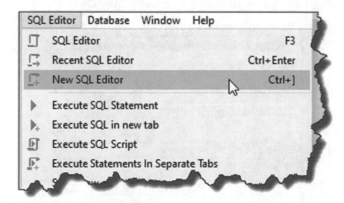

Figure 7-31. *Add new Query window*

---

[5]You do not need to provide a value for ID when you add data to the database; this is auto-created by PostgreSQL for us.

This will not surprisingly open a new query window. We then need to set the "active" database so that when we write a query, DBeaver knows which one we want to use. Simply right-click the database you want to set as the active one (in our case **CmdAPI**), and select "Set as default":

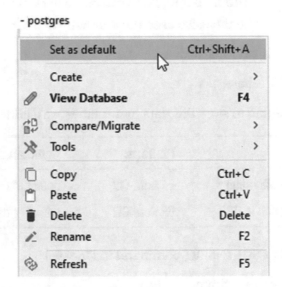

Figure 7-32. *Set Default Database*

This should change the name of the database to "bold."

Figure 7-33. *Our Default DB has been set*

In the query window, type the following SQL to insert both of our command-line snippets into the database:

```
insert into "CommandItems" ("HowTo", "Platform", "CommandLine")
values ('Create an EF migration', 'Entity Framework Core Command Line',
'dotnet ef migrations add');

insert into "CommandItems" ("HowTo", "Platform", "CommandLine")
VALUES ('Apply Migrations to DB', 'Entity Framework Core Command Line',
'dotnet ef database update');
```

After that, press Ctrl+Enter, or select "Execute SQL Statement" from the SQL Editor menu to run the SQL – this should insert the lines into our database. To check this, clear the SQL from the window (otherwise, if you execute it again, it'll insert two more rows, effectively duplicating the data), and type

```
select * from "CommandItems";
```

This should return something like the following.

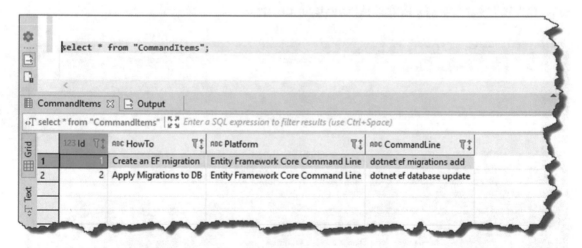

Figure 7-34. *Our two new rows of "real" data*

If you read my blog post on Entity Framework,[6] you'll have noticed by now that the commands used in that tutorial are different to those used here. That's because in that

---

[6]https://dotnetplaybook.com/introduction-to-entity-framework/

online tutorial, we're using the "Package Manager Console" in Visual Studio to issue commands for Entity Framework (not Entity Framework Core/.NET Core Command line) – quite confusing I know!

I think, therefore, just to labor that point, let's add two new command-line prompts in our DB.

HowTo	Platform	CommandLine
Create an EF Migration	Entity Framework Package Manager Console	add-migration <name of migration>
Apply Migrations to DB	Entity Framework Package Manager Console	update database

📑 **Learning Opportunity**   You'll need to write the SQL to insert these additional command snippets to our DB!

After executing the SQL INSERT commands, perform another SELECT "all" (i.e., SELECT * ...), and you should see the following.

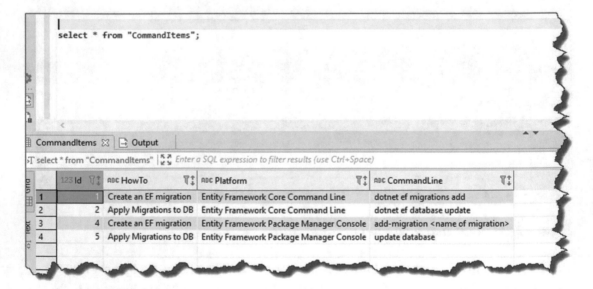

Figure 7-35. *Commands in the DB*

Hopefully, you can see that as you build out the data in our table, this API will become useful; if like me, your memory is not as good as it once was!

To round out this chapter, let's update our existing API Actions to return this data!

Tying It Altogether

A quick progress check to see where we are with our architecture, and this time I've just highlighted the *interaction* that we **have not yet** implemented.

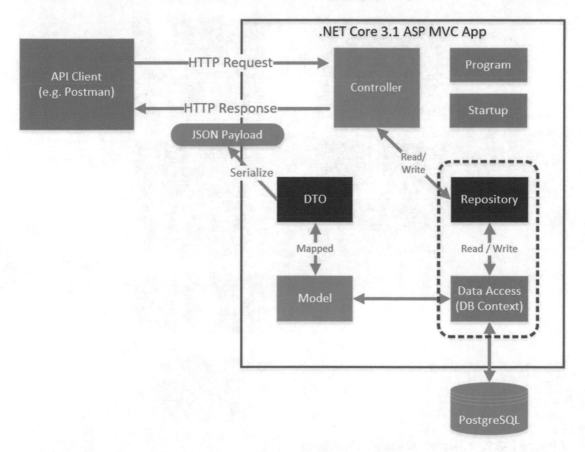

Figure 7-36. *We need to make use of our DB Context Class*

Currently, we are using our repository to return data using a mock implementation, so what we need to do next to make use of our "real" data (and, therefore, DB Context) is

- Create a new implementation of our repository interface (to use the DB Context).

- "Swap" out our existing mock implementation for our new one.

I've depicted our current state with our desired end state in Figure 7-37.

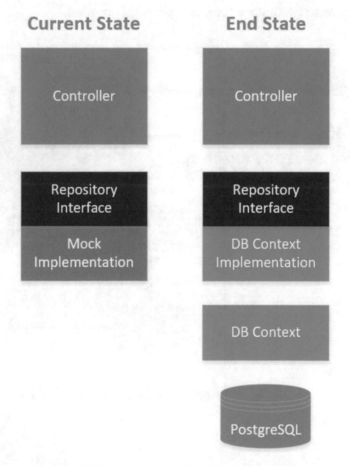

Figure 7-37. *Current State vs. End State*

Create a New Repository Implementation

The first thing we want to do is create a new *concrete implementation* of our ICommandAPIRepo interface, so add a new file to the *Data* folder in our API project, and call it *SqlCommandAPIRepo.cs* as shown in Figure 7-38.

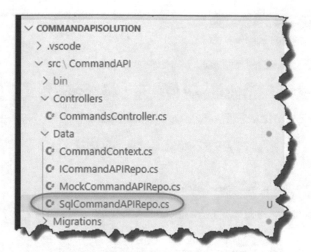

Figure 7-38. *New Concrete implementation class*

Add the following code to that file:

```
namespace CommandAPI.Data
{
    public class SqlCommandAPIRepo : ICommandAPIRepo
    {

    }
}
```

As you've done before with our mock implementation in Chapter 6, place your cursor "in" the ICommandAPIRepo statement, and press

CTRL + .

To auto-generate the template implementation code for our API, see Figure 7-39.

```csharp
using System.Collections.Generic;
using CommandAPI.Models;

namespace CommandAPI.Data
{
    public class SqlCommandAPIRepo : ICommandAPIRepo
    {
        public void CreateCommand(Command cmd)
        {
            throw new System.NotImplementedException();
        }

        public void DeleteCommand(Command cmd)
        {
            throw new System.NotImplementedException();
        }

        public IEnumerable<Command> GetAllCommands()
        {
            throw new System.NotImplementedException();
        }

        public Command GetCommandById(int id)
        {
            throw new System.NotImplementedException();
        }

        public bool SaveChanges()
        {
            throw new System.NotImplementedException();
        }

        public void UpdateCommand(Command cmd)
        {
            throw new System.NotImplementedException();
        }
    }
}
```

Figure 7-39. *Auto-generated interface implementation code*

For now, we're just going to implement the same two methods that we implemented in out mock implementation:

- GetAllCommands

- GetCommandById

To begin, we're going to use Constructor Dependency Injection to inject our DB Context into our `SqlCommandAPIRepo` class (so we can use it). Remember that we registered our DB Context class with the Service Container in the `Startup` class so it is available for "injection."

```
public void ConfigureServices(IServiceCollection services)
{
    services.AddDbContext<CommandContext>(opt => opt.UseNpgsql
    (Configuration.GetConnectionString("PostgreSqlConnection")));

    services.AddControllers();

    services.AddScoped<ICommandAPIRepo, MockCommandAPIRepo>();
}
```

Figure 7-40. *We registered our DB Context Class with the Service Container in the startup class*

So, to inject our DB Context into our new concrete repository class, add the following class constructor to `SqlCommandAPIRepo`:

```
using System.Collections.Generic;
using CommandAPI.Models;

namespace CommandAPI.Data
{
    public class SqlCommandAPIRepo : ICommandAPIRepo
    {
        private readonly CommandContext _context;

        public SqlCommandAPIRepo(CommandContext context)
        {
            _context = context;
        }
        .
        .
        .
```

Again, this pattern should be familiar to you now:

- A DB Context instance is injected in via our constructor (as context).

- We then assign context to a private read-only field (_context) that we can use in the rest of the SqlCommandAPIRepo class.

We then need to update our two methods as shown by the code here(making sure to add the using statement to using System.Linq at the top of the file):

```
using System.Linq;
.

.

.


public IEnumerable<Command> GetAllCommands()
{
  return _context.CommandItems.ToList();
}

public Command GetCommandById(int id)
{
  return _context.CommandItems.FirstOrDefault(p => p.Id == id);
}
```

To put the changes in context, I've shown them here.

```
using System.Collections.Generic;
using System.Linq;
using CommandAPI.Models;

namespace CommandAPI.Data
{
    public class SqlCommandAPIRepo : ICommandAPIRepo
    {
        private readonly CommandContext _context;          1

        public SqlCommandAPIRepo(CommandContext context)
        {
            _context = context;
        }

        public void CreateCommand(Command cmd)
        {
            throw new System.NotImplementedException();
        }

        public void DeleteCommand(Command cmd)
        {
            throw new System.NotImplementedException();
        }

        public IEnumerable<Command> GetAllCommands()      2
        {
            return _context.CommandItems.ToList();
        }
                                                          3
        public Command GetCommandById(int id)
        {
            return _context.CommandItems.FirstOrDefault(p => p.Id == id);
        }

        public bool SaveChanges()
```

Figure 7-41. *Concrete Implementation of our Repository*

To review

1. Class constructor utilizing the injection of or DB Context.

2. We reference "CommandItems" on our DB Context (_context) and return as a List of Command objects.

3. We call the FirstOrDefault method on our "CommandItems" to return a Command object (if one exists) that matches our desired ID.

As you can see, we can reference our object collections (in this case, we just have Commands) via our DB Context with relative ease (this is the power of the "ORM").

That's our new repository implementation complete (for now – we'll complete the other methods later). All that remains to do is to change our Service Container registration in the Startup class as shown next – it goes without saying that you should make these changes in your own code too.

```
public void ConfigureServices(IServiceCollection services)
{
    services.AddDbContext<CommandContext>(opt => opt.UseNpgsql
    (Configuration.GetConnectionString("PostgreSqlConnection")));

    services.AddControllers();

    //services.AddScoped<ICommandAPIRepo, MockCommandAPIRepo>();

    services.AddScoped<ICommandAPIRepo, SqlCommandAPIRepo>();
                                                    New Registration
}

public void Configure(IApplicationBuilder app, IWebHostEnvironment env)
```

Figure 7-42. *We swap out our mock implementation for our new Implementation*

And that's it! That's how easy it is to swap out implementations of our repository – we didn't have to change a single line of code in our Controller. While our codebase is quite small, you can imagine in situations where we're making use of our repository elsewhere in our code just how powerful (and convenient) this is.

Let's save everything and test to see if this is working, so

```
dotnet build
```

Assuming all is well, let's run

```
dotnet run
```

And let's trigger some calls in Postman.

Get All Command Items

Using the URI `http://localhost:5000/api/commands/` along with GET in Postman
yields the following.

Figure 7-43. *Our API working with database derived data*

Get A Single Command (Existing)

Using the URI `http://localhost:5000/api/commands/1` along with GET in Postman
yields the following.

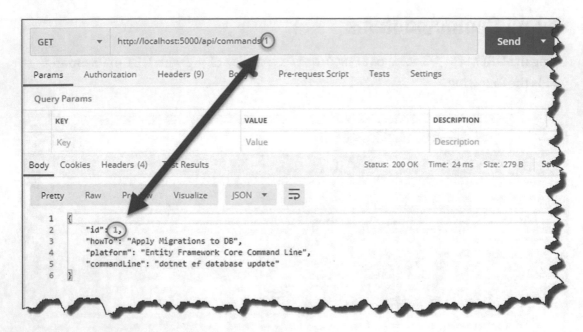

Figure 7-44. *Returning a Single Resource*

Get A Single Command (Not Existing)

Using the URI http://localhost:5000/api/commands/67 along with GET in Postman yields the following.

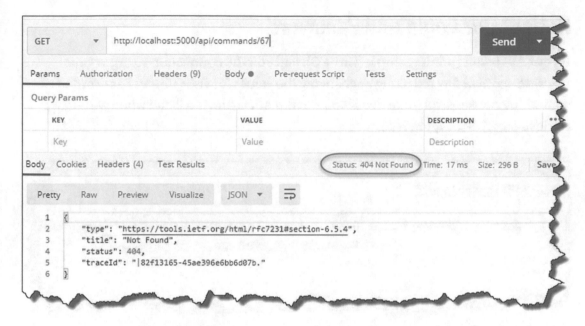

Figure 7-45. *404 Not Found Error*

🎂 **Celebration Checkpoint**   Possibly the most significant celebration in the whole book – well done! You've basically built a data drive API in .NET Core!

We've covered a lot of material in this chapter. To be honest, I was going to try and make it smaller, but then I felt the flow would not be as good.

Wrapping Up the Chapter

As we have our code under source control, we want to

- Add untracked (aka "new") files to source control/Git.

- Commit to those changes.

- Push our code up to GitHub **[WARNING before you do this!!!!]**.

Why am I warning you about pushing our code up to our public GitHub repository?

That's right, we have placed the user login and password to our database in the **appsettings.json** file – this will become publicly available if we push our code.

Redact Our Login and Password

If your API is still running, stop it (Ctrl + C), and edit the connection string in your
appsettings.json file, redacting or changing the values for User ID and Password to
something nonsensical (note that if you run the API again, it will fail when we come to
retrieve data!). See Figure 7-46.

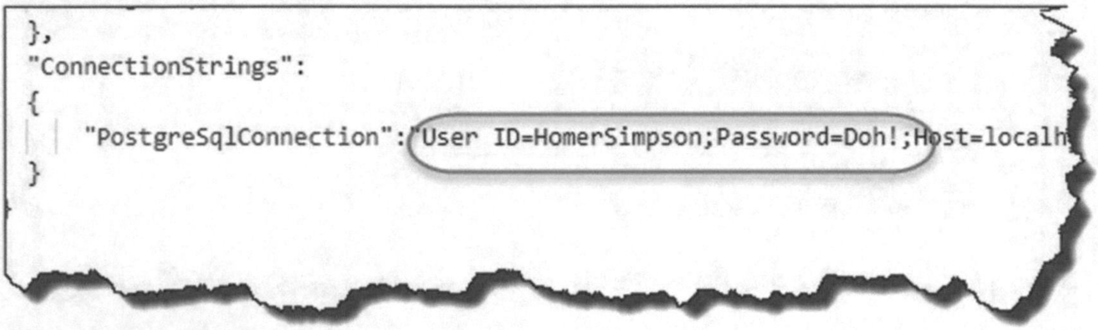

```
    },
    "ConnectionStrings":
    {
        "PostgreSqlConnection": "User ID=HomerSimpson;Password=Doh!;Host=localh
    }
```

Figure 7-46.   Nonsense User ID and Password

Save the file, then perform the three steps to Add/Track, Commit, and Push your
code to GitHub (remember to do this at the Solution level: *CommandAPISolution*
folder).

Go over to GitHub, and look at the *appsetting.json* file there.

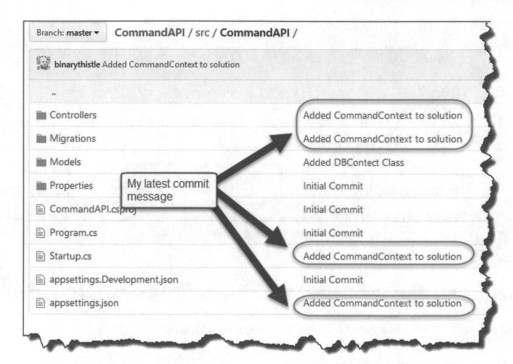

Figure 7-47. *Latest Commits*

See the ***appsettings.json*** file as it exists publicly on GitHub.

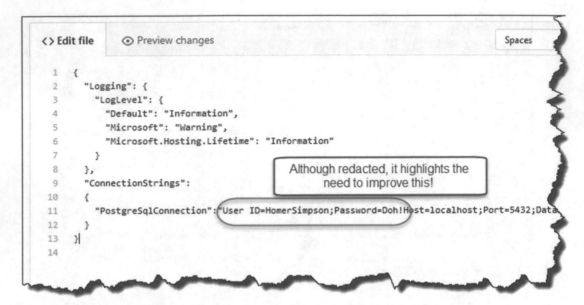

Figure 7-48. *Redacted User ID and Password on GitHub*

We have two major problems now:

- It's terribly insecure (even if we have put in temporary "fake" values).

- Our code does not work now! (We'll get authentication errors.)

Clearly, we can't publish user IDs and password to GitHub; even if we made the GitHub repository private, this is still terrible practice. We need a way of keeping these details secret.

## CHAPTER 8

Environment Variables and User Secrets

Chapter Summary

In this chapter we discuss what runtime environments are and how to configure them; we'll then discuss what user secrets are and how to use them.

When Done, You Will

- Understand what runtime environments are.
- How to set them via the ASPNETCORE_ENVIRONMENT variable.
- Understand the role of *launchSettings.json* and *appsettings.json* files.
- What *user secrets* are.
- How to use user secrets to solve the problem we had at the end of the last chapter.

Environments

When developing anything, you typically want the freedom to try new code, refactor existing code, and basically feel free to fail without impacting the end user. Imagine if you had to make code changes directly to a live customer environment? That would be

- Stressful for you as a developer

© Les Jackson 2020
L. Jackson, *The Complete ASP.NET Core 3 API Tutorial*, https://doi.org/10.1007/978-1-4842-6255-9_8

- Showing great irresponsibility as an application owner

- Potentially impactful to the end user

Therefore, to avoid such a scenario, most, if not all organizations, will have some kind of "Development" environment where developers can roam free and go for it, without fear of screwing up.

Les' Personal Anecdote   If you've ever worked as part of a development team, you'll know the preceding statement is not quite true. Yes, you can break things in the development environment without fear of impacting customers, but if you break the build, you will have the wrath of the other members of your team to deal with!

I know this from bitter experience.

Anyway, you'll almost always have a *Development* environment, but what other environments can you have? Well, jumping to the other end of the spectrum, you'll always have a *Production* environment. This is where the live production code sits and runs as the actual application, be it a customer-facing web site or in our case an API available for use by other applications.

You will typically never make code changes directly in production; indeed deployments and changes to production should be done, where possible, in as automated (and trackable) a way as possible, where the "human hand" doesn't intervene to any large extent.

So, are they the only two environments you can have? Of course not, and this is where you'll find the most differences in the real world. Most usually you will have some kind of "intermediate" environment (or environments) that sits in between Development and Production; it's primary use is to "stage" the build in as close to a Production environment as possible to allow for integration and even user testing. Names for this this environment vary, but you'll hear Microsoft refer to it as the "Staging" environment; I've also heard it called PR or "Production Replica."

Les' Personal Anecdote   Replicating a Production environment accurately can be tricky (and expensive), especially if you work in a large corporate environment with lots of "legacy" systems that are maintained by different third-party vendors – coordinating this can be a nightmare.

There are of course ways to simulate these legacy systems, but again, there is really no substitute for the real thing. If you're not simulating the legacy systems *your app* is interacting with precisely, that's when you find those lovely bugs in production.

I remember being caught out with SQL case sensitivity on an Oracle DB while on site at a customer deployment. An easy fix when I realized the issue, but something as simple as that can be stressful and also damaging to your own reputation!

Our Environment Setup

We are going to dispense with the Staging or Production Replica environment and use only Development and Production – this is more than sufficient to demonstrate the necessary concepts we need to cover. Refer to the following diagram to see my environmental setup (yours should mirror this to a large extent).

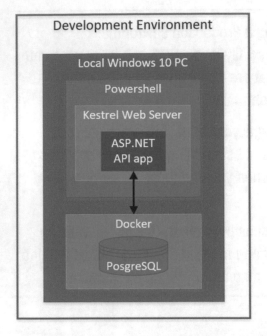
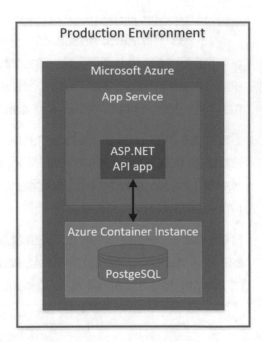

Figure 8-1. *Development and Production Environments*

As you can see, the "components" that are there are effectively the same; it's really only the underlying platform that is different (a local Windows PC vs. Microsoft Azure).

We'll park further discussion on the Production Environment for now and come back to that in later chapters; for now, we'll focus on our Development environment.

The Development Environment

How does our app know which environment it's in? Quite simply – we tell it!

This is where "Environment Variables" come into play, specifically the ASPNETCORE_ENVIRONMENT variable. Environment variables can be specified, or set, in a number of different ways depending on the physical environment (Windows, OSX, Linux, Azure, etc.). So, while they can be set at the OS level, our discussion will focus setting them in the *launchSettings.json* file (this can be found in the *Properties* folder of your project) for now.

ℹ️   Environment variables set in the *launchSettings.json* file will override environment variables set at the OS layer; that is why for the purposes of our discussion, we'll just focus on setting out values in the *launchSettings.json* file.

A fuller discussion on multiple environments in ASP.NET Core can be found here.[1]

Opening the *launchSettings.json* file in the API project; you should see something similar to the following.

```json
{
  "iisSettings": {
    "windowsAuthentication": false,
    "anonymousAuthentication": true,
    "iisExpress": {
      "applicationUrl": "http://localhost:12662",
      "sslPort": 44343
    }
  },
  "profiles": {
    "IIS Express": {
      "commandName": "IISExpress",
      "launchBrowser": true,
      "environmentVariables": {
        "ASPNETCORE_ENVIRONMENT": "Development"
      }
    },
    "CommandAPI": {
      "commandName": "Project",
      "launchBrowser": true,
      "applicationUrl": "https://localhost:5001;http://localhost:5000",
      "environmentVariables": {
        "ASPNETCORE_ENVIRONMENT": "Development"
      }
    }
  }
}
```

Figure 8-2. *LaunchSettings.json File*

---

[1]https://docs.microsoft.com/en-us/aspnet/core/fundamentals/environments

When you issue dotnet run at the .NET CLI the first *profile* with "commandName" : "Project" is used. The value of commandName specifies the webserver to launch. commandName can be any one of the following:

- IISExpress

- IIS

- Project (which launches the Kestrel web server)

In the preceding highlighted profile section, there are also additional details that are specified including the "applicationUrl" for both http and https and well as our environmentVariables; in this instance we only have one: ASPNETCORE_ENVIRONMENT, set to: Development.

So, when an application is launched (via dotnet run)

- *launchSettings.json* is read (if available).

- environmentVariables settings override system/OS-defined environment variables.

- The hosting environment is displayed.

For example, see Figure 8-3.

```
PROBLEMS    OUTPUT    DEBUG CONSOLE    TERMINAL

PS D:\APITutorial\NET Core 3.1\CommandAPISolution\src\CommandAPI> dotnet run
info: Microsoft.Hosting.Lifetime[0]
      Now listening on: https://localhost:5001
info: Microsoft.Hosting.Lifetime[0]
      Now listening on: http://localhost:5000
info: Microsoft.Hosting.Lifetime[0]
      Application started. Press Ctrl+C to shut down.
info: Microsoft.Hosting.Lifetime[0]
      Hosting environment: Development
info: Microsoft.Hosting.Lifetime[0]
      Content root path: D:\APITutorial\NET Core 3.1\CommandAPISolution\src\CommandAPI
```

Figure 8-3. *Our environment is set to Development*

So What?

At this stage I hear you all saying, *"Yeah that's great and everything, but so what?"*

Good question; I'm glad you asked that question![2]

Looking back at our simple environment setup, we need to connect to our Development database and eventually our Production database, and in almost all instances, they will be different, with different

- Endpoints (e.g., Server Name/IP address, etc.)

- Different log-in credentials, etc.

Therefore, depending on our *environment*, we'll want to change our *configuration*.

I'm using the database connection string as an example here, but there are many other configurations that will change depending on the environment. That is why it is so important we are aware of our environment.

Make the Distinction

OK, so what approach should you take within your application to make determinations on configuration based on the development environment (e.g., *use this* connection string for Development and *this one* for Production)? Well there are a number of different answers to that; to my mind there are two broad approaches:

1. "Manually" determine the environment in your code, and take the necessary action.

2. Leverage the power and behavior of the .NET Core *Configuration API.*

We're going to go with option 2. While option 1 is a possibility (indeed this pattern is used in many of the default .NET Core Projects – see the following example), I personally prefer to decouple code from configuration where possible, although it's not always possible – that is why we'll go with option 2.

---

[2]Beware when you get this response from either Salesman, an Executive, or Politician – it usually means that they don't know the answer and will either deflect the question somewhere else or lay on some major bullsh!t.

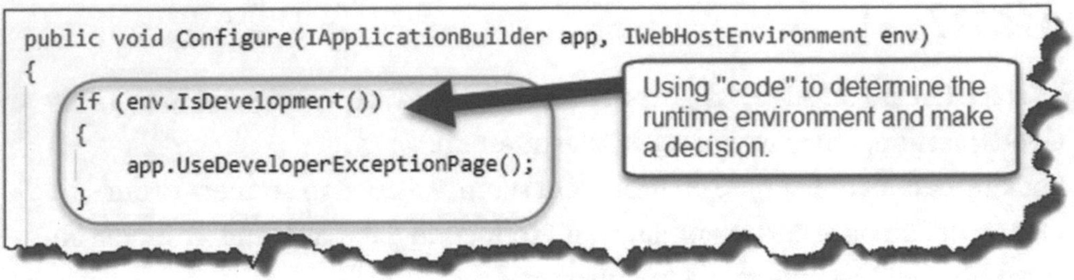

```
public void Configure(IApplicationBuilder app, IWebHostEnvironment env)
{
    if (env.IsDevelopment())
    {
        app.UseDeveloperExceptionPage();
    }
}
```

Using "code" to determine the runtime environment and make a decision.

Figure 8-4. *Code-based determination of environment*

The preceding snippet is taken from our very own Startup class, where the default project template uses the IsDevelopment parameter to determine which exception page to use.

Order of Precedence

OK, so we're going to leverage from the behavior of the .NET Core *Configuration API* to change the config as required for our two different environments (we've already made use of this when we configured the connection string for the DB Context).

Let's quickly revisit the Program Class startup sequence for our app as covered in Chapter 4.

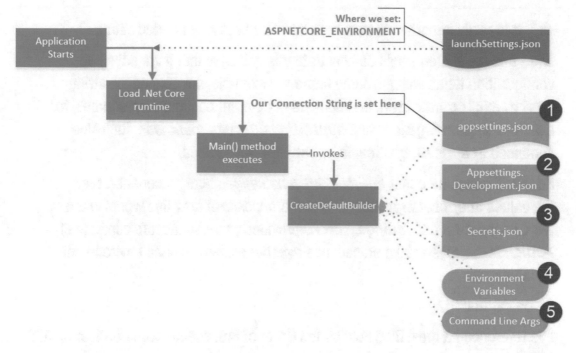

Figure 8-5. *Configuration sources and order of preference*

You'll see I've added some extra detail:

- The ***launchSettings.json*** file is loaded when we issue the `dotnet run` command and set the value for ASPNETCORE_ENVIRONMENT.

- A number of configuration sources that are used by the `CreateDefaultBuilder` method.

- By default these sources are loaded in the precedence order specified previously, so ***appsettings.json*** is loaded first, followed by ***appsettings.Development.json,*** and so on.

⚠   It is really important to note here that **The Last Key Loaded Wins.**

What this means (and we'll demonstrate this below) is that if we have two configuration items with the same name, for example, our connection string, `PostgreSqlConnection`, that appears in different configuration sources, for example, ***appsettings.json*** and ***appsettings.Development.json***, the value contained in ***appsettings.Development.json*** will be used.

So, you'll notice here that *Environment Variables* will take precedence over the values in ***appsettings.json***. This is the *opposite* of how this works when we talk about ***launchSettings.json***. As previously mentioned, the contents of ***launchSettings.json*** take precedence *over* our system-defined environment variables.

So be careful!

I've referenced a great Blog Post on the Order of Precedence with Configuring ASP. NET Core here,[3] for a further overview.

It's Time to Move

OK, let's put a bit of this theory into practice and demonstrate what we mean.

- Go into your ***appsettings.json*** file, and *copy* the `ConnectionStrings` key-value pair that contains our `PostgreSqlConnection` connection string.

- Make sure you have the **correct values**[4] for User ID and Password.

- Insert this JSON segment into the ***appsettings.Development.json*** file – see Figure 8-6.

---

[3]https://devblogs.microsoft.com/premier-developer/order-of-precedence-when-configuring-asp-net-core/

[4]Remember we had changed them at the end of the last chapter to avoid publishing them to GitHub.

This means we will have the *same configuration* element in *both **appsettings.json*** and ***appsettings.Development.json***.

Figure 8-6. *Appsettings.Development.json*

Again, if you're unsure that your JSON is well-formed, use something like `http://jsoneditoronline.org/` to check.

Save the files you've made any changes to, run your API, and make the same call – it all still works as usual.

Let's Break It

OK, so to prove the point we were previously making

- Stop your API from running (Ctrl + c).

- Go back into ***appsettings.Development.json*** file, and edit the `Password` parameter in the connection string so that authentication to the PostgreSQL Server will fail – see Figure 8-7.

- Save your file.

```
C# Commands.cs        {} appsettings.Development.json ×

src > CommandAPI > {} appsettings.Development.json > ...
  1   {
  2       "Logging": {
  3         "LogLevel": {
  4           "Default": "Information",
  5           "Microsoft": "Warning",
  6           "Microsoft.Hosting.Lifetime": "Information"
  7         }
  8       },
  9       "ConnectionStrings":
 10       {
 11           "PostgreSqlConnection":"User ID=cmddbuser;Password=somewrongpaassword;Host=
 12       }
 13   }
 14
```

Figure 8-7. *The wrong credentials*

OK, now run the app again, and try to make the API Call.

Looking at the terminal output, you'll see you get a database connection error; this is because the last value for our connection string was invalid.

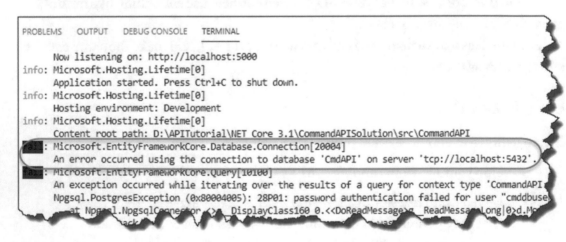

```
PROBLEMS   OUTPUT   DEBUG CONSOLE   TERMINAL

      Now listening on: http://localhost:5000
info: Microsoft.Hosting.Lifetime[0]
      Application started. Press Ctrl+C to shut down.
info: Microsoft.Hosting.Lifetime[0]
      Hosting environment: Development
info: Microsoft.Hosting.Lifetime[0]
      Content root path: D:\APITutorial\NET Core 3.1\CommandAPISolution\src\CommandAPI
fail: Microsoft.EntityFrameworkCore.Database.Connection[20004]
      An error occurred using the connection to database 'CmdAPI' on server 'tcp://localhost:5432'.
fail: Microsoft.EntityFrameworkCore.Query[10100]
      An exception occurred while iterating over the results of a query for context type 'CommandAPI
      Npgsql.PostgresException (0x80004005): 28P01: password authentication failed for user "cmddbuse
         at Npgsql.NpgsqlConnector.<>c__DisplayClass160_0.<<DoReadMessage>g__ReadMessageLong|0>d.M
```

Figure 8-8. *As expected, we can't connect*

Fix It Up

OK, so let's fix this:

- Edit your ***appsettings.Development.json*** file, and correct the value for the `Password` parameter

- ***Delete*** the `ConnectionStrings` json from the ***appsettings.json*** file.

This means that *only* our ***appsettings.Development.json*** file now contains our connection string; your ***appsettings.json*** file should now look like that in Figure 8-9.

```
{} appsettings.json  ×     {} appsettings.Development.json

src > CommandAPI > {} appsettings.json > ⊡ AllowedHosts
 1   {
 2       "Logging": {
 3         "LogLevel": {
 4           "Default": "Information",
 5           "Microsoft": "Warning",
 6           "Microsoft.Hosting.Lifetime": "Information"
 7         }
 8       },
 9       "AllowedHosts": "*"
10   }
11
```

Figure 8-9.   *Cleaned up Appsettings.json*

This means that currently, we only have a valid source for our connection string when running in a *Development* environment.

☞ **Learning Opportunity**   What will happen if you edit the ***launchSettings. json*** file and change the value of `ASPNETCORE_ENVIRONMENT` to "Production"?

Do this, run your app, and explain why you get this result.

We will cover our Production connection string in the Chapter 13.

User Secrets

We've covered the different environments you can have and why you have them and have even reconfigured our app to have a *development environment-only* connection string. But we still have not solved the issue we were left with at the end of the previous chapter – that being that, our User ID and Password are still in plaintext and are therefore available to anyone who has access to our source code – for example, someone looking at our repo in GitHub.

We solve that here.

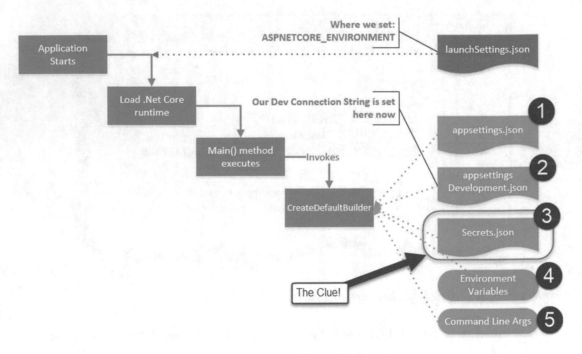

Figure 8-10. *Secrets.json in the scheme of things*

What Are User Secrets?

Well I gave you a bit of a clue in this chapter already.

In short, they are another location where you can store configuration elements; some points to note

- User Secrets are "tied" to the individual developer – that is, you!

- They are abstracted away from our source code and are not checked into any code repository.

- They are stored in the "*secrets.json*" file.

- The *secrets.json* file is *unencrypted* but is stored in a file system-protected user profile folder on the local dev machine.

This means that individual users can store (among other things) the credentials that they use to connect to a database. As the file is secured by the local file system, they remain secure (assuming no one has log-in access to your PC).

In terms of what you can store, this can be anything; it's just string data. We're now going to set up User Secrets for our *development connection* string.

Setting Up User Secrets

We need to make use of something called *The Secret Manager Tool* in order to make use of user secrets; this tool works on a project-by-project basis and therefore needs a way to uniquely identify each project. For this we need to make use of GUIDs.

☞ **Learning Opportunity**   Find out what GUID stands for, and do a little bit of reading on what they are and where they can be used (assuming you don't know this already!)

Cast your mind back to Chapter 2 where we set up our development lab, and one of the extensions we suggested for VS Code was *Insert GUID* – well now we get to use it!

In VS Code open your **CommandAPI.csproj** file, and in the <PropertyGroup> xml element, place the xml highlighted in the following:

```
<Project Sdk="Microsoft.NET.Sdk.Web">

  <PropertyGroup>
    <TargetFramework>netcoreapp3.1</TargetFramework>
    <UserSecretsId></UserSecretsId>
  </PropertyGroup>

  <ItemGroup>
```

```
<PackageReference Include="Microsoft.EntityFrameworkCore"
Version="3.0.0" />
.
.
.
</Project>
```

- Place your cursor in between the opening `<UserSecretsId>` and the closing `</UserSecretsId>` elements.

- Open the VS Code "Command Palette":

  - Press F1

  - Or Ctrl + Shift + P

  - Or View ➤ Command Palette

- Type "Insert."

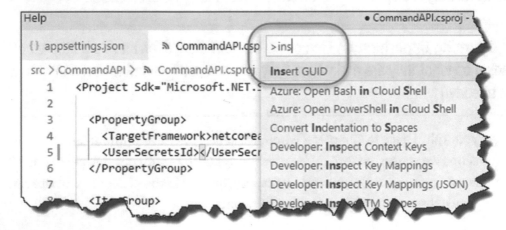

Figure 8-11. *Insert GUID*

- Insert GUID should appear; select it and select the first GUID Option.

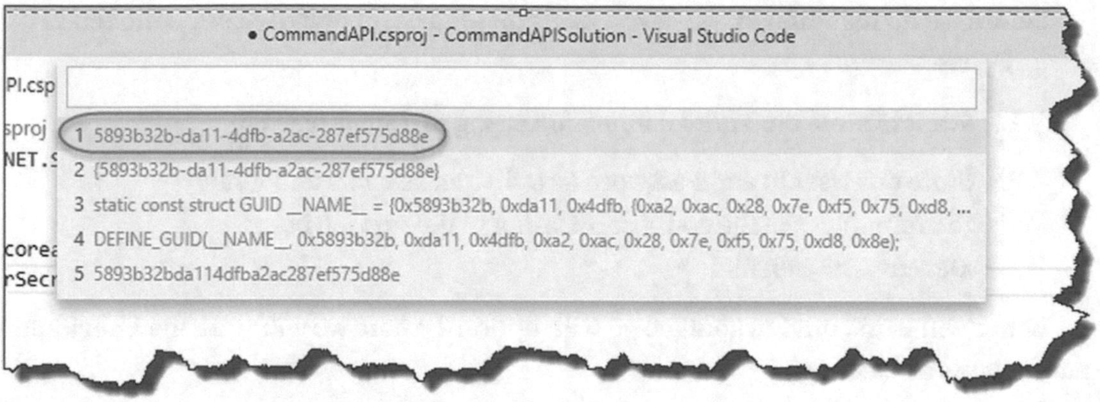

● CommandAPI.csproj - CommandAPISolution - Visual Studio Code

1 5893b32b-da11-4dfb-a2ac-287ef575d88e

2 {5893b32b-da11-4dfb-a2ac-287ef575d88e}

3 static const struct GUID __NAME__ = {0x5893b32b, 0xda11, 0x4dfb, {0xa2, 0xac, 0x28, 0x7e, 0xf5, 0x75, 0xd8, ...

4 DEFINE_GUID(__NAME__, 0x5893b32b, 0xda11, 0x4dfb, 0xa2, 0xac, 0x28, 0x7e, 0xf5, 0x75, 0xd8, 0x8e);

5 5893b32bda114dfba2ac287ef575d88e

Figure 8-12. *Select this GUID Format*

- This should place the auto-generated GUID into the xml elements
  specified; see the following example.

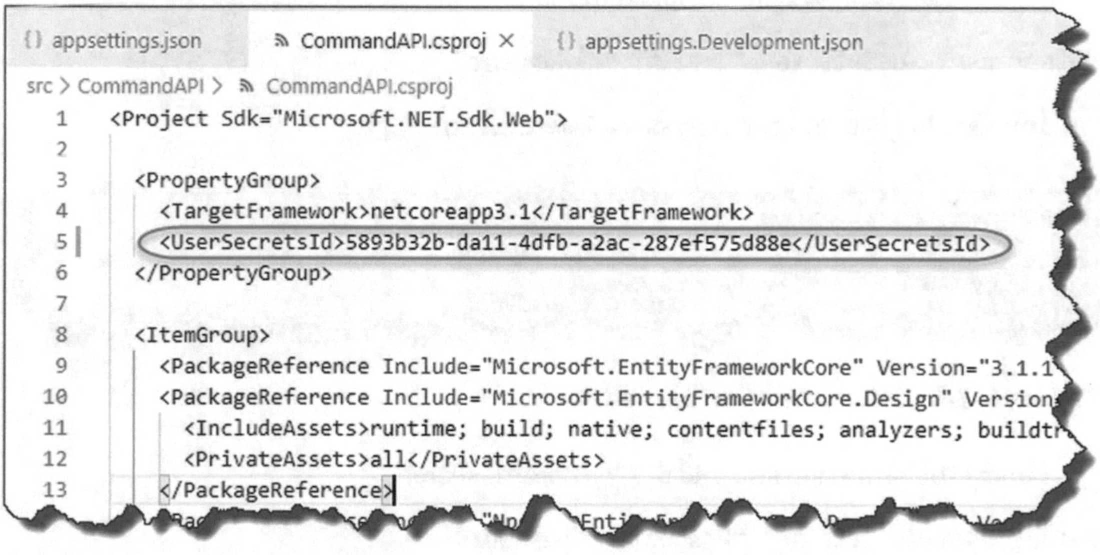

```
{} appsettings.json        ⋈ CommandAPI.csproj ×    {} appsettings.Development.json

src > CommandAPI > ⋈ CommandAPI.csproj
 1    <Project Sdk="Microsoft.NET.Sdk.Web">
 2
 3      <PropertyGroup>
 4        <TargetFramework>netcoreapp3.1</TargetFramework>
 5        <UserSecretsId>5893b32b-da11-4dfb-a2ac-287ef575d88e</UserSecretsId>
 6      </PropertyGroup>
 7
 8      <ItemGroup>
 9        <PackageReference Include="Microsoft.EntityFrameworkCore" Version="3.1.1
10        <PackageReference Include="Microsoft.EntityFrameworkCore.Design" Version
11          <IncludeAssets>runtime; build; native; contentfiles; analyzers; buildtr
12          <PrivateAssets>all</PrivateAssets>
13        </PackageReference>
```

Figure 8-13. *GUID Inserted into the .CSPROJ File*

Now save your file.

Deciding Your Secrets

Now we come to actually adding our secrets via The Secret Manager Tool, which will
generate a ***secrets.json*** file.

Before we do that though, we have a decision to make in regard to our connection string. Do we

1. Want to store our entire connection string as a single secret.

2. Store our User Id and Password as individual secrets and retain the remainder of the connection string in the ***appsettings. Developent.json*** file.

Either will work, but I'm going to go with option 2 where we will store the individual components as "secrets."

So, to add our two secrets:

• Ensure you have generated the GUID as described earlier, and save the .csproj file.

• At a terminal command (and make sure you're "inside" the ***CommandAPI*** project folder), type

```
dotnet user-secrets set "UserID" "cmddbuser"
```

You should get a "Successfully saved UserID..." message.

```
content root path: D:\APITutorial\NET Core 3.1\CommandAPISolution\src\CommandAPI
info: Microsoft.Hosting.Lifetime[0]
      Application is shutting down...
PS D:\APITutorial\NET Core 3.1\CommandAPISolution\src\CommandAPI> dotnet user-secrets set "UserID" "cmddbuser"
Successfully saved UserID = cmddbuser to the secret store.
PS D:\APITutorial\NET Core 3.1\CommandAPISolution\src\CommandAPI> []
```

Figure 8-14. *Adding our first user secret*

Repeat the same step and add the "Password" secret

```
dotnet user-secrets set "Password" "pa55w0rd!"
```

Again, you should get a similar success message.

Where Are They?

So where did our secrets end up? That's right, in our ***secrets.json*** file. You can find this file in a system-protected user profile folder on your local machine at the following location:

- Windows: `%APPDATA%\Microsoft\UserSecrets\<user_secrets_id>\secrets.json`

- Linux/OSX: `~/.microsoft/usersecrets/<user_secrets_id>/secrets.json`

So, on my machine, it can be found here.[5]

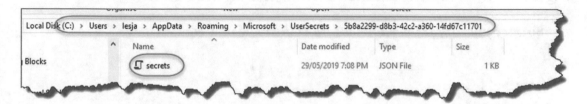

Figure 8-15. *Location of Secrets.Json on Windows*

Open this file, and have a look at the contents:

```
{
  "UserID": "cmddbuser",
  "Password": "pa55w0rd!"
}
```

It's just a simple, non-encrypted JSON file.

Code It Up

OK, so now to the really exciting bit where we'll actually use these secrets to build out our full connection string.

Step 1: Remove User ID and Password

We want to remove the "offending articles" from our existing connection string in our ***appsettings.Development.json*** file.

---

[5]On Windows you may need to ensure that you can see "Hidden items"; there is a tick box on the View ribbon on Windows Explorer where you can set this.

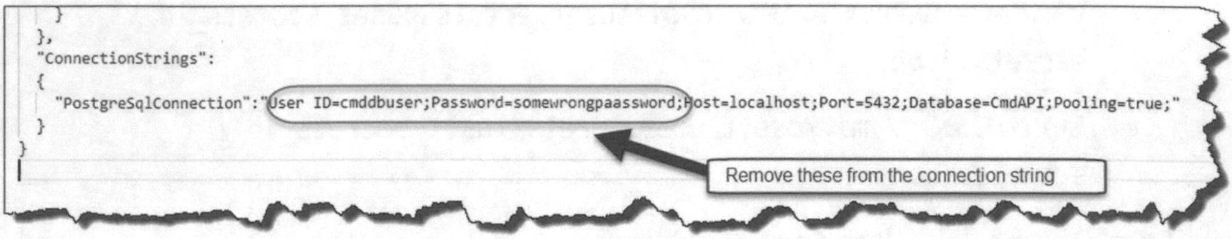

Figure 8-16. *Removal of sensitive connection string attributes*

So our ***appsettings.Development.json*** file should now contain only

```
{
  "Logging": {
    "LogLevel": {
      "Default": "Debug",
      "System": "Information",
      "Microsoft": "Information"
    }
  },
  "ConnectionStrings":
  {
    "PostgreSqlConnection":
      "Host=localhost;Port=5432;Database=CmdAPI;Pooling=true;"
  }
}
```

Make sure you save your file.

Step 2: Build Our Connection String

Move over into our Startup class, and add the following code to the ConfigureServices method (noting the inclusion of the new using statement at the top):

.

.

.

using Npgsql;

```
namespace CommandAPI
{
    public class Startup
    {
        public IConfiguration Configuration {get;}
        public Startup(IConfiguration configuration) => Configuration =
        configuration;

        public void ConfigureServices(IServiceCollection services)
        {
            var builder = new NpgsqlConnectionStringBuilder();
            builder.ConnectionString =
              Configuration.GetConnectionString("PostgreSqlConnection");
            builder.Username = Configuration["UserID"];
            builder.Password = Configuration["Password"];

            services.AddDbContext<CommandContext>
                (opt => opt.UseNpgsql(builder.ConnectionString));

            services.AddControllers();
            services.AddScoped<ICommandAPIRepo, SqlCommandAPIRepo>();
        }
    .
    .
    .
```

Again, for clarity I've circled the new/updated sections below:

```
using Microsoft.EntityFrameworkCore;
using Npgsql;

namespace CommandAPI
{
    public class Startup
    {
        public IConfiguration Configuration {get;}
        public Startup(IConfiguration configuration)
        {
            Configuration = configuration;
        }

        public void ConfigureServices(IServiceCollection services)
        {
            var builder = new NpgsqlConnectionStringBuilder();
            builder.ConnectionString =
                Configuration.GetConnectionString("PostgreSqlConnection");
                builder.Username = Configuration["UserID"];
                builder.Password = Configuration["Password"];


            services.AddDbContext<CommandContext>(opt => opt.UseNpgsql(builder.ConnectionString));

            services.AddControllers();

            services.AddScoped<ICommandAPIRepo, SqlCommandAPIRepo>();
        }
```

Figure 8-17. *Updated Startup class*

1. We need to add a reference to Npqsql in order to use
   NpgsqlConnectionStringBuilder.

2. This is where we

   a. Create a NpgsqlConnectionStringBuilder object, and pass in our
      "base" connection string PostgreSqlConnection from our ***appsettings.
      Development.json*** file.

   b. Continue to "build" the string by passing in both our UserID and Password
      secret from our ***secrets.json*** file.

3. Replace the original connection string with the newly constructed
   string using our builder object.

Save your work, build it, then run it. Fire up Postman, and issue our GET request to
our API. You should get a success!

🎂 **Celebration Checkpoint**   You have now dynamically created a connection string using a combination of configuration sources, one of which is User Secrets from our ***secrets.json*** file!

Just cast your mind back to the following diagram.

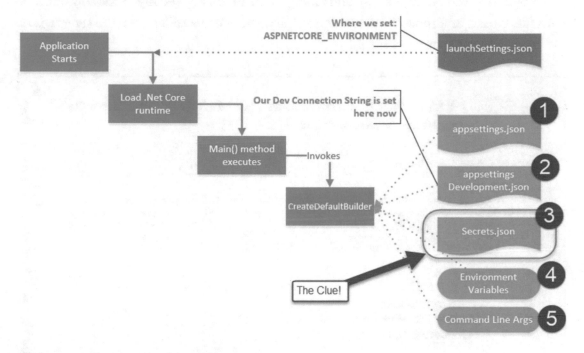

Figure 8-18. *Revisit of precedence*

The .NET Configuration layer by default provides us access to the configuration sources as shown in Figure 8-18; in this case we used a combination of 2 + 3.

Wrap It Up

Again, we covered a lot in this chapter; the main points are

- We moved our connection string to a development-only config file: ***appsetting.Development.json***.

- We removed the sensitive items from our connection string.

- We moved the sensitive items (User ID and Password) to *secrets.json* via The Secret Manager Tool.

- We constructed a fully working connection string using a combination of configuration sources.

All that's left to do is commit all our changes to Git then push up to GitHub!

Moving over to our repository and taking a look in the **appsettings.Development. json** file, we see an innocent connection string without user credentials (the *secrets.json* file is not added to source control)!

Figure 8-19. *Clean Appsettings.json on GitHub*

CHAPTER 9

Data Transfer Objects

Chapter Summary

In this chapter we'll complete the final piece of our architectural puzzled and introduce Data Transfer Objects.

When Done, You Will

- Understand what Data Transfer Objects (DTOs) are.
- Understand why you should use DTOs.
- Have started to implement DTOs in our solution.

Architecture Review

Outlining what we've either (a) started to implement or (b) fully implemented, our architectural is evolving nicely.

© Les Jackson 2020
L. Jackson, *The Complete ASP.NET Core 3 API Tutorial*, https://doi.org/10.1007/978-1-4842-6255-9_9

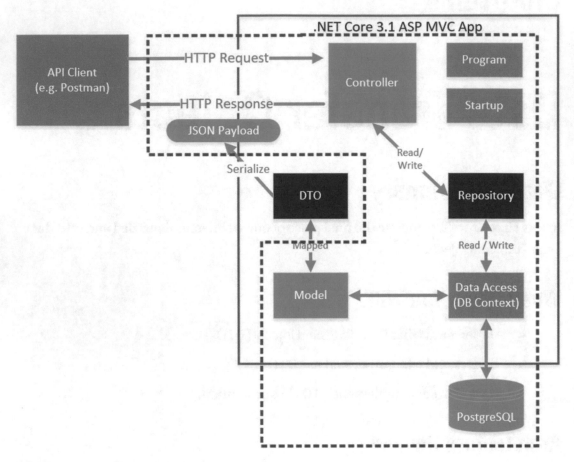

Figure 9-1. *Architecture Progress*

To summarize, we've

- Fully implemented our Model

- Fully implemented our *Repository Interface*

- Partially implemented our Concrete *Repository Implementation* (using the DB Context)

- Fully implemented our DB Context

- Fully implemented our Database

- Partially completed our Controller (we still have four actions to complete)

We have not yet started on the DTOs, so that is what we'll turn our attention to in this chapter.

The What and Why of DTOs

To answer both what DTOs are and why you'd use them, let's take a look at what we have implemented so far:

- We have implemented two Controller Actions that return serialized Command objects to the consumer.

What's wrong with that?

We are basically exposing "internal" domain detail out to our consumers; this has the following potential consequences:

- We may be exposing "sensitive" information.

- We may be exposing irrelevant information.

- We may be exposing information in the wrong format.

- We have "coupled" our internal implementation to our external contract, so changing our internals will be difficult if we want to maintain our contract (or we break the contract altogether – not advised).

This is not a great situation – so what is the answer?

Decouple Interface from Implementation (Again)

Again (similar to what we did with our repository), we want to decouple our external contract (our interface) from our internal implementation (our Domain model). This is where DTOs come in; observe the following diagram:

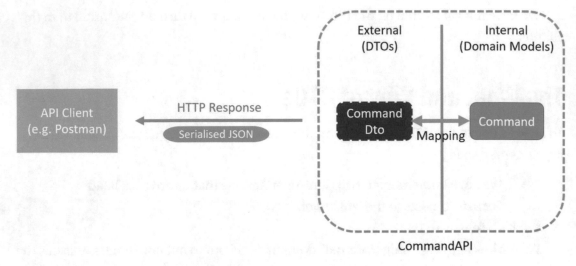

Figure 9-2. *Example of Read DTO*

DTOs are "mapped" to our internal Domain Model classes and represented externally as part of the contract, thus decoupling our implementation from our interface. We can then benefit from

- Change Agility: We can feel free to change our internal implementation, and as long as we perform the appropriate mapping back to our DTO, our interface remains intact.

- We can remove both sensitive and irrelevant implementation detail from our DTOs

- As part of our "mapping" operation, we can augment our internal representations and present them in an entirely new way (e.g., combining First and Last name and presenting externally as Full Name).

Taking it further, depending on what type of operation we are performing (Read, Create, Update, etc.), we may employ different variants of our DTO to cater for each, as shown below.

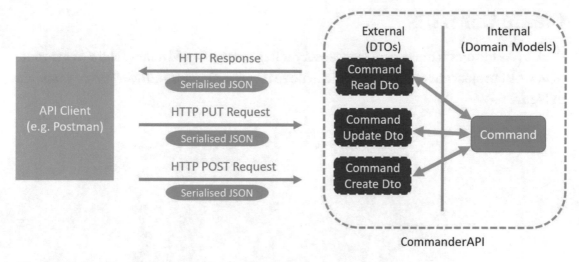

Figure 9-3. *We can have DTOs for different actions*

I'll explain this concept as we start to implement; just bear it in mind for now. With that I think we should move on to coding.

Implementing DTOs

To implement DTOs, we need to do the following:

- Create our DTO classes.

- Figure out how to perform the "mapping" mentioned previously.

The first point is actually very straightforward, but it is the second point that introduces more options and/or complexity. We could simply perform the mapping operations manually in code we write ourselves, and while this *may* be ok for small objects, as our models grow in size and complexity, this would become

- Tiresome

- Error-prone

Therefore, we are going to employ an automation framework (called AutoMapper) to perform the mapping function for us. While this does require a little bit more upfront effort, believe me it's worth it! Before we get involved with AutoMapper, let's start with implementing our DTO classes.

Create Our DTOs

Back in API Project (make sure the webserver has stopped), add a new folder to the root of our API project called **Dtos**, and add a file to it called **CommandReadDto.cs** as shown in Figure 9-4.

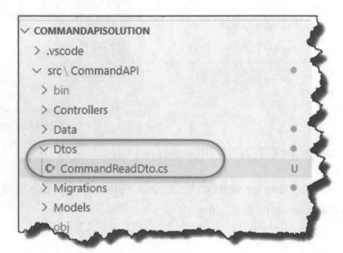

Figure 9-4. *New Dtos Folder and CommandReadDto.cs file*

As the name suggests, we will use this DTO when we perform any read operation, so in effect this is the object that will be serialized and sent back to the client whenever they perform a GET request.

Now at this point, you may ask yourself the question: Won't the DTO be *exactly* the same as our Command model? And to be honest, yes it will, but is nonetheless still a valid use case. With that in mind, complete the code for our DTO as follows:

```
namespace CommandAPI.Dtos
{
    public class CommandReadDto
    {
        public int Id {get; set;}

        public string HowTo {get; set;}

        public string Platform {get; set;}
```

```
        public string CommandLine {get; set;}
    }
}
```

You can see this has more than a passing resemblance to our Command model. You will notice though that in this case, there are no Data Annotations (we will be utilizing them again, just not for this DTO).

And that's essentially it for our first DTO class – I told you it was simple. We now need to move on to setting up AutoMapper.

Setting Up AutoMapper

The first thing we need to do is install another package in our API Project, so ensure the webserver is not running (CTRL + C if it is), and at a command prompt "in" the API project folder (***CommandAPI***), enter the following:

```
dotnet add package AutoMapper.Extensions.Microsoft.DependencyInjection
```

This will install the AutoMapper package; confirm this by checking the ***.csproj*** file for the API project, and you should see something similar to Figure 9-5.

```
<Project Sdk="Microsoft.NET.Sdk.Web">

  <PropertyGroup>
    <TargetFramework>netcoreapp3.1</TargetFramework>
    <UserSecretsId>cabd2435-bee0-47b0-8990-0889111a5d36</UserSecretsId>
  </PropertyGroup>

  <ItemGroup>
    <PackageReference Include="AutoMapper.Extensions.Microsoft.DependencyInjection" Version="7.0.0" />
    <PackageReference Include="Microsoft.EntityFrameworkCore" Version="3.1.4" />
    <PackageReference Include="Microsoft.EntityFrameworkCore.Design" Version="3.1.4">
      <IncludeAssets>runtime; build; native; contentfiles; analyzers; buildtransitive</IncludeAssets>
      <PrivateAssets>all</PrivateAssets>
    </PackageReference>
    <PackageReference Include="Npgsql.EntityFrameworkCore.PostgreSQL" Version="3.1.3" />
  </ItemGroup>

</Project>
```

Figure 9-5. *Reference to Automapper*

To use AutoMapper we move over to our Startup class and register it in our Service Container by adding the following lines (making it available to us throughout our application via our old friend *Dependency Injection*):

.

using AutoMapper;

.

.

.

```
services.AddControllers();
```

```
//Add the line below
```

services.AddAutoMapper(AppDomain.CurrentDomain.GetAssemblies());

```
services.AddScoped<ICommandAPIRepo, SqlCommandAPIRepo>();.
```

To put it in context, I've highlighted those new inclusions in Figure 9-6.

```
using Microsoft.Extensions.Hosting;
using Microsoft.EntityFrameworkCore;
using Npgsql;
using AutoMapper;

namespace CommandAPI
{
    public class Startup
    {
        public IConfiguration Configuration {get;}
        public Startup(IConfiguration configuration)
        {
            Configuration = configuration;
        }

        public void ConfigureServices(IServiceCollection services)
        {
            var builder = new NpgsqlConnectionStringBuilder();
            builder.ConnectionString =
                Configuration.GetConnectionString("PostgreSqlConnection");
                builder.Username = Configuration["UserID"];
                builder.Password = Configuration["Password"];

            services.AddDbContext<CommandContext>(opt => opt.UseNpgsql(builder.ConnectionString));

            services.AddControllers();

            services.AddAutoMapper(AppDomain.CurrentDomain.GetAssemblies());

            services.AddScoped<ICommandAPIRepo, SqlCommandAPIRepo>();
```

Figure 9-6. *AutoMapper service registered*

> **Note**   The registration of Automapper can really be placed anywhere in the
> `ConfigureServices` method; I've just chosen to place it here in case you're
> wondering. For more detail on how to use AutoMapper with Dependency Injection
> in .NET Core, refer to the AutoMapper Docs.[1]

That's our setup of AutoMapper complete – see, it wasn't that bad; we now need to
move onto using it.

Using AutoMapper

In order to use AutoMapper, we need *somewhere* to configure the mapping of our
Model to our DTO, in this case mapping Command to CommandReadDto, and we do
that via a "profile." To start using AutoMapper profiles, create another folder in the
root of our ***CommandAPI*** project called ***Profiles***, and in there create a file called
CommandsProfile.cs as so.

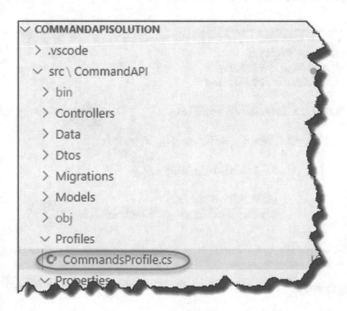

Figure 9-7. *New Profiles folder and CommandsProfile.cs file*

---

[1]https://docs.automapper.org/en/stable/Dependency-injection.html#asp-net-core

Now add the following code to the file:

```
using AutoMapper;
using CommandAPI.Dtos;
using CommandAPI.Models;

namespace CommandAPI.Profiles
{
    public class CommandsProfile : Profile
    {
        public CommandsProfile()
        {
            CreateMap<Command, CommandReadDto>();
        }
    }
}
```

The class can be explained in Figure 9-8.

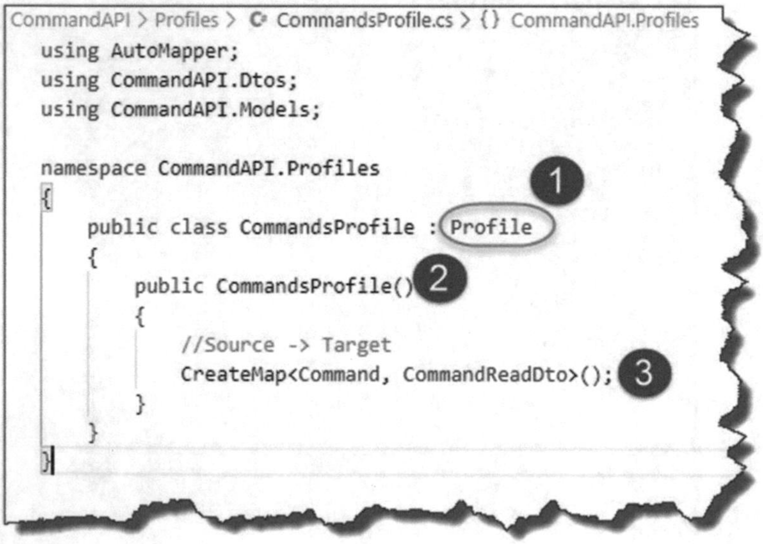

Figure 9-8. *Our first AutoMapper Mapping*

1.   Our class inherits from `Automapper.Profile`.

2.   We add a simple class constructor.

3. We use the `CreateMap` method to map our source object (`Command`)
    to our target object (`CommandReadDto`).

And that's our mapping complete. It's so straightforward in our case as the property names of both classes are identical; AutoMapper can derive the mappings easily.

Finally, we want to update our Controller to return our DTO representation (`CommandReadDto`) instead of `Command` Model for both our GET Actions. Before we do that though, we need to make AutoMapper "available" to our Controller. Any ideas how we do that?

For those of you that said *Constructor Dependency Injection*, well done! That's exactly what we're going to do. So over in our Controller, add the following highlighted code:

.

.

```
using AutoMapper;
using CommandAPI.Dtos;

namespace CommandAPI.Controllers
{
  [Route("api/[controller]")]
  [ApiController]
  public class CommandsController : ControllerBase
  {
    private readonly ICommandAPIRepo _repository;
    private readonly IMapper _mapper;

    public CommandsController(ICommandAPIRepo repository, IMapper mapper)
    {
      _repository = repository;
      _mapper = mapper;
    }
```

.

.

.

To explain what we've done, have a look at the changes in context in Figure 9-9.

```
using System.Collections.Generic;
using AutoMapper;                    1
using CommandAPI.Dtos;
using CommandAPI.Data;
using CommandAPI.Models;
using Microsoft.AspNetCore.Mvc;

namespace CommandAPI.Controllers
{
    [Route("api/[controller]")]
    [ApiController]
    public class CommandsController : ControllerBase
    {
        private readonly ICommandAPIRepo _repository;
        private readonly IMapper _mapper;              2            3

        public CommandsController(ICommandAPIRepo repository, IMapper mapper)
        {
            _repository = repository;
            _mapper = mapper;              4
        }

        [HttpGet]
```

Figure 9-9. *Injecting AutoMapper into the controller*

1. Added our two new using directives.

2. Created a new read-only field to hold an instance of IMapper.

3. An instance of IMapper will be injected by the DI system into our constructor.

4. We assign our injected instance to the private member _mapper for further use.

This pattern should be very familiar to you now as we have used it multiple times within our API; the only point of note is that you can see we can inject *multiple instances* into our Constructor.

We can now update our two existing controller actions to make use of AutoMapper and return our DTO representation to our consumers as shown by the highlighted code in the following:

.

.

```
[HttpGet]
```

```csharp
public ActionResult<IEnumerable<CommandReadDto>> GetAllCommands()
{
  var commandItems = _repository.GetAllCommands();

  return Ok(_mapper.Map<IEnumerable<CommandReadDto>>(commandItems));
}

[HttpGet("{id}")]
public ActionResult<CommandReadDto> GetCommandById(int id)
{
  var commandItem = _repository.GetCommandById(id);
  if (commandItem == null){
    return NotFound();
  }
  return Ok(_mapper.Map<CommandReadDto>(commandItem));
}
.
.
.
```

The changes are shown and explained in Figure 9-10.

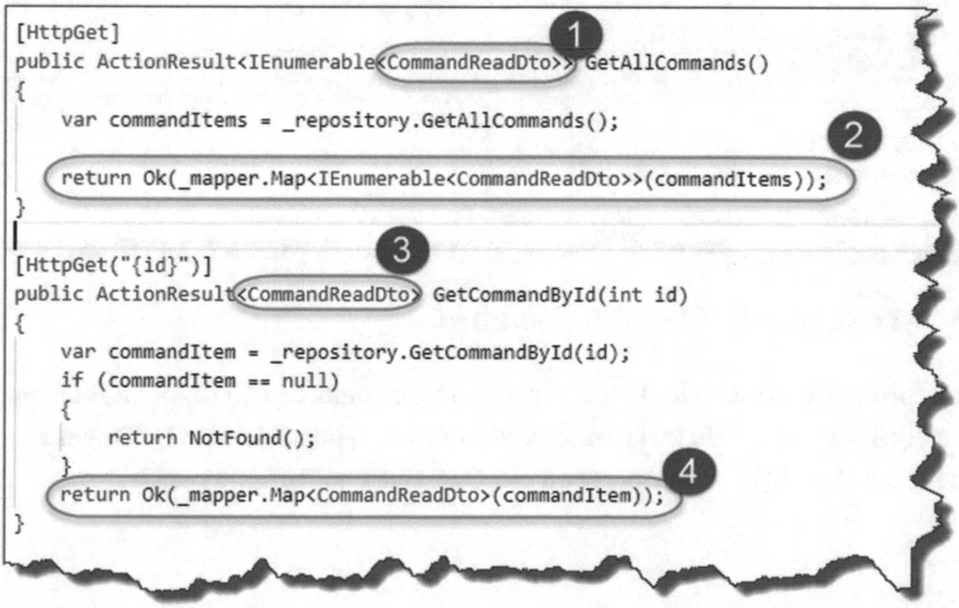

Figure 9-10. *Use of Automapper in our 2 GET Controller Actions*

1. We ensure our ActionResult return type is changed from Command to CommandReadDto.

2. We call the Map method on our _mapper instance. It maps our collection of Command objects to an IEnumerable of CommaneReadDtos that we return in our OK method.

3. We ensure our ActionResult return type is changed from Command to CommandReadDto.

4. Does the same thing as #1, except we are working with a single Command object as the source and returning (if available) a single CommandReadDto object in our OK method.

Save all your code and run as before.

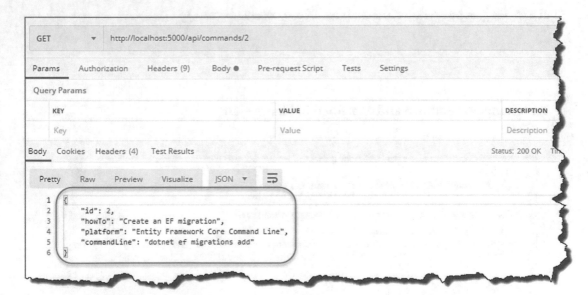

Figure 9-11. *CommandReadDTO Returned*

The "problem" is that it looks exactly the same as before (well it's not a *problem*; technically it's working). So just to demonstrate what is possible with DTOs, let's comment out the Platform property on our CommandReadDto, as shown here:

```
namespace CommandAPI.Dtos
{
  public class CommandReadDto
  {
    public int Id {get; set;}

    public string HowTo {get; set;}

    //Comment out the line below
    //public string Platform {get; set;}

    public string CommandLine {get; set;}
  }
}
```

Once you've saved your changes, restart the webserver and rerun your Postman query.

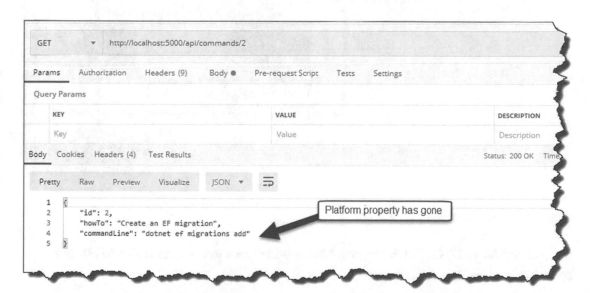

Figure 9-12. *CommandReadDto returned with platform removed*

You'll see that our DTO representation has in fact been returned! Once you're happy, *revert those changes* so we're returning the full object.

A quick look at our application architecture and you can see that we have now completed the groundwork for all our architectural components (although some components are only partially complete as depicted in Figure 9-13):

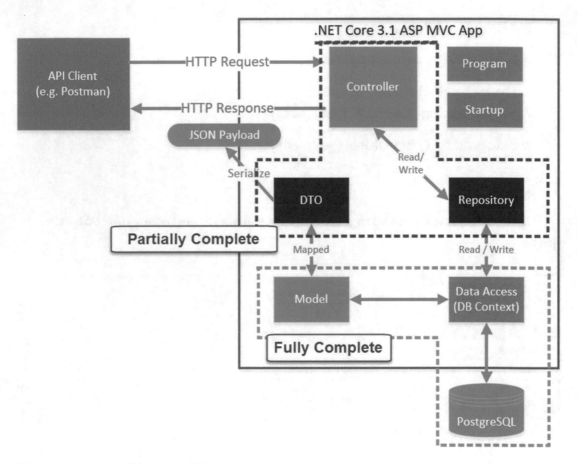

Figure 9-13. *Architecture Check*

We can leave DTOs there for now, but we will return to them as we build out our remaining controller actions next.

## CHAPTER 10

Completing Our API Endpoints

Chapter Summary

In the last few chapters, we have put a lot of work into the underlying architectural fabric of our API, but we've only implemented two of our endpoints (controller actions). In this chapter we address this and move up a gear to finalize our remaining four endpoints.

When Done, You Will

- Understand how data changes are persisted by Entity Framework Core.

- Have fully implemented our Create (POST) resource endpoint.

- Have fully implemented our two Update (PUT and PATCH) resource endpoints.

- Have fully implemented our Delete (DELETE) resource endpoint.

- Understand more about REST best practice.

Persisting Changes in EF Core

So far, we have used an EF Core DB Context (via our Repository) to read data from our PostgreSQL database and return it to our consumer (using DTOs). These endpoints are considered "safe" as they cannot change the data in our database; they can only read it.

L. Jackson, *The Complete ASP.NET Core 3 API Tutorial*, https://doi.org/10.1007/978-1-4842-6255-9_10

Our four remaining endpoints, (shown below) are slightly more *dangerous* in that they are able to *change* the data in our database, or to use a slightly more dramatic term – they are considered "unsafe."

Verb	URI	Operation	Description
POST	/api/commands	Create	Create a new resource
PUT	/api/commands/{Id}	Update (full)	Update all of a single resource (by Id)
PATCH	/api/commands/{Id}	Update (partial)	Update part of a single resource (by Id)
DELETE	/api/commands/{Id}	Delete	Delete a single resource (by Id)

The reason I'm calling out this fairly obvious point is because I want to shine a little light on how changes to data occur in EF Core and in particular when using a DB Context, as it becomes relevant in the sections that follow.

DB Context Tracks Changes

Let's take a simple example of adding a new Command resource to the PostgreSQL DB; using our DB Context, we will

1. Obtain the Command object to be added (don't worry where we get this for now).

2. Add that Command object to the CommandItems DBSet in our DB Context.

3. Save the changes *pending* on the DB Context.

4. Changes will then be reflected in the PostgreSQL database.

The point I'm making here is that just by adding (or removing/updating) objects on our DB Context does not mean those changes will be automatically reflected down on the PostgreSQL database. We need to further *Save* the pending changes for that to happen.

What you can take from this is that the DB Context tracks (multiple) changes to the data "internally," be they create, update, or delete operations, but will only persist those changes to the DB when we explicitly tell it to – by *Saving Changes.*

Again, I wanted to call that out here, as it becomes relevant in a couple of areas as we move into implementing our remaining endpoints.

The Create Endpoint (POST)

The next endpoint we want to implement is the "Create" endpoint, which gives us the ability to add resources to our DB. A quick reminder of our high-level definition is shown here.

Verb	URI	Operation	Description
POST	/api/commands	Create	Create a new resource

We'll also introduce some other attributes that will help us understand, build, and ultimately test our endpoint; they are shown in the following table.

Attribute	Description

Inputs (x1)	The "command" object to be created.
	 This will be added to the request body of our POST request; an example is shown here:
	 {
	   "howTo": "Example how to",
	   "platform": "Example platform",
	   "commandLine": "Example command line"
	 }

Process	Will attempt to add a new command object to our DB
Success Outputs	• HTTP 201 Created Status • Newly Created Resource (response body) • URI to newly created resource (response header)
Failure Outputs	• HTTP 400 Bad Request • HTTP 405 Not Allowed
Safe	No – Endpoint can alter our resources
Idempotent	No – Repeating the same operation will incur a different result

Most of this should make sense, but there are probably three callouts for me before we move onto coding.

Input Object

You'll notice that the object we can expect to attach to the request body in order to create a resource *does not* contain an "Id" attribute – why is that? Simply because the responsibility for creating a unique id has been devolved down to our PostgreSQL Database. When a new row is inserted to our CommandItems table, it is at that point that a new (unique) id will be created for us. (You should remember this when we manually added data to our DB via SQL commands in Chapter 7.)

📖 **Learning Opportunity**   As our input command object is different to our *internal domain command model*, what technique could we use to deal with this?

Success Outputs

The issuing of a 201 Created Http Status code is self-explanatory, but what you may not have expected is that we should pass back both:

- The newly created resource (with Id)

- A URI (or "route") to where we can obtain that resource again if needed

The second point in particular is to allow us to align with the REST architectural principles, so we'll follow it here in our API. Further discussion on this can be found in this article on REST.[1]

Idempotency

I've already mentioned "safety" in the opening to this chapter, but I've also included whether this endpoint is "idempotent." What is idempotency?

An operation is idempotent when performing the same operation again gives the same result.

So, in the case of our create endpoint, the first time we fire off a request (assuming it's successful), we'll get the newly created resource returned. If we perform the *exact same*

---

[1]https://en.wikipedia.org/wiki/Representational_state_transfer

request again, we'll get a *different result*. Why? Because we'll have created a whole new resource (with a new Id) in addition to the first one. Our create endpoint is therefore *not* idempotent.

Compare that with one of our existing GET requests; we can perform the same request time and time again and get the *same result* – these *are* idempotent.

Why have I included this? Simply because I've seen the use of the term increase dramatically over the short term (although the concept is not new), so I would be doing you a disservice if I didn't introduce it to you here.

Enough theory – lets code.

Updating the Repository

Let's work from "the ground up" and return to our repository. Refer to Figure 10-1 that details the repository interface definition ICommandAPIRepo.

```
public interface ICommandAPIRepo
{
    bool SaveChanges();

    IEnumerable<Command> GetAllCommands();
    Command GetCommandById(int id);
    void CreateCommand(Command cmd);
    void UpdateCommand(Command cmd);
    void DeleteCommand(Command cmd);
}
```

Figure 10-1. *CreateCommand Repository Method*

We can see that for the highlighted repository method, we simply require a Command object to be passed in (and, as inferred, added to our DB Context – and ultimately our PostgreSQL database). We don't expect anything returned back. Moving over to our concrete implementation, SqlCommandAPIRepo, add the following code to the CreateCommand method (making sure to include the using System namespace):

```
using System
    .
    .
    .
```

```
public void CreateCommand(Command cmd)
{
  if(cmd == null)
  {
    throw new ArgumentNullException(nameof(cmd));
  }
  _context.CommandItems.Add(cmd);
}
```

To put these in context, see Figure 10-2.

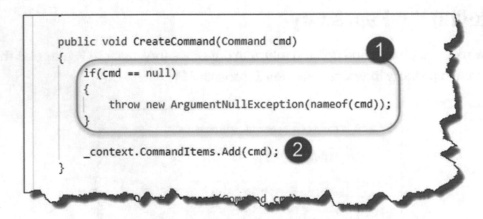

Figure 10-2. *Implementation of CreateCommand*

1. We check to see if the object passed in is null, and if so throw an exception (this case will be caught in our controller when it comes to validate the command model we have; however, we don't know where else our repository implementation may be used, so it's good practice to put code like this in any way).

2. Using our DB Context instance (_context), we reference our CommandItems DB Set and call the Add method, passing in our Command object.

Going back to our discussion on how data is persisted in EF Core, you'll be aware that just calling this method *will not persist our changes down to the DB*; at this point we only have the Command object added to the DB Context/DB Set.

Implement SaveChanges

Returning once again to our repository interface definition, ICommandAPIRepo, you'll remember a mysterious method definition (well probably not *that* mysterious anymore).

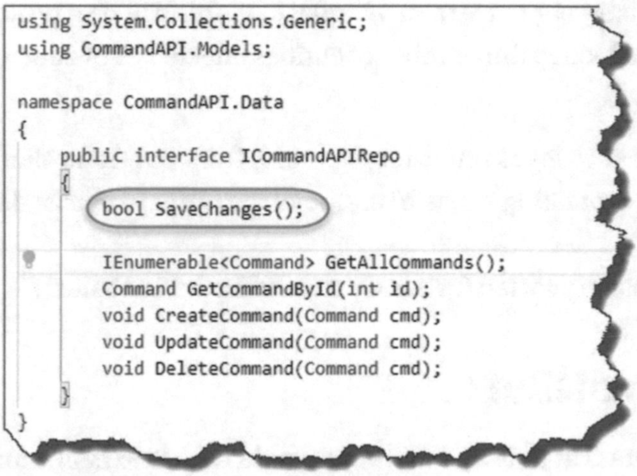

```
using System.Collections.Generic;
using CommandAPI.Models;

namespace CommandAPI.Data
{
    public interface ICommandAPIRepo
    {
        bool SaveChanges();

        IEnumerable<Command> GetAllCommands();
        Command GetCommandById(int id);
        void CreateCommand(Command cmd);
        void UpdateCommand(Command cmd);
        void DeleteCommand(Command cmd);
    }
}
```

Figure 10-3. *The SaveChanges Interface method*

Well we need to implement that now in our concrete implementation, so back over in SqlCommandAPIRepo, add the following code to the SaveChanges method:

```
public bool SaveChanges()
{
  return (_context.SaveChanges() >= 0);
}
```

In context, these changes look like this.

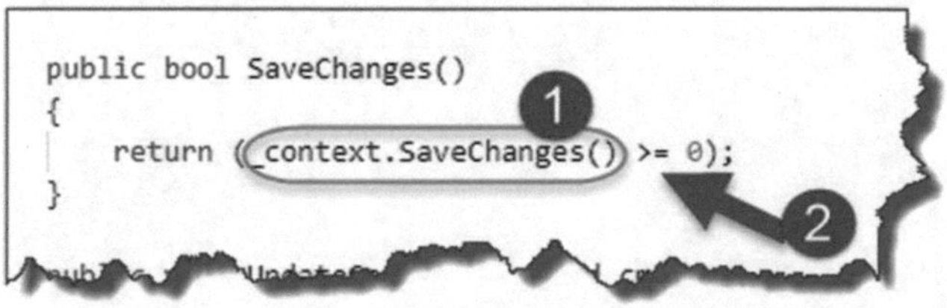

```
public bool SaveChanges()
{
    return (_context.SaveChanges() >= 0);
}
```

Figure 10-4. *Implementation of SaveChanges*

213

1. Call the SaveChanges method on our DB Context; this replicates
    all pending changes on the DB Context down to the PostgreSQL
    DB and persists them.

2. We use this comparison operator to return true if the result of
    save changes is greater than or equal to 0 (this will be a positive
    integer reflecting the number of entities affected or of course 0 if
    none are[2]).

We'll use the SaveChanges repository operator from our Controller, and we'll use
it for all four of our remaining "unsafe" endpoints in order to persist data (not just our
Create endpoint).

That's our repository sorted for our Create method, what's next?

CommandCreateDto

Earlier in this chapter I asked what *technique* could we use to deal with the fact that
the representation of the command resource we expect from our POST request will be
different to our internal command model? For those of you that answered with "DTOs,"
give yourself a pat on the back – yes we're going to use a DTO to represent the input for
our command resource and, using AutoMapper, map it back to an internal command
model we can pass over to our repository, I've shown a slightly simplified version of this
scenario in Figure 10-5.

---

[2]https://docs.microsoft.com/en-us/dotnet/api/microsoft.entityframeworkcore.
dbcontext.savechanges

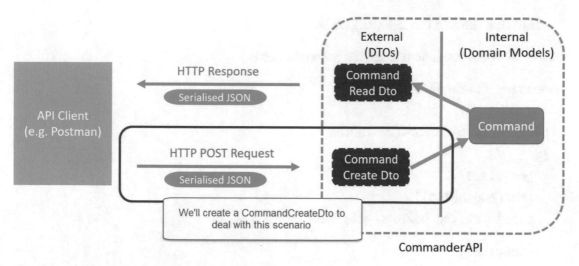

Figure 10-5. *CommandCreate DTO Example*

Create the New DTO

Back over in our project, create a file called ***CommandCreateDto.cs*** in the ***Dtos*** folder
as so.

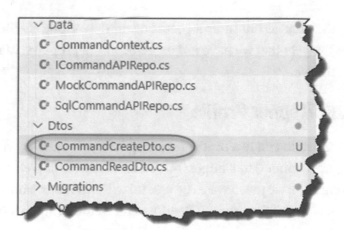

Figure 10-6. *CommandCreateDTO.cs created*

Into that file add the following code:

```
using System.ComponentModel.DataAnnotations;

namespace CommandAPI.Dtos
{
  public class CommandCreateDto
  {
    [Required]
    [MaxLength(250)]
    public string HowTo { get; set; }

    [Required]
    public string Platform { get; set; }

    [Required]
    public string CommandLine { get; set; }

  }
}
```

This is exactly the same as our internal command model (noting we have included the use of annotations), except that we have *not included* the Id property. Make sure you remember to save the file.

Update the AutoMapper Profile

You'll remember we had to create a profile mapping for our first DTO, which mapped our "source" (a command model) to a target (our CommandReadDto). Well we have to do the exact same thing here; we just have to be careful with what our "source" is vs. what our "target" is. So over in the ***CommandsProfile.cs*** file in the ***Profiles*** folder, add the following mapping:

```
public class CommandsProfile : Profile
{
  public CommandsProfile()
  {
    //Source ➤ Target
    CreateMap<Command, CommandReadDto>();
```

```
CreateMap<CommandCreateDto, Command>();
  }
}
```

I won't display the usual "code in context" image for explanation purposes as I feel this is straightforward, but in essence our "source" is the CommandCreateDto (as will be supplied in our POST request body), and the target is our internal Command model.

So with

- The new CommandCreateDto created

- An updated AutoMapper mapping profile

We can move on to implementing our controller action (our Create endpoint).

Updating the Controller

So fair warning, although the code for our next action is not particularly large in volume, there are a lot of concepts in this section. Thinking about the best way to present it to you, I'd decided to include all the code in one go (rather than layering it up which I feel would not translate well to the written page and be more confusing than helpful). Don't worry, we go through it all line by line by way of explanation afterward.

So over in our CommandsController class, add the following code to create our new controller action:

```
[HttpPost]
public ActionResult <CommandReadDto> CreateCommand
  (CommandCreateDto commandCreateDto)
{
  var commandModel = _mapper.Map<Command>(commandCreateDto);
  _repository.CreateCommand(commandModel);
  _repository.SaveChanges();

  var commandReadDto = _mapper.Map<CommandReadDto>(commandModel);

  return CreatedAtRoute(nameof(GetCommandById),
    new {Id = commandReadDto.Id}, commandReadDto);
}
```

217

To put those changes in context, see Figure 10-7.

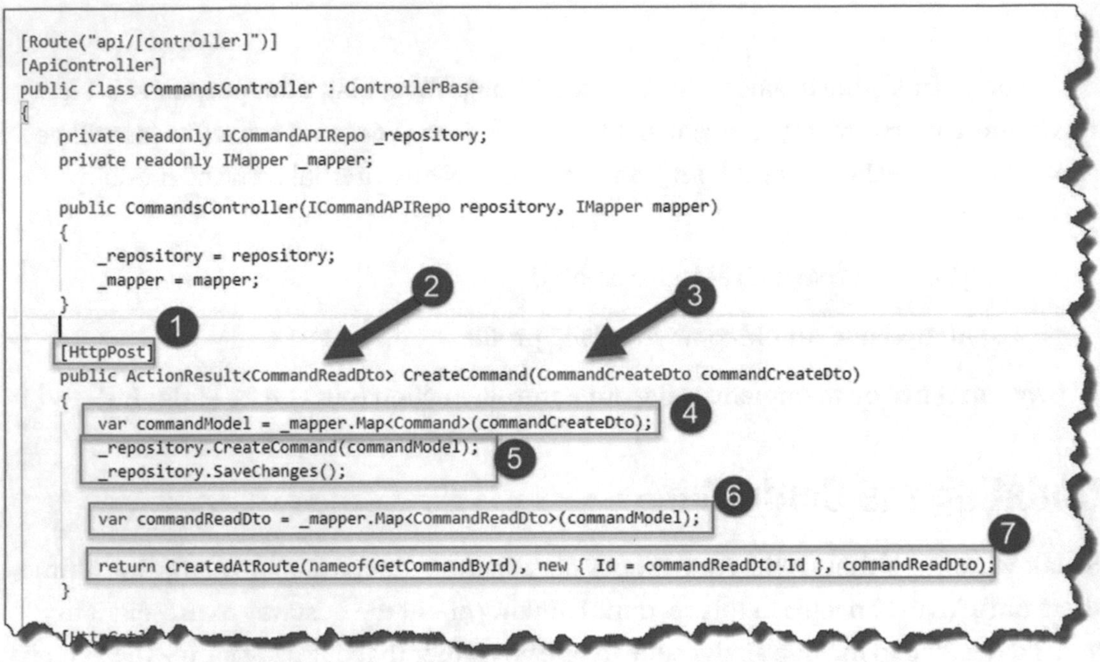

Figure 10-7. CreateCommand Implementation

Let's go through this:

1. HttpPost

We decorate the action with [HttpPost], which I feel is straightforward enough. As mentioned before, this action will respond to the Class-wide route of

`api/commands`

with the POST verb, which in combination makes it unique to this Controller.

2. Return DTO Type

As described in the endpoint attributes, we expect to return the newly created resource as part of our response back to the consumer. In this instance (as with our existing two GET actions), we return a CommandReadDto.

3. Input DTO Type

Our action expects `CommandCreateDto` as input, fair enough, but where does that come from? As mentioned, *when* we come to using Postman to test this, we'll place a "CommandCreateDto" in the body of the request, as shown next.

Important   ***Don't*** test this Action yet as we still have some more code changes to make before it'll work; I've just shown the Body payload in Figure 10-8 to illustrate this point.

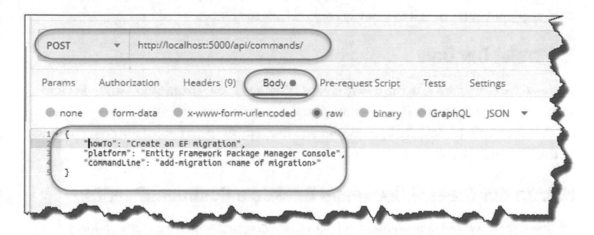

Figure 10-8. *POST Request in Postman*

But that still doesn't answer the question of how does our action "know" to get this data from the Body of the request and pass it in as the `commandCreateDto` parameter.

The answer to that is *Binding Sources*.

A controller action can derive its inputs from a number of Binding Sources:

- From the Query String

- From the Route (we obtain the `Id` attribute in our URI form here)

- From the Request Body

- From Form fields

- From the Request Header

We can explicitly tell our action where to locate this data or we can fall back on the default behaviors provided to us. For controllers that are decorated with the [ApiController] attribute (as ours is), the default location of *model objects* is the request *Body*.

Therefore, the commandCreateDto parameter of our action will be populated with the object we provide in our POST request body.

For a deeper discussion in this, I'd refer you to the <u>Microsoft docs.</u>[3]

4. Map Our CommandCreateDto to a Command Object

In this step we make use of our AutoMapper profile mapping and, taking our input commandCreateDto, map it to a newly created Command object.

5. Persist Our Data

In these two steps, we take the newly created Command model from step 4 and pass it to the CreateCommand method of our repository.

We then call the SaveChanges method on our repository to persist the changes down to the PostgreSQL DB.

6. Map Our Created Command Back to a CommandReadDto

We have already said that we need to pass back a CommandReadDto as part of our endpoint specification, so we do this once again using AutoMapper, to map the newly created Command object back to a CommandReadDto. What is of note here is that as we have persisted the Command to the PostgreSQL DB; we now have access to the Id attribute (by reference), which is needed going forward – see step 7.

7. Created at Route

Then finally we return CreatedAtRoute (see definition on Microsoft Docs[4]) where we:

- Specify the "route" where our Created resource resides (more on this below).

---

[3]https://docs.microsoft.com/en-us/aspnet/core/mvc/models/
model-binding?view=aspnetcore-3.1

[4]https://docs.microsoft.com/en-us/dotnet/api/system.web.http.apicontroller.
createdatroute

- The Id of the resource (used to generate the route).

- Content value of the body returned.

To summarize, this method will

- Return a 201 – Created Http status code.

- Pass back the created resource in the body response.

- Pass back the URI (or route if you prefer) in the response header.

It basically fulfills the desired behavior of our Create endpoint. If we take a look at this method again, we need to explore one item a little further.

```
[HttpPost]
public ActionResult<CommandReadDto> CreateCommand(CommandCreateDto commandCreateDto)
{
    var commandModel = _mapper.Map<Command>(commandCreateDto);
    _repository.CreateCommand(commandModel);
    _repository.SaveChanges();

    var commandReadDto = _mapper.Map<CommandReadDto>(commandModel);

    return CreatedAtRoute(nameof(GetCommandById), new { Id = commandReadDto.Id }, commandReadDto);
}
```

Figure 10-9. *CreatedAtRoute Route Name Parameter*

The first parameter of CreatedAtRoute is the routeName which in our case is just the existing GET action that returns a single resource based on a supplied Id: GetCommandById. In order for the call to CreatedAtRoute to work, we need to return to the GetCommandById action and "name" it.

So, staying in our controller code, make the necessary highlighted changes to the GetCommandById action:

```
[HttpGet("{id}", Name="GetCommandById")]

public ActionResult<CommandReadDto> GetCommandById(int id)
{
    var commandItem = _repository.GetCommandById(id);
    if (commandItem == null)
```

```
  {
    return NotFound();
  }
  return Ok(_mapper.Map<CommandReadDto>(commandItem));
}
```

I've highlighted what's changed in Figure 10-10.

```
[HttpGet("{id}", Name="GetCommandById")]
public ActionResult<CommandReadDto> GetCommandById(int id)
{
    var commandItem = _repository.GetCommandById(id);
    if (commandItem == null)
    {
        return NotFound();
    }
    return Ok(_mapper.Map<CommandReadDto>(commandItem));
}
```

Figure 10-10. *Naming our GetCommandById method*

We have explicitly named our action so the call from `CreatedAtRoute` resolves correctly.

Phew! I told you there was a lot to this action – don't worry the remaining actions are not that complex.

All that remains to do is perform some manual tests.

Manually Testing the Create Endpoint

Before you do anything else, make sure you save all your code (we've made quite a few changes), and perform a `dotnet build` just to check for errors. Assuming all is well, run up your server and move over to Postman.

Successful Test Case

Here we'll supply the necessary inputs to generate a successful outcome; take a look at my Postman setup in Figure 10-11.

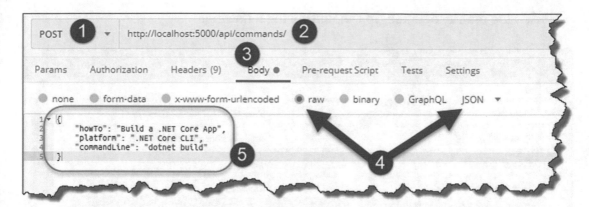

Figure 10-11. *Test our CreatCommand Endpoint*

1. Ensure POST is the selected verb.

2. Make sure the route is correct (note there is no Id passed).

3. Select "Body" for the request.

4. Set "Raw" and "JSON" for the request body data type.

5. Supply a valid JSON object that adheres to our
   CommandCreateDto.

With all that set up, click Send and you should get the following response.

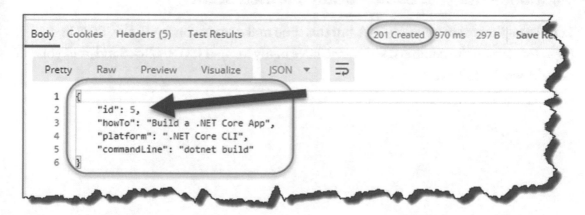

Figure 10-12. *Successful 201 Result*

- 201 Http Created Status Code.

- The newly created resource with Id.

Selecting the Headers Tab, you should get the following.

Figure 10-13. *URI of our newly created resource is returned in the header*

Looks good!

🎓 **Learning Opportunity**   What else can you do to check that the resource has been created?

Unsuccessful test Case – Badly Formed JSON

Let's issue that exact same request, but this time make some change to the JSON body (e.g., remove all the commas) so that we have badly formed JSON. Click Send, and you should see the following.

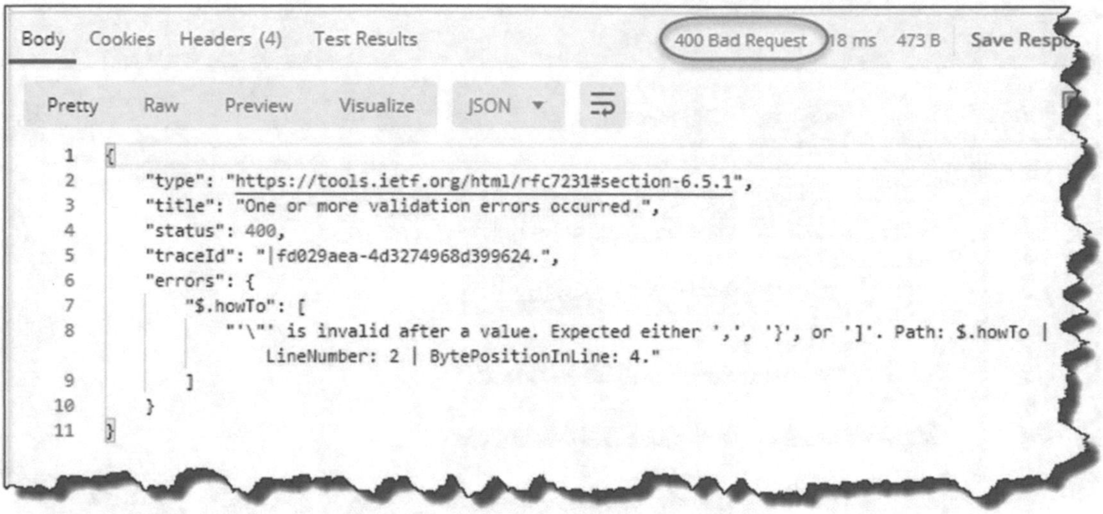

Figure 10-14. *Bad request*

We get a Http 400 – Bad request along with some helpful guidance on what's wrong. We didn't specifically code this behavior in our controller action – we get this behavior by default as we have decorated our controller with the [ApiController] attribute – see how useful it is!

Unsuccessful Test Case – Contradict Our Annotations

The last unsuccessful test case I want to run is making sure we violate the data annotations we've placed on our CommandCreateDto, specifically the [Required] attribute on one of our properties. To test, reformat the JSON so it's valid, and remove the Platform property. Click Send again and you should get the following.

We get another 400 Bad Request Http response, with some detail about the validation error.

```
Body   Cookies   Headers (4)   Test Results                    400 Bad Request   23 ms

  Pretty    Raw    Preview    Visualize    JSON  ▼   ⇉

   1   {
   2        "type": "https://tools.ietf.org/html/rfc7231#section-6.5.1",
   3        "title": "One or more validation errors occurred.",
   4        "status": 400,
   5        "traceId": "|fd029aeb-4d3274968d399624.",
   6        "errors": {
   7            "Platform": [
   8                "The Platform field is required."
   9            ]
  10        }
  11   }
```

Figure 10-15. *Bad Request with validation detail*

☞ **Learning Opportunity**   Test what will happen if you remove the
[Required] attribute from the Platform property on our CommandCreateDto,
and rerun the same request.

We'll return to testing all our endpoints further in Chapter 11, but for now let's move
on to implementing our Update endpoints.

The Update Endpoint #1 (PUT)

The next endpoint we want to implement is the first "Update" action which gives us the
ability to *fully update* a single resource in our DB using a PUT request. A quick reminder
of our high-level definition is shown in the table.

Verb	URI	Operation	Description
PUT	/api/commands/{Id}	Update (Full)	Update all of a single resource (by Id)

As before, I've introduced some other attributes that will help us understand, build, and test our endpoint more effectively.

Attribute	Description

Inputs (x2)	The Id of the resource to be updated. This will be present in the URI of our PUT request.
	The full "command" object to be updated.
	This will be added to the `request` body of our PUT request; an example is shown here:
	
	``
	{
	    "howTo": "Example how to",
	    "platform": "Example platform",
	    "commandLine": "Example command line"
	}
	``

Process	Will attempt to fully update an existing command object in our DB
Success Outputs	• HTTP 204 No Content response code
Failure Outputs	• HTTP 400 Bad Request • HTTP 404 Not Found • HTTP 405 Not Allowed
Safe	No – Endpoint can alter our resources
Idempotent	Yes – Repeating the same operation will not incur a different result

Again, quite straight forward, but I'd call out the following points of note.

Input Object

This is identical to our Create endpoint – does this mean we can reuse our CommandCreateDto? Theoretically we could, but in the interests of true decoupling, we're going to create a separate CommandUpdateDto, just to future-proof our solution should these objects diverge in the future.

The other point of note is that this object does not contain the Id attribute. We do require it for this operation (otherwise, how would we know which object to update), but in this case, we get this value from the URI (which is another stipulation of REST), so we don't need to double up on it here.

Success Outputs

Very simple in this case, we just supply a 204 No Content http result.

Idempotent

This method is idempotent as you can repeat it multiple times and the result will be the same.

Les' Personal Anecdote   The PUT request has fallen out of favor when compared to the PATCH request these days, mainly due to the fact you have to supply *all* the object attributes to be updated, even the ones that are not changing!

This is really inefficient for large objects. Say you have an object with 20 properties and you only need to change 1, you still have to supply all 20 to the PUT request, ensuring that you provide the correct (same) value for each of the 19 that are *not changing*.

If you inadvertently provide the wrong value or omit it altogether for 1 of the 19, you could end up in real strife! *Cough, cough; I have never done that.*

Not only is it problematic/inefficient in this respect; from a network perspective it's not optimal; you're essentially sending potentially large amounts of redundant data over the wire (or through the air).

The only reason I've included it here is for completeness and because I'm a nice guy.

Updating the Repository

Again, starting at the repository level, let's take a look at the update method signature in our ICommandRepoAPI interface.

```
public interface ICommandAPIRepo
{
    bool SaveChanges();

    IEnumerable<Command> GetAllCommands();
    Command GetCommandById(int id);
    void CreateCommand(Command cmd);
    void UpdateCommand(Command cmd);
    void DeleteCommand(Command cmd);
}
```

Figure 10-16. *UpdateCommand Interface Method*

We accept a Command object (update the database if required), and don't expect to pass anything back. You'll notice my choice of words: "update the database *if* required"; the reason I've chosen these will become clearer below.

What I'd like to remind you about our repository interface is that it is *technology-agnostic* – meaning that it is an interface specification we could use against different persistence providers, for example, Entity Framework Core, nHibernate, Dapper, etc. We just so happen to be using it with Entity Framework Core, and we therefore have to provide a specific, concrete implementation for that ORM. And this is where it gets weird.

Moving over to our SqlCommandAPIRepo implementation class, update the UpdateCommand method as follows:

```
public void UpdateCommand(Command cmd)
{
  //We don't need to do anything here
}
```

Yes, that's right – it contains "no implementation" – just a smart-arsed comment from me. I've not gone mad, let me explain.

Remember How Our DB Context Works

Cast your mind back to the lengthy explanation of how EF Core persists data at the start of this chapter; not only was that just generally useful information to know, but it was done in expectation of this explanation. This is the payoff.

We will actually perform the *update* of our existing Command object *in our Controller action*, so we don't need to put any code in our repository implementation. It will probably become clearer when we come to code it up, but let me explain further how this will work:

1. The Update action will be called (with the CommandUpdateDto object in the request Body).

2. **In our controller**: Based on the Id in the request URI, we'll search the DB Context to see if we have an existing Command object with that Id.

3. **If it doesn't exist**: We return a 404 Not Found Result and return.

4. **If it does exist**: We'll "Map" the CommandUpdateDto received in the request body to the Command object we just received from our DB Context in Step 2. **It is at this point the Command object is updated in the DB Context**. We therefore don't need any implementation code in our SqlCommandAPIRepo repository.

5. We call the SaveChanges method on our repository, and the changes will be persisted to the database.

You may then ask the very valid question: If we *don't need* implementation code here, why not remove it altogether from our repository interface? The answer to that is to once again remind you that the repository interface is technology agnostic, so while we don't require an implementation *in this instance*, if we choose to switch our persistence provider, they *may require* a coded implementation.

So logically speaking it makes sense to specify an Update method signature in our interface, even if in this instance we *don't* need to implement it.

Anyway, with that we're done with the repository "implementation" and can move on to the DTO.

CommandUpdateDto

As recently described, we're going to expect a CommandUpdateDto in our request body and map it over to the Command retrieved from our DB Context. To enable this, create a file in the *Dtos* folder called *CommandUpdateDto.cs*, and add the following code:

```
using System.ComponentModel.DataAnnotations;

namespace CommandAPI.Dtos
{
  public class CommandUpdateDto
  {
    [Required]
    [MaxLength(250)]
    public string HowTo {get; set;}

    [Required]
    public string Platform {get; set;}

    [Required]
    public string CommandLine {get; set;}
  }
}
```

This is exactly the same as our CommandCreateDto, but we'll maintain a separate instance for future-proofing purposes. Save the file, and move on to updating out AutoMapper profile mappings.

Update the AutoMapper Profile

We need to add a mapping with the CommandUpdateDto as the mapping source and the Command model as the target, so update the CommandsProfile class with the following mapping entry:

```
using AutoMapper;
using CommandAPI.Dtos;
using CommandAPI.Models;

namespace CommandAPI.Profiles
{
  public class CommandsProfile : Profile
  {
    public CommandsProfile()
    {
```

```
    //Source ➤ Target
    CreateMap<Command, CommandReadDto>();
    CreateMap<CommandCreateDto, Command>();
    CreateMap<CommandUpdateDto, Command>();
  }
 }
}
```

I don't believe at this stage we require any further explanation on this!

Updating the Controller

Moving back to our controller, we need to add a new controller action to host our new endpoint, so in the CommandsController class, add the following code to achieve this:

```
[HttpPut("{id}")]
public ActionResult UpdateCommand(int id, CommandUpdateDto
commandUpdateDto)
{
  var commandModelFromRepo = _repository.GetCommandById(id);
  if (commandModelFromRepo == null)
  {
    return NotFound();
  }
  _mapper.Map(commandUpdateDto, commandModelFromRepo);

  _repository.UpdateCommand(commandModelFromRepo);

  _repository.SaveChanges();

  return NoContent();
}
```

Let's walk through the code.

Figure 10-17. UpdateCommand Controller Action Implementation

1. HttpPut

We decorate the UpdateCommand method with the [HttpPut] attribute (no real controversy there), but we also expect an Id as part of the route; this means this endpoint will respond to the class-wide route plus the Id, so

api/commands/{id}

2 Inputs

The UpdateCommand method expects two parameters:

1. **id**: this is the id passed in from the route, which equates to the unique id of the resource we want to attempt update.

2. **commandUpdateDto**: this is the object passed in in the request body.

3. Attempt Command Resource Retrieval

We make use of the id passed in from the route and, using our existing repository method, GetCommandById, attempt to retrieve it. Irrespective of the result, we place the result of this operation in commandModelFromRepo.

4. Return 404 Not Found

Not much more to say here; if the "object" we attempted to retrieve from the repository is null, then we just return with a 404 Not Found Http response.

5. Update our Command

This is where the actual update occurs! We use a slightly different form of the Map method on our _mapper instance to map the DTO to our Command. By reference the Command object is updated in the DB Context. Again, this is not yet reflected down to our PostgreSQL DB.

6. Update Nothing

This is a controversial one! You probably think I've definitely gone mad now.

This line does nothing,(at the moment). But remember, we may at any point in time swap out our Entity Framework Core implementation for another provider that *may need* a call to the UpdateCommand method in our repository. This is essentially the same reason for keeping the definition in the repository interface in the first place.

By keeping this call here (even though it's currently redundant), if we do swap out our repository implementation (that requires a call to UpdateCommand), we won't need to change our Controller code, which is kind of the point of doing all this!

Personal Perspective   This is probably the single most contentious part of the build and the one that I do get questioned on quite a lot. If you feel more comfortable *not including* step 6, that is your choice; the code will still work in *this* instance.

I personally find that the embedding of knowledge and understanding comes from your own practical approaches and experiments - so go with what you feel works best for you. However, just remember this section if you do ever have to rework your code in the future.

---

7. Save Changes

An obvious one, don't think I need to go on here.

8. Return 204 No Content

Nice and simple, we return a 204 No Content. You'll also notice that the
UpdateCommand method does not have a return type.

OK, save your work, start your engines, and let's move on to performing a few
manual tests.

Manually Testing the Update (PUT) EndPoint

Successful Test Case

Here we supply the necessary inputs to generate a successful outcome as reflected in the
Postman setup in Figure 10-18.

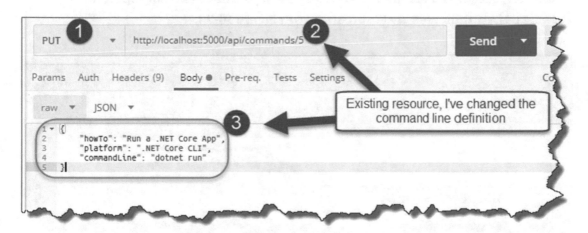

Figure 10-18. *Testing the Put Action Result*

1. Ensure PUT is selected.

2. The route to the resource you want to update needs to be valid.

3. I've just updated howTo and commandLine, but I've also had to
   supply the Platform even though this is not changing.

Click Send and you should get a similar result to the one in Figure 10-19.

Figure 10-19. *Success – 204 No Content Returned*

Fairly basic, just a 204 No Content Http Response. I'll leave it to you to check if this actually did update the resource in the DB.

Unsuccessful Test Case - Contradict Our Annotations

In this test, case we'll attempt to update an existing resource and not supply a [Required] attribute; see my Postman setup in Figure 10-20.

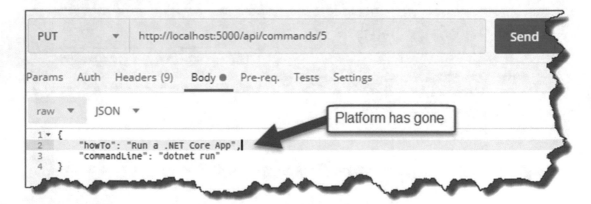

Figure 10-20. *Force a validation error*

Click send and you'll see something like the following.

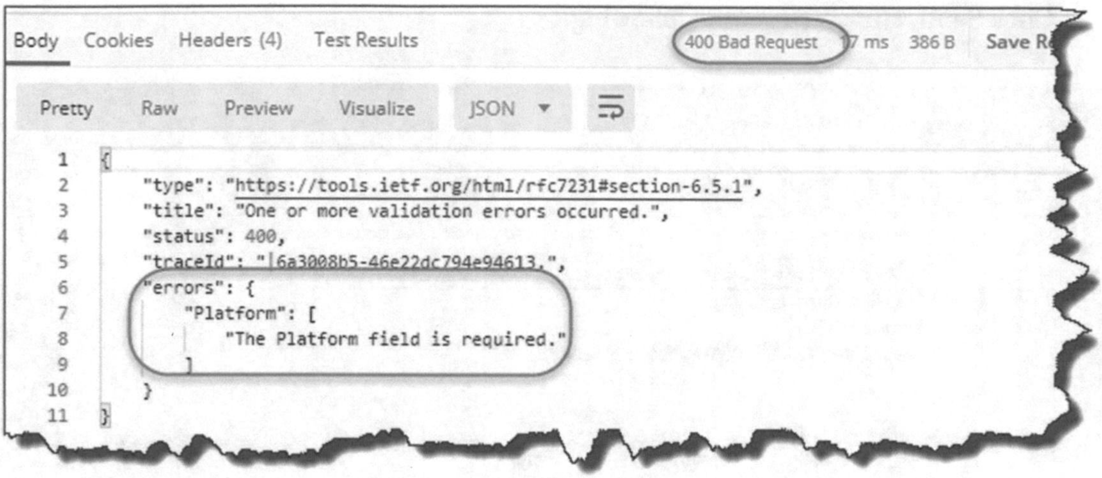

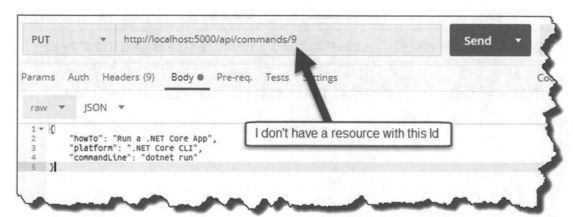

Figure 10-21. Validation Error Returned

This demonstrates the usefulness of data annotations. But I hear you cry: I thought you said we needed to supply all attributes in a PUT request anyway?

Great question, the answer to that is yes you do if you want them to be updated (or remain the same). Taking the [Required] annotation out the equation, if we *could supply a null* value for Platform and don't supply it in our PUT request – that will work. What will happen though is that the existing value for Platform will not be persisted as is; it will revert to the default value, and if it doesn't have one, then null!

Unsuccessful Test Case – Invalid Resource ID

Here, we just supply an Id for a resource that does not exist.

Figure 10-22. Test with nonexistent resource

237

Click Send, and you'll get the following.

Figure 10-23. *404 Not Found Returned*

So, looks like everything is working as per our requirements; let's move on to the arguably more interesting PATCH update endpoint.

The Update Endpoint #2 (PATCH)

The next endpoint we want to implement is the second "Update" endpoint (using the PATCH verb), which gives us the ability to perform partial updates on a resource. This addresses many of the inefficiencies of the PUT endpoint that we noted in the last section. A quick reminder of our high-level definition is shown in the table.

Verb	URI	Operation	Description
PATCH	/api/commands/{Id}	Update (partial)	Update part of a single resource (by Id)

To further flesh out our definition, I've included some addition attributes here.

Attribute	Description

Inputs (x2)	The Id of the resource to be updated. This will be present in the URI of our PATCH request.
	The change-set or "patch document" to be applied to the resource
	This will be added to the `request` body of our PATCH request; an example is shown here:
	<pre>[
	  {
	    "op": "replace",
	    "path": "/howto",
	    "value": "Some new value"
	  },
	  {
	    "op": "test",
	    "path" : "commandline",
	    "value" : "dotnet new"
	  }
	]</pre>

Process	Will attempt to perform the updates as specified in the patch document Note: If there is more than one update, all those updates need to be successful. If one fails, then they all fail.
Success Outputs	• HTTP 204 Not Content HTTP Status
Failure Outputs	• HTTP 400 Bad Request • HTTP 404 Not Found • HTTP 405 Not Allowed
Safe	No – Endpoint can alter our resources
Idempotent	No – Repeating the same operation *may* incur a different result

There are a few new concepts here so let's go through them.

Input Object

Instead of supplying a representation of the resource we want to update, we supply a series of changes that we want to perform against that resource. We call this a Patch Document or Change Set.

Our Patch Document can perform the following *operations*:

- **Add**: Adds a new property to our object (this requires "dynamic" objects which we won't be using).

- **Remove**: Again, requires dynamic objects and allows us to remove a property from our resource.

- **Replace**: Allows us to change an existing property (this is the one we'll be using).

- **Copy**: As the name suggests, this allows us to copy a resource property value to another.

- **Move**: The same as combining Copy and Remove operations.

- **Test**: Allows us to test the value of a given resource property.

In addition to specifying what operation we want to perform against a property, we need to supply

- A path to that resource property

- The new value we want to assign

Refer to the example in Figure 10-24 for clarity.

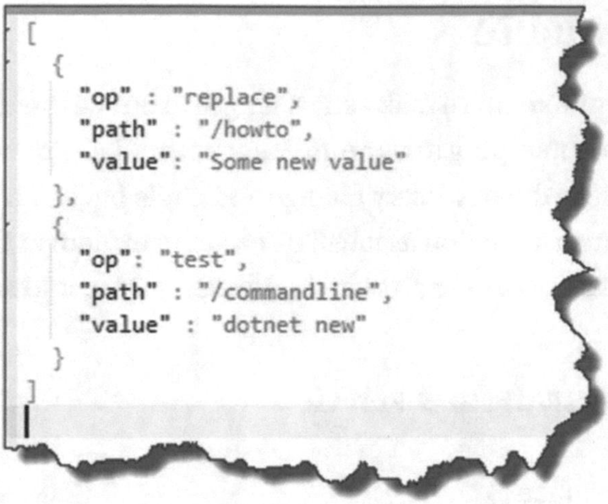

```
[
    {
      "op" : "replace",
      "path" : "/howto",
      "value": "Some new value"
    },
    {
      "op": "test",
      "path" : "/commandline",
      "value" : "dotnet new"
    }
]
```

Figure 10-24. *Example of a simple patch document*

The Patch Document is attempting to perform two operations:

1. Replace the value of the howto property with the value "Some new value."

2. Test to see if the commandline property contains the value "dotnet new"

For this Patch Document to be successful, both of these operations will need to succeed.

For more information on the PATCH specification, refer to the RFC 6902 standard.[5]

Idempotent

The PATCH operation is not idempotent as running the same request multiple times may yield different results.

Updating the Repository

There is no requirement to perform further update on our repository.

---

[5]https://tools.ietf.org/html/rfc6902

241

CommandUpdateDto

While there isn't a requirement to make any changes to our `CommandUpdateDto`, we do need to add one further mapping to our AutoMapper Profiles. I'm not going to explain why here; we'll just make the necessary change and circle back to it when we come to implementing the controller action as it will be easier to explain at that point.

So, open the `CommandsProfile` class in the **Profiles** folder, and add the following (final) mapping:

```
public class CommandsProfile : Profile
{
  public CommandsProfile()
  {
    //Source ➤ Target
    CreateMap<Command, CommandReadDto>();
    CreateMap<CommandCreateDto, Command>();
    CreateMap<CommandUpdateDto, Command>();
    CreateMap<Command, CommandUpdateDto>();
  }
}
```

You should be comfortable of *what* is happening here; we'll cover off the *why* below.

Install Dependencies for PATCH

Unlike the other endpoints we've covered, PATCH requests require some further package dependencies to be installed in order for PATCH requests to work correctly. So at a command prompt (and making sure you are "in" the **CommandAPI** project folder), issue the following commands:

```
dotnet add package Microsoft.AspNetCore.JsonPatch
dotnet add package Microsoft.AspNetCore.Mvc.NewtonsoftJson
```

The first adds support for the PATCH request; the second is required to correctly work with Patch Documents in our controller.

To make sure the dependencies were installed, check the **.csproj** file for our project.

```
<ItemGroup>
    <PackageReference Include="AutoMapper.Extensions.Microsoft.DependencyInjection" Version="7.0.0" />
    <PackageReference Include="Microsoft.AspNetCore.JsonPatch" Version="3.1.4" />
    <PackageReference Include="Microsoft.AspNetCore.Mvc.NewtonsoftJson" Version="3.1.4" />
    <PackageReference Include="Microsoft.EntityFrameworkCore" Version="3.1.4" />
    <PackageReference Include="Microsoft.EntityFrameworkCore.Design" Version="3.1.4">
      <IncludeAssets>runtime; build; native; contentfiles; analyzers; buildtransitive</IncludeAssets>
      <PrivateAssets>all</PrivateAssets>
    </PackageReference>
    <PackageReference Include="Npgsql.EntityFrameworkCore.PostgreSQL" Version="3.1.3" />
</ItemGroup>

</Project>
```

Figure 10-25. *Packages required to support Patch*

Updating the Startup Class

To make use of the second package we added earlier, we need to make a minor addition to our Startup class as shown below (make sure to include the using statement too):

.
.
.

```
using Newtonsoft.Json.Serialization;
```

.
.

```
services.AddControllers().AddNewtonsoftJson(s =>
{
  s.SerializerSettings.ContractResolver = new
  CamelCasePropertyNamesContractResolver();
});
```

.
.

To put those changes in context (for brevity I've *not* shown the new using statement below), see Figure 10-26.

```
public void ConfigureServices(IServiceCollection services)
{
    var builder = new NpgsqlConnectionStringBuilder();
    builder.ConnectionString =
        Configuration.GetConnectionString("PostgreSqlConnection");
        builder.Username = Configuration["UserID"];
        builder.Password = Configuration["Password"];


    services.AddDbContext<CommandContext>(opt => opt.UseNpgsql(builder.ConnectionString));

    services.AddControllers().AddNewtonsoftJson(s => {
        s.SerializerSettings.ContractResolver = new CamelCasePropertyNamesContractResolver();
    });
```

Figure 10-26. *Serializer settings on our controllers*

As you can see, we require the use of NewtonSoftJson package within our controller; this allows for the correct parsing of our Patch document.

With that set up, we're now ready to move over to our controller.

Updating the Controller

As we did with our create action, I'm just going to get you to enter the entire code for this action, and we'll then step through the code line by line by way of explanation.

```
using Microsoft.AspNetCore.JsonPatch;


[HttpPatch("{id}")]
public ActionResult PartialCommandUpdate(int id,
    JsonPatchDocument<CommandUpdateDto> patchDoc)
{
    var commandModelFromRepo = _repository.GetCommandById(id);
    if(commandModelFromRepo == null)
    {
        return NotFound();
    }

    var commandToPatch = _mapper.Map<CommandUpdateDto>(commandModelFromRepo);
    patchDoc.ApplyTo(commandToPatch, ModelState);
```

```
if(!TryValidateModel(commandToPatch))
{
  return ValidationProblem(ModelState);
}

_mapper.Map(commandToPatch, commandModelFromRepo);

_repository.UpdateCommand(commandModelFromRepo);

_repository.SaveChanges();

return NoContent();
}
```

Quite a lot to take in there, so let's go through the code before we come on to testing it.

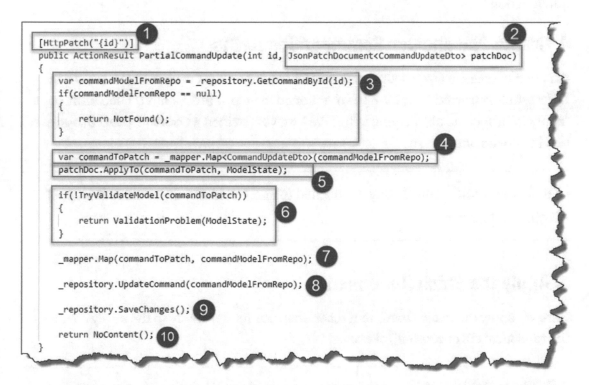

Figure 10-27. *Patch Controller Action*

1. HttpPatch

Shouldn't be any surprises here; we need to decorate with [HttpPatch] and specify that we expect a resource Id in the route.

2. JsonPatchDocument

We expect a JsonPatchDocument in the request body that "applies" to a CommandUpdateDto. This feeds into the validations that are performed below. (We need to specify the object type the JsonPatchDocument "applies to" in order to deduce if it's valid.)

3. Attempt Command Resource Retrieval

This is exactly the same code that we had in our PUT action; it doesn't require further qualification.

4. Create Placeholder CommandUpdateDto

We need to create a CommandUpdateDto object based on the Command object we've just successfully retrieved. Why? Well as mentioned in Step 1, the JsonPatchDocument has to "apply to" a specific object type; in this case we've specified a CommandUpdateDto, so we need to create one for use.

ℹ Circle Back   This is why we needed to add our fourth and final AutoMapper Profile mapping.

---

5. Apply the Patch Document

Here we apply the Patch Document received in our request body to the newly created CommandUpdateDto: commandToPatch.

ℹ Circle Back   Had we not included and used the Microsoft.AspNetCore. Mvc.NewtonsoftJson package, we would not be able to correctly perform this operation.

---

6. Validate Model Changes

Following the application of the desired changes in our Patch Document, we then attempt to see if the model validation (via our Data Annotations) is valid. For example, if the Patch Document requested a Replace operation on the HowTo property that was greater than 250 characters, it would be picked up here.

7. Map Updated Dto to Command and Return

Our CommandUpdateDto (commandToPatch) has been successfully updated at this point. We now use AutoMapper to map it back to our Command object in our DB Context.

Note   From this point onward, the code is identical to our previous PUT action, so to save on duplicating that explanation, please just refer to the recent explanation.

And with that – we're done with coding this controller action; make sure you save everything, and we'll move on to some manual tests.

Manually Testing the Update (PATCH) EndPoint

Successful Test Case

The most important thing to get right here is the Patch Document; to begin with I'm keeping it simple and updating the HowTo property of an existing resource as shown in my Postman setup.

1.   PATCH Verb is selected.

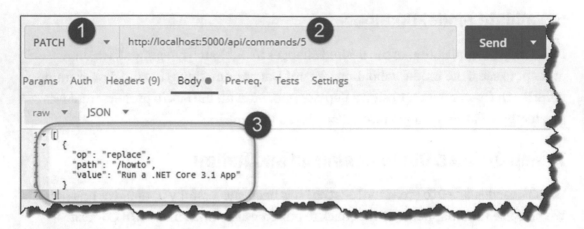

Figure 10-28. *Test our Patch ActionResult*

2. URI to an existing resource.

3. Our Patch Document with a single operation.

⚠ **Warning!**   You'll note that even though our Patch Document has only one operation, we still need to enclose it in square parenthesis [].

Remembering from our discussion on JSON, square brackets [] denote an array.

🎓 **Learning Opportunity**   I'll refrain from detailing our failing or unsuccessful test cases here and leave it to you to explore these – have fun! (They're not much different from the ones we ran for PUT.)

The Delete Endpoint (DELETE)

The final endpoint we want to implement is the "Delete" endpoint, which gives us the ability to remove resources from our DB. A quick reminder of our high-level definition is shown here.

Verb	URI	Operation	Description
DELETE	/api/commands/{Id}	Delete	Delete a single resource (by Id)

Further details of how this Endpoint should operate are listed here.

Attribute	Description
Inputs (x1)	The Id of the resource to be deleted. This will be present in the URI of our DELETE request
Process	Will attempt to delete an existing command object to our DB
Success Outputs	• HTTP 204 No Content HTTP result
Failure Outputs	• HTTP 404 Not Found HTTP result
Safe	No – Endpoint can alter our resources
Idempotent	Yes – Repeating the same operation will incur the same result

There's not much to call out here, so let's move on to what we need to code.

Updating the Repository

Refer back to our repository interface as detailed in Figure 10-29.

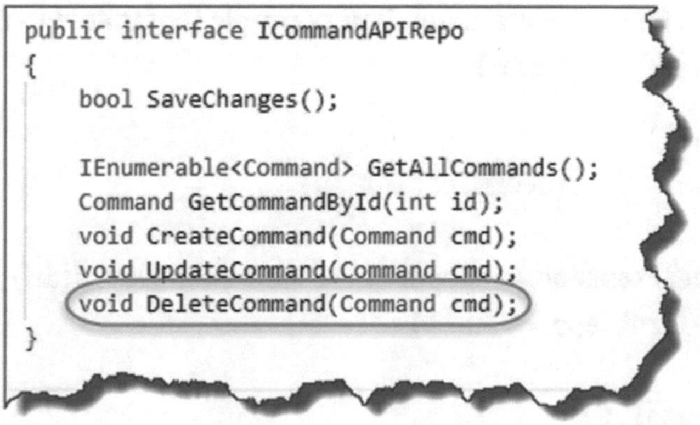

```
public interface ICommandAPIRepo
{
    bool SaveChanges();

    IEnumerable<Command> GetAllCommands();
    Command GetCommandById(int id);
    void CreateCommand(Command cmd);
    void UpdateCommand(Command cmd);
    void DeleteCommand(Command cmd);
}
```

Figure 10-29. *Delete Interface Method*

We expect the Command object to be deleted and do not expect anything to be passed back.

Moving over to our implementation class SqlCommandAPIRepo, update the DeleteCommand method as follows:

```
public void DeleteCommand(Command cmd)
{
  if(cmd == null)
  {
    throw new ArgumentNullException(nameof(cmd));
  }
  _context.CommandItems.Remove(cmd);
}
```

The code is pretty straightforward, so I don't feel further explanation is needed. Just remember that calling this method only marks the Command for deletion in the DB Context; we still need to call SaveChanges to effect a change in the database.

CommandDeleteDto

There is no requirement for a CommandDeleteDto.

Updating the Controller

Thankfully the code for our delete action is very simple (compared to the last three Endpoints we've done); it's shown here:

```
[HttpDelete("{id}")]
public ActionResult DeleteCommand(int id)
{
  var commandModelFromRepo = _repository.GetCommandById(id);
  if(commandModelFromRepo == null)
  {
    return NotFound();
  }
```

```
_repository.DeleteCommand(commandModelFromRepo);
_repository.SaveChanges();

return NoContent();
}
```

☞ **Learning Opportunity**   I feel at this stage there is little benefit in me adding extra narrative on both what this code is doing and how to manually test it!

We've covered significantly more complex use-cases, so I think you can round off the manual testing of this Endpoint yourself.

Wrap Up

🎂 **Celebration Checkpoint**   We have fully implemented our API now! Congratulations!

We covered a lot of code in this chapter; I did consider splitting it across multiple chapters but thought that may have interrupted the flow of what we were tackling.

Once again, let us return to our application architecture as shown in Figure 10-30.

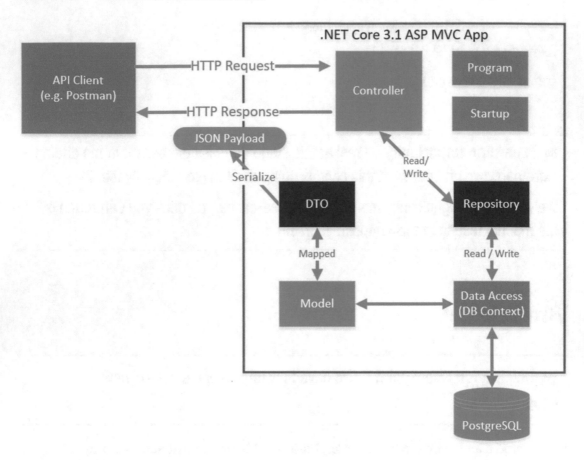

Figure 10-30. *Architecture Checkpoint*

You can see that we have now implemented everything – great job! Don't celebrate too quickly though as we are not done just yet. In the chapters that follow, I take you through

- Automating Testing for our API

- Deploying the API to Production using a CI/CD Pipeline

- Securing our API from unwanted guests

Before you move on, remember to save everything and commit locally to GitHub.

## CHAPTER 11

Unit Testing Our API

Chapter Summary

In this chapter we'll introduce you to Unit Testing, what it is, and why you'd use it. We'll then create unit tests to test the core functionality of our API Controller, providing us with an automated regression suite (don't worry if you don't know what that means!).

When Done, You Will

- Understand what Unit Testing is and why you should use it.

- Understand the power of the Repository Interface once again!

- Understand how to use a mocking or isolation framework in unit testing.

- Write Unit Tests using *xUnit* to test our API functionality.

What Is Unit Testing

Probably the best way to describe what Unit Testing is is to put it in context of the other general types of "testing" you will encounter, so I refer you to the "Testing Pyramid" in Figure 11-1.

© Les Jackson 2020

L. Jackson, *The Complete ASP.NET Core 3 API Tutorial*, https://doi.org/10.1007/978-1-4842-6255-9_11

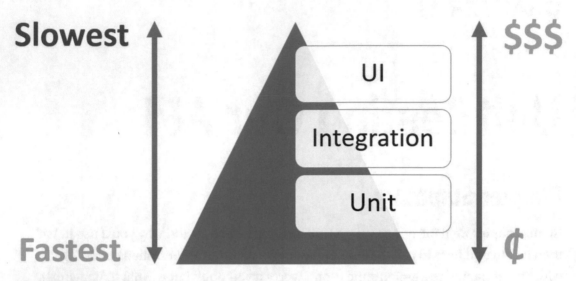

Figure 11-1. *Testing Pyramid*

Unit tests are

- **Abundant**: There should be more of them than other types of test.

- **Small**: They should test one thing only, that is, a "unit" (as opposed to full end-to-end "scenarios" or use cases).

- **Cheap**: They are both written and executed first. This means any errors they catch should be easier to rectify when compared to those you catch much later in the development life cycle.

- Quick to both write and execute

Unit tests are written by the developer (as opposed to a tester or business analyst), so that is why we'll be using them here to test our own code.

OK, so aside from the fact that they are quick and cheap, what other advantages do you have in using them?

Protection Against Regression

Because you'll have a suite of unit tests that are built up over time, you can run them again every time you introduce new functionality (which you should also build tests for). This means that you can check to see if your new code had introduced errors to the existing code base (these are called *regression defects*). Unit testing therefore gives you confidence that you've not introduced errors or, if you have, give you an early heads up so you can rectify.

Executable Documentation

When we come to write some unit tests, you'll see that the way we name them is descriptive and speaks to what is being tested and the expected outcome. Therefore, assuming you take this approach, your unit test suite essentially becomes documentation for your code.

ℹ When naming your unit test methods, they should follow a construct similar to

`<method name>_<expected result>_<condition>`

For example:

`GetCommandItem_Returns200OK_WhenSuppliedIDIsValid`

Note: There are variants on the convention, so find the one the one that works best for you.

Characteristics of a Good Unit Test

I've taken the following list of unit test characteristics from the Unit Testing Best Practices[1] guide by Microsoft; it's well worth a read, but again we cover more than enough here to get you going. So, the characteristics of a good unit test are

- **Fast:** Individual tests should execute quickly (required as we can have 1000's of them), and when we say quick, we're talking in the region of milliseconds.

- **Isolated:** Unit tests should not be dependent on external factors, for example, databases, network connections, etc.

- **Repeatable:** The same test should yield the same result between runs (assuming you don't change anything between runs).

- **Self-checking:** Should not require human intervention to determine whether it has passed or failed.

---

[1]https://docs.microsoft.com/en-us/dotnet/core/testing/unit-testing-best-practices

- **Timely:** The unit test should not take a disproportionately long time to run compared with the code being tested.

I'd also add

- **Focused:** A unit test (as the name suggests and as mentioned earlier) should test only one thing.

We'll use these factors as a touchstone when we come to writing our own tests.

What to Test?

OK, so we know what they are, why we have them, and even the characteristics of a "good" test, but the $1,00,000 question is what should we actually test? The characteristics detailed earlier should help drive this choice, but ultimately it comes down to the individual developer and what they are happy with.

Some developers may only write a small number of unit tests that only test really novel code; others may write many more that test more standard, trivial functionality. As our API is simple, we'll be writing tests that are pretty basic, and test quite obvious functionality. I've taken this approach to get you used to unit testing more than anything else.

Note   You would generally *not test functionality that is inherent in the programming language*: for example, you would not write unit tests to check basic arithmetic operations– that would be overkill and not terribly useful. Taking this further, unit testing code you cannot change (i.e., code you did not write) may be somewhat pointless: discuss.

Unit Testing Frameworks

I asked a question at the start of the book about what xUnit is. Well xUnit is simply a unit testing framework; it's open source and was used heavily in the creation of .NET Core, so it seems like a pretty good choice for us.

There are alternatives of course that do pretty much the same thing; performing a dotnet new at the command line, you'll see the unit test projects available to us.

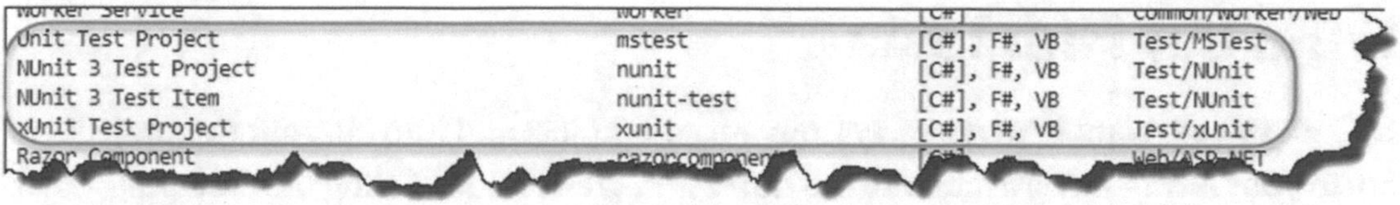

Figure 11-2. *Unit Testing .NET Core Project templates*

The others we could have used are

- MSTest

- NUnit

We'll be sticking with xUnit though, so if you want to find out about the others, you'll need to do your own reading.

Arrange, Act, and Assert

Irrespective of your choice of framework, all unit tests follow the same pattern (xUnit is no exception).

Arrange

This is where you perform the "setup" of your test. For example, you may set up some objects and configure data used to drive the test.

Act

This is where you execute the test to generate the result.

Assert

This is where you "check" the *actual result* against the *expected result*. How that assertion goes will depend on whether your test passes or fails.

Going back to the characteristics of a good unit test, the "focused" characteristic comes in to play here, meaning that we should really have only *one assertion per test*. If you assert multiple conditions, the unit tests become diluted and confusing – what are you testing again?

So, enough theory – let's practice!

Write Our First Tests

OK, so we now want to move away from our API project and into our unit test project. So, in your terminal, navigate into the **Command.Tests** folder, listing the contents of that folder you should see.

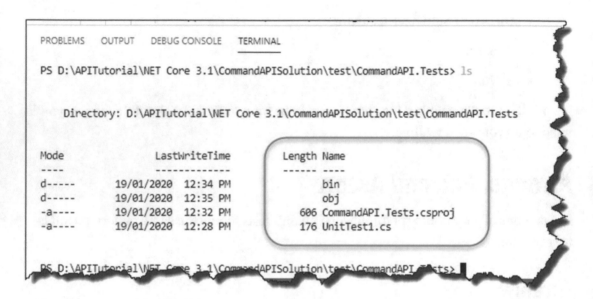

Figure 11-3. *Anatomy of a xUnit Project*

We have

- **bin** folder

- **obj** folder

- **CommandAPI.Tests.csproj** project file

- **UnitTest1.cs** default class

You should be familiar with the first three of these, as they are the same artifacts we had in our API project. With regard to the project file, **CommandAPI.Tests.csproj**, you'll recall we added a reference to our API project in here so we can "test" it.

The fourth and final artifact here is a default class set up for us when we created the project; open it, and take a look.

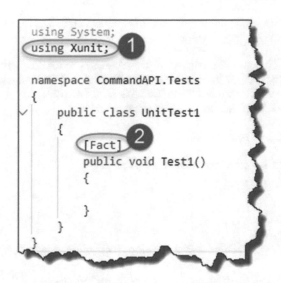

Figure 11-4. *Simple xUnit Test Case*

This is just a standard class definition, with only two points of note:

1. A reference to xUnit

2. Our class method Test1 is decorated with the [Fact] attribute.
   This tells the xUnit test runner that this method is a test.

You'll see at this stage our Test1 method is empty, but we can still run it nonetheless; to do so, return to your terminal (ensure you're in the *CommandAPI.Tests* folder), and type

```
dotnet test
```

This will run our test which should "pass," although it's empty and not really doing anything.

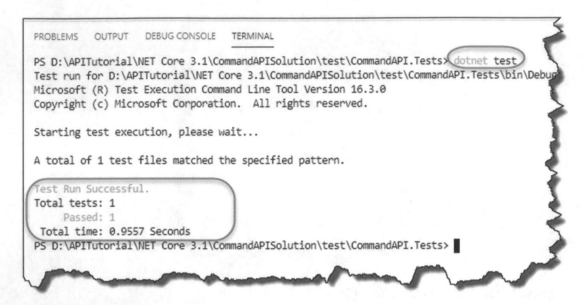

Figure 11-5. *Running Tests in xUnit*

OK, we know our testing setup is good to go, so let's start writing some tests.

Les' Personal Anecdote   When running through the code again myself (yes I actually followed the book all the way through to make sure it made sense!), I got a warning at this stage complaining that `Microsoft.EntityFrameworkCore.Relational` was at a different version in the xUnit project compared to the main API project.

Note that this package *was not* explicitly listed in the package references in our xUnit projects .csproj file.

To rectify this I installed the `Microsoft.EntityFrameworkCore.Relational` package in my xUnit project:

```
dotnet add package Microsoft.EntityFrameworkCore.
Relational --version 3.1.4
```

noting that I did specify a version this time to ensure both packages across both projects were in alignment. If you encounter this same behavior, take note of the version that gets complained about, and act accordingly.

Even though I believe this warning was benign, I don't like warnings lingering in the background.

Testing Our Model

Our first test is really at the trivial end of the spectrum to such an extent you *probably wouldn't unit test this* outside the scope of a learning exercise. However, *this is a learning exercise*, and even though it is a simple test, it covers all the necessary mechanics to get a unit test up and running.

Thinking about our model, what would we want to test? As a refresher, here's the model class in our API project.

```
using System.ComponentModel.DataAnnotations;

namespace CommandAPI.Models
{
    public class Command
    {
        [Key]
        [Required]
        public int Id {get; set;}

        [Required]
        [MaxLength(250)]
        public string HowTo {get; set;}

        [Required]
        public string Platform {get; set;}

        [Required]
        public string CommandLine {get; set;}
    }
}
```

Figure 11-6. *Revisiting the model*

How about

- *We can change the value of each of the class attributes.*

There are probably others we could think of, but let's keep it simple to start with. To set this up we're going to create a new class that will contain tests only for our Command model, so

- Create a new file called ***CommandTests.cs*** in the root of our ***CommandAPI.Tests*** Project.

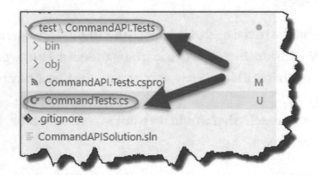

Figure 11-7. *Tests for our Model*

Add the following code to this class:

```
using System;
using Xunit;
using CommandAPI.Models;

namespace CommandAPI.Tests
{
    public class CommandTests
    {
        [Fact]
        public void CanChangeHowTo()
        {

        }
    }
}
```

> ℹ This is such a trivial test (we're not even testing a method); we can't really use the unit test naming convention mentioned earlier:
>
> <method name>_<expected result>_<condition>
>
> So, in this instance, we're going with something more basic.

The following sections are of note.

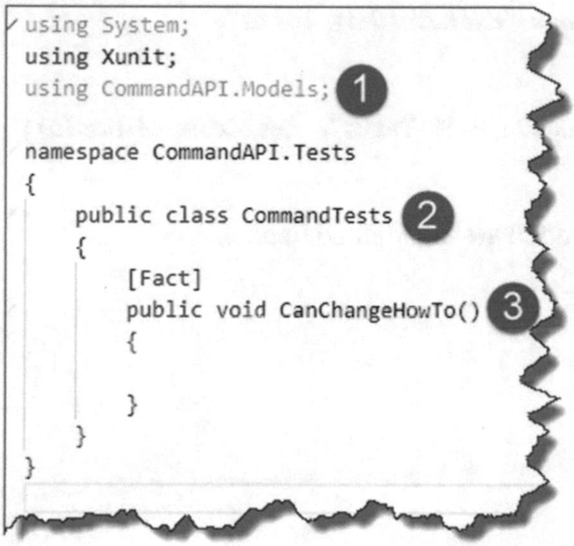

```
using System;
using Xunit;
using CommandAPI.Models;   ①

namespace CommandAPI.Tests
{
    public class CommandTests   ②
    {
        [Fact]
        public void CanChangeHowTo()   ③
        {

        }
    }
}
```

Figure 11-8. *Our First Model test*

1. We have a reference to our Models in the ***CommandAPI*** project.

2. Our Class is named after what we are testing (i.e., our Command model).

3. The naming convention of our test method is such that it tells us what the test is testing for.

OK, so now time to write our Arrange, Act, and Asset code; add the following highlighted code to the CanChangeHowTo test method:

```
[Fact]
public void CanChangeHowTo()
{
```

```
//Arrange
var testCommand = new Command
{
  HowTo = "Do something awesome",
  Platform = "xUnit",
  CommandLine = "dotnet test"
};

//Act
testCommand.HowTo = "Execute Unit Tests";

//Assert
Assert.Equal("Execute Unit Tests", testCommand.HowTo);
}
```

The sections we added are highlighted here.

```
using System;
using Xunit;
using CommandAPI.Models;

namespace CommandAPI.Tests
{
    public class CommandTests
    {
        [Fact]
        public void CanChangeHowTo()
        {
            //Arrange                                    1
            var testCommand = new Command
            {
                HowTo = "Do something awesome",
                Platform = "xUnit",
                CommandLine = "dotnet test"
            };

            //Act                                        2
            testCommand.HowTo = "Execute Unit Tests";

            //Assert                                     3
            Assert.Equal("Execute Unit Tests", testCommand.HowTo);
        }
    }
}
```

Figure 11-9. *Arrange, Act, and Assert*

1. **Arrange**: Create a testCommand and populate with initial values.

2. **Act**: Perform the action we want to test, that is, change the value of HowTo.

3. **Assert**: Check that the value of HowTo matches what we expect.

Steps 1 and 2 are straightforward, so it's really step 3 and the use of the xUnit Assert class to perform the "Equal" operation that are possibly new to you. Whether this step is true or false determines whether the test passes or fails.

Let's run our very simple test to see if it passes or fails:

- Ensure you save your **CommandTests.cs** file.

- **dotnet build:** This will just check your tests are syntactically correct.

- **dotnet test:** Will run our test suite.

The test should pass and you'll see something like the following.

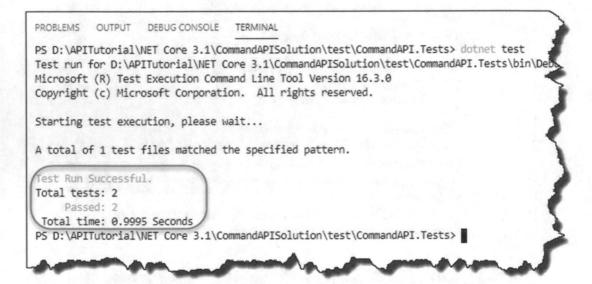

PROBLEMS   OUTPUT   DEBUG CONSOLE   TERMINAL

```
PS D:\APITutorial\NET Core 3.1\CommandAPISolution\test\CommandAPI.Tests> dotnet test
Test run for D:\APITutorial\NET Core 3.1\CommandAPISolution\test\CommandAPI.Tests\bin\Deb
Microsoft (R) Test Execution Command Line Tool Version 16.3.0
Copyright (c) Microsoft Corporation.  All rights reserved.

Starting test execution, please wait...

A total of 1 test files matched the specified pattern.

Test Run Successful.
Total tests: 2
    Passed: 2
Total time: 0.9995 Seconds
PS D:\APITutorial\NET Core 3.1\CommandAPISolution\test\CommandAPI.Tests> █
```

Figure 11-10. *We have two passing tests?*

It says two tests have passed? Where is the other test? That's right we still have our original UnitTest1 class with an empty test method, so that's where the second test is being picked up. Before we continue, lets' **delete that class**.

We can also "force" this test to fail. To do so, change the "expected" value in our Assert.Equal operation to something random, for example.

```
[Fact]
public void CanChangeHowTo()
{
    //Arrange
    var testCommand = new Command
    {
        HowTo = "Do something awesome",
        Platform = "xUnit",
        CommandLine = "dotnet test"
    };

    //Act
    testCommand.HowTo = "Execute Unit Tests";

    //Assert
    Assert.Equal("Test will fail", testCommand.HowTo);
}
```

Figure 11-11. *Forcing test Failure*

Save the file, and rerun your tests; you'll get a failure response with some verbose messaging.

```
Starting test execution, please wait...

A total of 1 test files matched the specified pattern.
[xUnit.net 00:00:00.58]    CommandAPI.Tests.CommandTests.CanChangeHowTo [FAIL]
  X CommandAPI.Tests.CommandTests.CanChangeHowTo [4ms]
  Error Message:
    Assert.Equal() Failure
            (pos 0)
Expected: Test will fail
Actual:   Execute Unit Tests
            (pos 0)
  Stack Trace:
      at CommandAPI.Tests.CommandTests.CanChangeHowTo() in D:\APITutorial\NET Core 3.

Test Run Failed.
Total tests: 2
     Passed: 1
     Failed: 1
 Total time: 1.0458 Seconds
PS D:\APITutorial\NET Core 3.1\CommandAP...   ...on\tes... ...andAPI.Tests>
```

Figure 11-12. *As expected, failed test*

Here, you can see the test has failed and we even get the reasoning for the failure. Revert the expected string back to a passing value before we continue.

☞ **Learning Opportunity**   We have two other attributes in our Command class that we should be testing for: `Platform` and `CommandLine` (the Id attribute is auto-managed so we shouldn't bother with this for now).

Write two additional tests to test that we can change these values too.

Don't Repeat Yourself

OK, so assuming that you completed the last Learning Opportunity, you should now have three test methods in your `CommandTests` class, with three passing tests. If you didn't complete that, I'd suggest you do it, or if you really don't want to – refer to the code on GitHub.[2]

One thing you'll notice is that the Arrange component for each of the three tests is identical and therefore a bit wasteful. When you have a scenario like this, that is, you need to perform some standard setup that multiple tests use; xUnit allows for that.

The xUnit documentation describes this concept as *Shared Context* between tests and specifies three approaches to achieve this:

- Constructor and Dispose (shared setup/clean-up code without sharing object instances)

- Class Fixtures (shared object instance across tests in a *single class*)

- Collection Fixtures (shared object instances across multiple test classes)

---

[2]https://github.com/binarythistle/Complete-ASP-NET-3-API-Tutorial-Book

We are going to use the first approach, which will set up a new instance of the testCommand object for each of our tests; you can alter your CommandsTests class to the following:

```
using System;
using Xunit;
using CommandAPI.Models;

namespace CommandAPI.Tests
{
  public class CommandTests : IDisposable
  {
    Command testCommand;

    public CommandTests()
    {
      testCommand = new Command
      {
        HowTo = "Do something",
        Platform = "Some platform",
        CommandLine = "Some commandline"
      };
    }

    public void Dispose()
    {
      testCommand = null;
    }

    [Fact]
    public void CanChangeHowTo()
    {
      //Arrange

      //Act
      testCommand.HowTo = "Execute Unit Tests";
```

```
        //Assert
        Assert.Equal("Execute Unit Tests", testCommand.HowTo);
    }

    [Fact]
    public void CanChangePlatform()
    {
        //Arrange

        //Act
        testCommand.Platform = "xUnit";

        //Assert
        Assert.Equal("xUnit", testCommand.Platform);
    }

    [Fact]
    public void CanChangeCommandLine()
    {
        //Arrange

        //Act
        testCommand.CommandLine = "dotnet test";

        //Assert
        Assert.Equal("dotnet test", testCommand.CommandLine);
    }
  }
}
```

For clarity of the sections, we have added Figure 11-13.

```
using System;
using Xunit;
using CommandAPI.Models;

namespace CommandAPI.Tests
{                                          1
    public class CommandTests : IDisposable
    {

        Command testCommand;        2

        public CommandTests()                3
        {
            testCommand = new Command
            {
                HowTo = "Do something",
                Platform = "Some platform",
                CommandLine = "Some commandline"
            };
        }

        public void Dispose()                4
        {
            testCommand = null;
        }

        [Fact]
        public void CanChangeHowTo()
        {                                        5
            //Arrange

            //Act
            testCommand.HowTo = "Execute Unit Tests";

            //Assert
            Assert.Equal("Execute Unit Tests", testCommand.HowTo);
        }
}
```

Figure 11-13. *Don't Repeat Yourself – refactored Model tests*

1. We inherit the IDisposable interface (used for code cleanup).

2. Create a "global" instance of our Command class.

3. Create a Class Constructor where we perform the setup of our testCommand object instance.

4. Implement a Dispose method, to clean up our code.

271

5. You'll notice that the Arrange section for each test is now empty; the class constructor will be called for every test (I've only shown one test here for brevity).

For more information, refer to the xUnit documentation.[3]

Run your tests again and you should see three passing tests.

```
PS D:\APITutorial\NET Core 3.1\CommandAPISolution\test\CommandAPI.Tests> dotnet
Test run for D:\APITutorial\NET Core 3.1\CommandAPISolution\test\CommandAPI.Test
Microsoft (R) Test Execution Command Line Tool Version 16.5.0
Copyright (c) Microsoft Corporation.  All rights reserved.

Starting test execution, please wait...

A total of 1 test files matched the specified pattern.

Test Run Successful.
Total tests: 3
     Passed: 3
 Total time: 0.9666 Seconds
PS D:\APITutorial\NET Core 3.1\CommandAPISolution\test\CommandAPI.Tests> []
```

Figure 11-14. 3 Passing Tests

Test Our Controller

OK, so testing our model was just an *amuse-bouche*[4] for what's about to come next: testing our Controller. We up the ante here as it's a decidedly more complex affair; although the concepts you learned in the last section still hold true, we just expand upon that here.

Revisit Unit Testing Characteristics

I think before we move on, it's worth revisiting our Unit Testing Characteristics:

- **Fast:** Individual tests should execute quickly (required as we can have 1000s of them), and when we say quick, we're talking in the region of milliseconds.

---

[3]https://xunit.net/docs/shared-context

[4]Bite-sized hors d'oeuvre, literally means "mouth amuser" in French. They differ from appetizers in that they are not ordered from a menu by patrons but are served free and according to the chef's selection alone.

- **Isolated:** Unit tests should not be dependent on external factors, for example, databases, network connections, etc.

- **Repeatable:** The same test should yield the same result between runs (assuming you don't change anything between runs).

- **Self-checking:** Should not require human intervention to determine whether it has passed or failed.

- **Timely:** The unit test should not take a disproportionately long time to run compared with the code being tested.

- **Focused:** A unit test (as the name suggests and as mentioned earlier) should test only one thing.

I often struggle with the **Focused** characteristic and frequently have to pull myself back to testing *just one thing*, rather than wandering into integration test territory (and attempting to test an end-to-end flow). But that's not the characteristic I'm most worried about in this instance.

When we come to Unit testing our controller, the **Isolation** characteristic will present as problematic. Why? Let's remind ourselves of our Controller constructor.

```
[Route("api/[controller]")]
[ApiController]
public class CommandsController : ControllerBase
{
    private readonly ICommandAPIRepo _repository;
    private readonly IMapper _mapper;

    public CommandsController(ICommandAPIRepo repository, IMapper mapper)
    {
        _repository = repository;
        _mapper = mapper;
    }

    [HttpDelete("{id}")]
```

Figure 11-15. Reminder of the dependencies injected into the constructor

Even though we are using Dependency Injection (which is awesome), they are still dependencies as far as our controller is concerned, so when we come to unit testing the controller – how do we deal with this? Dependency Injection again? Stick a pin in that for now – I just want to plant the seed.

As before, I think the best way to learn about this is to get coding, so let's turn our attention back to our very first controller action: GetAllCommands.

GetAllCommands Unit Tests and Groundwork

GetAllCommands Overview

Let's remind ourselves of how GetAllCommands is supposed to be called.

Verb	URI	Operation	Description
GET	/api/commands	Read	Read all command resources

Additionally, I've provided some of the more detailed attributes of GetAllCommands that should help drive our testing.

Attribute	Description
Inputs	None; we simply make a GET request to the URI in the preceding table
Process	Attempt to retrieve a collection of command resources
Success Outputs	• HTTP 200 OK Status
Failure Outputs	N/A: If this endpoint exists, it can't really be called "incorrectly"
Safe	Yes – Endpoint cannot alter our resources
Idempotent	Yes – Repeating the same operation will provide the same result

GetAllCommands Unit Tests

What to test can be somewhat subjective, and from a test perspective, this is probably our simplest controller action, so I've settled on the following test cases.

Test ID	Arrange and action	Assert
Test 1.1	Request Resources when 0 exist	Return 200 OK HTTP Response
Test 1.2	Request Resources when 1 exists	Return a Single Command Object
Test 1.3	Request Resources when 1 exists	Return 200 OK HTTP Response
Test 1.4	Request Resources when 1 exists	Return the correct "type"

You'll see that tests 1.2, 1.3, and 1.4 have the same Arrange and Action:

- Request a Resource when one exists.

So why not roll these into one test and perform the three assertions there? Well again that would break our **Focused** characteristic – we should be testing for one thing only per test.

Groundwork for Controller Tests

As with our Command model, we want to create a separate test class in our unit test project to hold the controller tests, so create a class called ***CommandsControllerTests.cs***, as shown in Figure 11-16.

Figure 11-16. *Tests for the Controller*

Place the following code into the ***CommandsControllerTests.cs*** file to get started:

```
using System;
using Xunit;
using CommandAPI.Controllers;
using Microsoft.AspNetCore.Mvc;

namespace CommandAPI.Tests
{
  public class CommandsControllerTests
  {
    [Fact]
    public void GetCommandItems_ReturnsZeroItems_WhenDBIsEmpty()
    {
      //Arrange
      //We need to create an instance of our CommandsController class
      var controller = new CommandsController( /* repository, AutoMapper */);
    }
  }
}
```

So straight away we want to start *arranging* our tests so that we have access to a
CommandsController class to work with, but how do we create one when it has two
dependencies (the repository and AutoMapper)? Dependency Injection – I hear you say!
But if you look back at the anatomy of our Unit Test project, there's no equivalent of the
Startup class in which to Register our services for injection. We could start to add one I
guess, but that would then lead to the problem of testing against our repository.

Even if we were to use Dependency Injection here, we'd still need to provide a
concrete implementation instance; which one would we use? SqlCommanAPIRepo?
That requires a DB Context, which in turn requires our Database. Argh! Not only is that
horrifically complicated, we're breaking the **Isolation** characteristic in a big way by
dragging all that stuff into our unit testing.

We could move back to MockCommandAPIRepo and implement test code in there that
wasn't dependent on external factors, a possibility, but still a hassle – don't worry there is
a better way!

Mocking Frameworks

Thankfully we can turn to something called "mocking," which means we can quickly create "fake" (or mock) copies of any required objects to use within our unit tests. It allows us to self-contain everything we need in our unit test project and adhere to the **Isolation** principle. We can certainly use mocking for our repository and *possibly* AutoMapper.

In order to use mocking, we need to turn to an external framework for this; the one I've chosen for us is called **Moq**. It's fairly well understood and used within the C# .NET Community, so I thought it was a good choice for us.

Install Moq and AutoMapper

Open a command prompt, and make sure you're "in" the ***CommandAPI.Tests*** folder, and issue the following commands:

```
dotnet add package Moq
dotnet add package AutoMapper.Extensions.Microsoft.DependencyInjection
```

Confirm that these dependencies have been added to the ***CommandAPITests.csproj*** file.

```
<ItemGroup>
  <PackageReference Include="AutoMapper.Extensions.Microsoft.DependencyInjection" Version="7.0.0" />
  <PackageReference Include="Microsoft.EntityFrameworkCore.Relational" Version="3.1.4" />
  <PackageReference Include="Microsoft.NET.Test.Sdk" Version="16.6.1" />
  <PackageReference Include="Moq" Version="4.14.1" />
  <PackageReference Include="xunit" Version="2.4.1" />
  <PackageReference Include="xunit.runner.visualstudio" Version="2.4.1" />
  <PackageReference Include="coverlet.collector" Version="1.2.1" />
</ItemGroup>

<ItemGroup>
  <ProjectReference Include="..\..\src\CommandAPI\CommandAPI.csproj" />
</ItemGroup>
```

Figure 11-17. *Package References for Moq*

You'll notice we've added AutoMapper in addition to Moq; we'll require this later.

Using Moq (Mock the Repository)

Returning to our CommandsControllerTests class, add the following code (taking note of our new using directives):

```
using System;
using System.Collections.Generic;
using Moq;
using AutoMapper;
using CommandAPI.Models;
using CommandAPI.Data;
using Xunit;
using CommandAPI.Controllers;
using Microsoft.AspNetCore.Mvc;

namespace CommandAPI.Tests
{
  public class CommandsControllerTests
  {
    [Fact]
    public void GetCommandItems_Returns200OK_WhenDBIsEmpty()
    {
      //Arrange
      var mockRepo = new Mock<ICommandAPIRepo>();

      mockRepo.Setup(repo =>
        repo.GetAllCommands()).Returns(GetCommands(0));

      var controller = new CommandsController(mockRepo.Object,
      /* AutoMapper*/ );
    }

    private List<Command> GetCommands(int num)
    {
      var commands = new List<Command>();
      if (num > 0){
        commands.Add(new Command
```

```
    {
        Id = 0,
        HowTo = "How to generate a migration",
        CommandLine = "dotnet ef migrations add <Name of Migration>",
        Platform = ".Net Core EF"
    });
    }
    return commands;
  }
 }
}
```

Or code is **still not runnable**, but I wanted to pause here and go through what we have added as there is quite a lot going on!

ℹ   Quick reminder, all this code is on GitHub[5] if you don't want to type this stuff in.

---
[5]https://github.com/binarythistle/Complete-ASP-NET-3-API-Tutorial-Book

```
[Fact]
public void GetCommandItems_Returns200OK_WhenDBIsEmpty()
{
    //Arrange
    var mockRepo = new Mock<ICommandAPIRepo>();          (1)

    mockRepo.Setup(repo =>                               (2)
        repo.GetAllCommands()).Returns(GetCommands(0));  (3)

    var controller = new CommandsController(mockRepo.Object, /* to do */);
                                                         (4)
}


private List<Command> GetCommands(int num)               (5)
{
    var commands = new List<Command>();
    if (num > 0)
    {
        commands.Add(new Command
        {
            Id = 0,
            HowTo = "How to genrate a migration",
            CommandLine = "dotnet ef migrations add <Name of Migration>",
            Platform = ".Net Core EF"
        });
    }
    return commands;
}
```

Figure 11-18. *Mocking our repository*

1. We set up a new "mock" instance of our repository; note that we only need to pass the interface definition.

2. Using our new mock repository, we use the Setup method to establish how it will "behave." Here, we specify the interface method we want to mock followed by what we want it to return (as described next).

3. Still in our Setup, we specify that the repository GetAllCommands method returns GetCommands(0) – see step 5.

4. We use the Object extension on our mock to pass in a mock *object instance* of ICommandAPIRepo.

5. We've mocked a private method: GetCommands that will return either an empty List or a List with one Command object depending on the value of the input parameter.

You can see how easy it is to set up mock objects using this type of framework, saving us a lot of the hassle of writing up our own mock classes. It also highlights the usefulness of our repository interface definition once again.

OK, so we've created a mock of our repository that we can use to create a `CommandsController` instance, but what about AutoMapper?

Mock AutoMapper?

While you *can* use Moq to mock-up AutoMapper, we're not going to do that here. Why? Well because in this particular instance, general consensus is that it is more effective (and useful) to use an actual instance of AutoMapper. Additionally, using this approach we get to test the AutoMapper Profiles we've set up in our API Project too.

Now I want to sense check here.

This may seem completely contrary to the **Isolation** and **Focused** principles, and to some extent it is. My response to that is one of pragmatism (you may call it a cop out!), but the Unit Test Characteristics are just that: *Characteristics*. They are not unbreakable rules.

As developers we're often faced with choices and challenges. I may take one path, and you may choose another – personally I think that's fine. Coding can be as much art as science.

What me must strive to do is solve a problem the best way we can, and sometimes that involves compromise or, as I prefer to call it, *pragmatism*. In this case (in my view), using an instance of AutoMapper (as opposed to a mocked instance of it) provides more benefits than downsides, so that is the approach I'm going to take.

But please feel free to disagree!

So back in our `CommandsControllerTest` class, add the following code to provide us with an instance of AutoMapper (taking care to note the new using directive to bring in our Profiles):

```
using System;
using System.Collections.Generic;
using Moq;
using AutoMapper;
using CommandAPI.Models;
using CommandAPI.Data;
using CommandAPI.Profiles;
```

```
using Xunit;
using CommandAPI.Controllers;
using Microsoft.AspNetCore.Mvc;

namespace CommandAPI.Tests
{
  public class CommandsControllerTests
  {
    [Fact]
    public void GetCommandItems_Returns200OK_WhenDBIsEmpty()
    {
      //Arrange
      var mockRepo = new Mock<ICommandAPIRepo>();

      mockRepo.Setup(repo =>
        repo.GetAllCommands()).Returns(GetCommands(0));

      var realProfile = new CommandsProfile();
      var configuration = new MapperConfiguration(cfg =>
        cfg.AddProfile(realProfile));
      IMapper mapper = new Mapper(configuration);

      var controller = new CommandsController(mockRepo.Object, mapper);
    }

    .
    .
    .
  }
}
```

To step through the changes (for brevity I've not shown the using directives below), see Figure 11-19.

```
[Fact]
public void GetCommandItems_Returns200OK_WhenDBIsEmpty()
{
    //Arrange
    var mockRepo = new Mock<ICommandAPIRepo>();

    mockRepo.Setup(repo =>
      repo.GetAllCommands()).Returns(GetCommands(0));     1

      var realProfile = new CommandsProfile();
      var configuration = new MapperConfiguration(cfg =>
        cfg.AddProfile(realProfile));
      IMapper mapper = new Mapper(configuration);          2


    var controller = new CommandsController(mockRepo.Object, mapper);   3

}
```

Figure 11-19. *Using AutoMapper in our tests*

1. We set up a CommandsProfile instance and assign it to a MapperConfiguration.

2. We create a concrete instance of IMapper and give it our MapperConfiguration.

3. We pass our IMapper instance to our CommandController constructor.

There is a lot of new content and groundwork there, but now we're set up; the rest of this chapter should be quite quick! Make sure you save your work, build to check for errors, commit to GitHub, and we'll move onto completing our first test!

Finish Test 1.1 – Check 200 OK HTTP Response (Empty DB)

Just to remind ourselves what we were wanting to test, see the following table.

Test ID	Arrange and action	Assert
Test 1.1	Request Resources when 0 exist	Return 200 OK HTTP Response

Back in the CommandsControllerTests, complete the code for our first test (make sure you include the using directive):

```
using CommandAPI.Dtos;

//Arrange
.
.
var controller = new CommandsController(mockRepo.Object, mapper);

//Act
var result = controller.GetAllCommands();

//Assert
Assert.IsType<OkObjectResult>(result.Result);
```

To put these in context, see Figure 11-20.

Figure 11-20. *Finalizing our Test*

1. We make a call to the GetAllCommands action on our Controller.

2. We Assert that the Result is an OkObjectResult (essentially equating to 200 OK).

As before, we can refactor our code to be a bit more reusable and place some of the common setup into a class constructor, as shown here:

```
public class CommandsControllerTests : IDisposable
{
  Mock<ICommandAPIRepo> mockRepo;
  CommandsProfile realProfile;
  MapperConfiguration configuration;
  IMapper mapper;

  public CommandsControllerTests()
  {
    mockRepo = new Mock<ICommandAPIRepo>();
    realProfile = new CommandsProfile();
    configuration = new MapperConfiguration(cfg => cfg.
    AddProfile(realProfile));
    mapper = new Mapper(configuration);
  }

  public void Dispose()
  {
    mockRepo = null;
    mapper = null;
    configuration = null;
    realProfile = null;
  }

  [Fact]
  public void GetCommandItems_Returns200OK_WhenDBIsEmpty()
  {
    //Arrange
    mockRepo.Setup(repo =>
    repo.GetAllCommands()).Returns(GetCommands(0));

    var controller = new CommandsController(mockRepo.Object, mapper);
```

```
//Act
var result = controller.GetAllCommands();
```

.

.

.

The only specific arrangement for this test case is the fact that we want the mock repository to return "0" resources.

If you want to "test your test," save your work, and build the project, and then perform a dotnet test (of course inside the xUnit Project) to make sure it passes.

Test 1.2 – Check Single Resource Returned

The second test checks to see that we get one resource returned.

Test ID	Arrange and action	Assert
Test 1.2	Request Resource when 1 exists	Return Single Resource

 Les' Personal Anecdote   I debated on whether to include this test at all. Depending on how you look at it, you may claim that this is not really testing our Controller but testing our Repository.

Nonetheless, I thought I'd include it to show you how to obtain this type of information.

In the code here, we configure our private GetCommands method to return one object. The "assertion" code looks a bit convoluted, but that is a consequence of how we have written our original controller action; here's the code, and we'll step through it here:

```
[Fact]
public void GetAllCommands_ReturnsOneItem_WhenDBHasOneResource()
{
  //Arrange
  mockRepo.Setup(repo =>
    repo.GetAllCommands()).Returns(GetCommands(1));
```

```
    var controller = new CommandsController(mockRepo.Object, mapper);

    //Act
    var result = controller.GetAllCommands();

    //Assert
    var okResult = result.Result as OkObjectResult;

    var commands = okResult.Value as List<CommandReadDto>;

    Assert.Single(commands);
}
```

To put in context, see Figure 11-21.

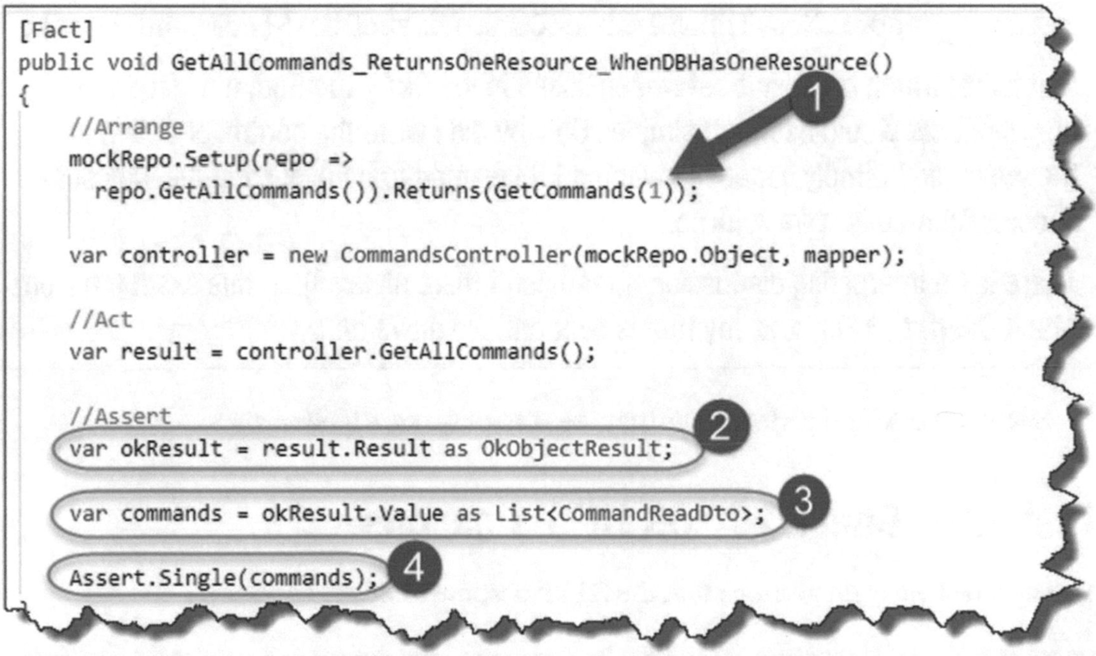

Figure 11-21. *Getting to the Value*

1. We arrange our mockRepo to return a single command resource.

2. In order to obtain the Value (see step 4), we need to convert our original result to an OkObjectResult object so we can then navigate the object hierarchy.

3. We obtain a list of CommandReadDtos (again we use the "as" keyword to assist here).

4. We assert that we have a Single result set on our commands List.

Les' Personal Anecdote   Personally, I hate this code and think it's way too complex. The reason for this complexity stems from the fact that in our GetAllCommands controller action, we return our result set as follows:

```
return Ok(_mapper.Map<IEnumerable<CommandReadDto>>
(commandItems));
```

Had we just used this

```
return _mapper.Map<IEnumerable<CommandReadDto>>(commandItems);
```

that is, returning our result set *not* enclosed in the Ok() method, navigation to our result set would be much simpler. So why did I write the controller action in the way I did? Simply because I wanted to! I wanted to be explicit in the way our successful results were returned.

There is an interesting discussion thread (isn't there always!) on this exact topic on Stack Overflow.[6] For now, my rant is over and we move on.

Save the code and perform a dotnet test to make sure it passes.

Test 1.3 – Check 200 OK HTTP Response

The next test we want to check that the HTTP Response code is correct.

Test ID	Arrange and action	Assert
Test 1.3	Request Resource when 1 exists	Return HTTP 200 OK

---

[6]https://stackoverflow.com/questions/51489111/how-to-unit-test-with-actionresultt

The code is quite straightforward, so don't think it requires much more explanation:

```
[Fact]
public void GetAllCommands_Returns200OK_WhenDBHasOneResource()
{
  //Arrange
  mockRepo.Setup(repo =>
    repo.GetAllCommands()).Returns(GetCommands(1));

  var controller = new CommandsController(mockRepo.Object, mapper);

  //Act
  var result = controller.GetAllCommands();

  //Assert
  Assert.IsType<OkObjectResult>(result.Result);

}
```

Test 1.4 – Check the Correct Object Type Returned

The final test is arguably the most useful one: it tests for the correct return *type*, in this case an ActionResult with an enumeration of CommandReadDtos.

Test ID	Arrange and action	Assert
Test 1.4	Request Resource when 1 exists	Return the correct "type"

```
[Fact]
public void GetAllCommands_ReturnsCorrectType_WhenDBHasOneResource()
{
  //Arrange
  mockRepo.Setup(repo =>
  repo.GetAllCommands()).Returns(GetCommands(1));

  var controller = new CommandsController(mockRepo.Object, mapper);

  //Act
  var result = controller.GetAllCommands();
```

```
//Assert
Assert.IsType<ActionResult<IEnumerable<CommandReadDto>>>(result);
}
```

Out of the four tests we've constructed for our first controller action, this is my favorite. Why? It's essentially testing our external contract. If we subsequently change how our controller behaves (and what it passes back to our consumers), this test will fail in regression. This is the mark of a valuable test for me!

Les' Personal Anecdote   Now, I had an internal debate with myself whether to include the rest of the unit test code in the book or whether just to reference you off to GitHub, and we'd close this chapter off here.

The reason I had that debate was

1. I said no fluff/filler content - and you could argue that given the repeated nature of unit tests that we are going into that territory.

2. Most of the code that follows doesn't require much more explanation as we have covered the concepts already. So, it's just ends up as code on a page.

However, I *did* decide to keep the code here in the book, which means that chapter continues on. Why? In one word: Completeness. I wanted to produce the best product that I could, and I felt if I didn't keep all the code here in the book, it wouldn't be a complete product.

I hope you agree.

GetCommandByID Unit Tests

GetCommandByID Overview

Again, we'll remind ourselves how this endpoint is supposed to be called.

Verb	URI	Operation	Description
GET	/api/commands/{id}	Read	Read a single resource (by Id)

And some further detail to help us with defining our tests.

Attribute	Description
Inputs	The Id of the resource to be retrieved. This will be present in the URI of our GET request
Process	Attempt to retrieve the resource with the specified identifier
Success Outputs	• 200 OK HTTP Response • Returned resource <CommandReadDto>
Failure Outputs	• 404 Not Found Response
Safe	Yes – Endpoint *cannot* alter our resources
Idempotent	Yes – Repeating the same operation will provide the same result

GetCommandByID Unit Tests

This action is ultimately about returning a single resource based on a unique Id, so we should test the following.

Test ID	Condition	Expected Result
Test 2.1	Resource ID is invalid (does not exist in DB)	404 Not Found HTTP Response
Test 2.2	Resource ID is valid (exists in the DB)	200 Ok HTTP Response
Test 2.3	Resource ID is valid (exists in the DB)	Correct Resource Type Returned

Test 2.1 – Check 404 Not Found HTTP Response

The code for this test is outlined here:

```
[Fact]
public void GetCommandByID_Returns404NotFound_WhenNonExistentIDProvided()
{
  //Arrange
  mockRepo.Setup(repo =>
    repo.GetCommandById(0)).Returns(() => null);
```

```
var controller = new CommandsController(mockRepo.Object, mapper);

//Act
var result = controller.GetCommandById(1);

//Assert
Assert.IsType<NotFoundResult>(result.Result);
}
```

Here we setup the GetCommandsById method on our mock repository to return null when an Id of "0" is passed in. This is a great demonstration of the real power of Moq. How simple was that to set up the behavior of our repository? The answer is very simple!

We then just check for the NotFoundResult type (equating to a 404 Not Found HTTP Response).

Test 2.2 – Check 200 OK HTTP Response

The code for this test is outlined here:

```
[Fact]
public void GetCommandByID_Returns200OK__WhenValidIDProvided()
{
  //Arrange
  mockRepo.Setup(repo =>
    repo.GetCommandById(1)).Returns(new Command { Id = 1,
    HowTo = "mock",
    Platform = "Mock",
    CommandLine = "Mock" });

  var controller = new CommandsController(mockRepo.Object, mapper);

  //Act
  var result = controller.GetCommandById(1);

  //Assert
  Assert.IsType<OkObjectResult>(result.Result);
}
```

The only novel code here is the way we set up the GetCommandByID method on our repository to return a valid object, again very simple and quick. The rest of the code doesn't require further discussion.

Test 2.3 – Check the Correct Object Type Returned

The code for this test is outlined here:

```
[Fact]
public void GetCommandByID_Returns200OK_WhenValidIDProvided()
{
  //Arrange
  mockRepo.Setup(repo =>
    repo.GetCommandById(1)).Returns(new Command { Id = 1,
    HowTo = "mock",
    Platform = "Mock",
    CommandLine = "Mock" });

  var controller = new CommandsController(mockRepo.Object, mapper);

  //Act
  var result = controller.GetCommandById(1);

  //Assert
  Assert.IsType<ActionResult<CommandReadDto>>(result);
}
```

This test checks to see if we returned a CommandReadDto. In terms of checking for the validity of our externally facing contract, I like this test very much. If we changed our Controller code to return a different type, this test would fail, highlighting a potential problem with our contract – very useful.

CreateCommand Unit Tests

CreateCommand Overview

Here are the characteristics of the CreateCommand endpoint.

Verb	URI	Operation	Description
POST	/api/commands	Create	Create a new resource

A reminder on the detailed behavior outlined here.

Attribute	Description

Inputs	The "command" object to be created
	This will be added to the request body of our POST request; an example is shown here:
	
	`{`
	   `"howTo": "Example how to",`
	   `"platform": "Example platform",`
	   `"commandLine": "Example command line"`
	`}`

Process	Will attempt to add a new command object to our DB
Success Outputs	• HTTP 201 Created Status • Newly Created Resource (response body) • URI to newly created resource (response header)
Failure Outputs	• HTTP 400 Bad Request • HTTP 405 Not Allowed
Safe	No – Endpoint can alter our resources
Idempotent	No – Repeating the same operation will incur a different result

CreateCommand Unit Tests

Test ID	Condition	Expected Result
Test 3.1	Valid Object Submitted for Creation	Correct Object Type Returned
Test 3.2	Valid Object Submitted for Creation	201 Created HTTP Response

Now these tests may look a little spartan for this controller; could we not be testing more? I had originally conceived of the following additional tests

1. Test before and after object count of our repository (increment by 1).

2. Test if the content of the object passed back was correct.

3. Test for the 400 Bad Request.

4. Test for the 405 Not Allowed.

So why didn't I? Well tests 1 and 2 are not really testing our controller; they're really testing our repository. So as

- That's not the focus of our testing here.

- Our Repository is mocked.

I chose not to write unit tests for those. These cases could be considered valid *integration* tests that *included* our controller, but again that's not what we are doing here. (This is the trap I said I could fall into around the **Focused** unit test principle.)

For tests 3 and 4, the behavior demonstrated here derived from the default behaviors we get from decorating our controller with the [ApiController] attribute. This is not code I (or you) wrote – so I'm not going to write a unit test for code that I have no control over.

If I subsequently decided to add my own code to handle these conditions, then I'd probably introduce testing for them.

Test 3.1 Check If the Correct Object Type Is Returned

The code for this test is outlined here:

```
[Fact]
public void CreateCommand_ReturnsCorrectResourceType_
WhenValidObjectSubmitted()
{
  //Arrange
  mockRepo.Setup(repo =>
    repo.GetCommandById(1)).Returns(new Command { Id = 1,
    HowTo = "mock",
    Platform = "Mock",
    CommandLine = "Mock" });

    var controller = new CommandsController(mockRepo.Object, mapper);

    //Act
    var result = controller.CreateCommand(new CommandCreateDto { });

    //Assert
    Assert.IsType<ActionResult<CommandReadDto>>(result);
}
```

Test 3.2 Check 201 HTTP Response

The code for this test is outlined here:

```
[Fact]
public void CreateCommand_Returns201Created_WhenValidObjectSubmitted()
{
  //Arrange
  mockRepo.Setup(repo =>
    repo.GetCommandById(1)).Returns(new Command { Id = 1,
    HowTo = "mock",
    Platform = "Mock",
    CommandLine = "Mock" });

    var controller = new CommandsController(mockRepo.Object, mapper);
```

```
//Act
var result = controller.CreateCommand(new CommandCreateDto { });

//Assert
Assert.IsType<CreatedAtRouteResult>(result.Result);
}
```

UpdateCommand Unit Tests

UpdateCommand Overview

Here are the characteristics of the UpdateCommand.

Verb	URI	Operation	Description
PUT	/api/commands/{Id}	Update (full)	Update all of a single resource (by Id)

Detailed behaviors are shown here.

Attribute	Description

Inputs (2)	The Id of the resource to be updated. This will be present in the URI of our PUT request
	The full "command" object to be updated
	This will be added to the request body of our PUT request; an example is shown here:
	`{`
	`    "howTo": "Example how to",`
	`    "platform": "Example platform",`
	`    "commandLine": "Example command line"`
	`}`

Process	Will attempt to fully update an existing command object in our DB
Success Outputs	• HTTP 204 No Content response code
Failure Outputs	• HTTP 400 Bad Request • HTTP 404 Not Found • HTTP 405 Not Allowed

297

Attribute	Description
Safe	No – Endpoint can alter our resources
Idempotent	Yes – Repeating the same operation will not incur a different result

UpdateCommand Unit Tests

Test ID	Condition	Expected result
Test 4.1	Valid object submitted for update	204 No Content HTTP Response
Test 4.2	Nonexistent resource ID submitted for update	404 Not Found HTTP Response

Not too may tests here; points of note

- As we are not returning any resources back as part of our update, there are no tests checking for resource type this time.

- I have opted to test for the 404 Not Found result as this is behavior we actually wrote – so I want to test it.

Test 4.1 Check 204 HTTP Response

The code for this test is outlined here:

```
[Fact]
public void UpdateCommand_Returns204NoContent_WhenValidObjectSubmitted()
{
  //Arrange
  mockRepo.Setup(repo =>
  repo.GetCommandById(1)).Returns(new Command { Id = 1,
  HowTo = "mock",
  Platform = "Mock",
  CommandLine = "Mock" });

  var controller = new CommandsController(mockRepo.Object, mapper);
```

```
//Act
var result = controller.UpdateCommand(1, new CommandUpdateDto { });

//Assert
Assert.IsType<NoContentResult>(result);
}
```

Here we ensure that the GetCommandById method will return a valid resource when we attempt to "update." We then check to see that we get the success 204 No Content Response.

Test 4.2 Check 404 HTTP Response

The code for this test is outlined here:

```
[Fact]
public void UpdateCommand_Returns404NotFound_
WhenNonExistentResourceIDSubmitted()
{
  //Arrange
  mockRepo.Setup(repo =>
    repo.GetCommandById(0)).Returns(() => null);

  var controller = new CommandsController(mockRepo.Object, mapper);
  //Act
  var result = controller.UpdateCommand(0, new CommandUpdateDto { });

  //Assert
  Assert.IsType<NotFoundResult>(result);
}
```

We setup our mock repository to return back null, which should trigger the 404 Not Found behavior.

PartialCommandUpdate Unit Tests
PartialCommandUpdate Overview

The behavior of the `PartialCommandUpdate` method is shown here.

Verb	URI	Operation	Description
PATCH	/api/commands/{Id}	Update (partial)	Update part of a single resource (by Id)

Detailed behavior here.

Attribute	Description

Inputs (2)	The Id of the resource to be updated. This will be present in the URI of our PATCH request
	The change-set or "patch document" to be applied to the resource
	This will be added to the `request` body of our PATCH request; an example is shown here:
	`[`
	`  {`
	`    "op": "replace",`
	`    "path": "/howto",`
	`    "value": "Some new value"`
	`  },`
	`  {`
	`    "op": "test",`
	`    "path" : "commandline",`
	`    "value" : "dotnet new"`
	`  }`
	`]`

Process	Will attempt to perform the updates as specified in the patch document Note: If there is more than one update, all those updates need to be successful. If one fails, then they all fail
Success Outputs	• HTTP 204 Not Content HTTP Status

Attribute	Description
Failure Outputs	<ul><li>HTTP 400 Bad Request</li><li>HTTP 404 Not Found</li><li>HTTP 405 Not Allowed</li></ul>
Safe	No – Endpoint can alter our resources
Idempotent	No – Repeating the same operation may incur a different result

PartialCommandUpdate Unit Tests

Test ID	Condition	Expected Result
Test 5.1	Nonexistent resource ID submitted for update	404 Not Found HTTP Response

Even fewer tests here! As mentioned, when we implemented this endpoint, there are addition external dependencies required to get PATCH endpoints up and running. This cascades into unit testing too. The cost vs. benefit proposition of including the necessary inclusions to perform one unit test (testing for a 204 No Content) did not stack up for me and I assumed for you too as the reader! I have therefore included only one test below – the 404 Not Found Response.

Test 5.1 Check 404 HTTP Response

The code for this test is outlined here:

```
[Fact]
public void PartialCommandUpdate_Returns404NotFound_
WhenNonExistentResourceIDSubmitted()
{
  //Arrange
  mockRepo.Setup(repo =>
    repo.GetCommandById(0)).Returns(() => null);

  var controller = new CommandsController(mockRepo.Object, mapper);
```

```
//Act
var result = controller.PartialCommandUpdate(0,
    new Microsoft.AspNetCore.JsonPatch.JsonPatchDocument<CommandUpdateDto>
{ });

//Assert
Assert.IsType<NotFoundResult>(result);
}
```

DeleteCommand Unit Tests

DeleteCommand Overview

An overview of our DeleteCommand is shown here.

Verb	URI	Operation	Description
DELETE	/api/commands/{Id}	Delete	Delete a single resource (by Id)

Further details of how this endpoint should operate are listed here.

Attribute	Description
Inputs	The Id of the resource to be deleted. This will be present in the URI of our DELETE request
Process	Will attempt to delete an existing command object to our DB
Success Outputs	• HTTP 204 No Content HTTP result
Failure Outputs	• HTTP 404 Not Found HTTP result
Safe	No – End point can alter our resources
Idempotent	Yes – Repeating the same operation will incur the same result

DeleteCommand Unit Tests

Test ID	Condition	Expected result
Test 6.1	Valid resource Id submitted for deletion	204 No Content HTTP Response
Test 6.2	Nonexistent resource Id submitted for deletion	404 Not Found HTTP Response

Test 6.1 Check for 204 No Content HTTP Response

The code for this test is outlined here:

```
[Fact]
public void DeleteCommand_Returns204NoContent_
WhenValidResourceIDSubmitted()
{
  //Arrange
  mockRepo.Setup(repo =>
    repo.GetCommandById(1)).Returns(new Command { Id = 1,
    HowTo = "mock", Platform = "Mock", CommandLine = "Mock" });

  var controller = new CommandsController(mockRepo.Object, mapper);

  //Act
  var result = controller.DeleteCommand(1);

  //Assert
  Assert.IsType<NoContentResult>(result);
}
```

Test 6.2 Check for 404 Not Found HTTP Response

The code for this test is outlined here:

```
[Fact]
public void DeleteCommand_Returns_404NotFound_
WhenNonExistentResourceIDSubmitted()
{
```

```
//Arrange
mockRepo.Setup(repo =>
  repo.GetCommandById(0)).Returns(() => null);

var controller = new CommandsController(mockRepo.Object, mapper);

//Act
var result = controller.DeleteCommand(0);

//Assert
Assert.IsType<NotFoundResult>(result);
}
```

Wrap It Up

We covered a lot in this chapter, and to be honest we really only scraped the surface. Hopefully though you learned enough to start to get you up to speed on unit testing.

The main takeaways are

- The power of Moq to help Isolate ourselves when unit testing

- The somewhat arbitrary nature of what to test (use the characteristics as pragmatic guidelines)

With that we move into looking at how we'll deploy to production using a CI/CD pipeline on Azure DevOps!

## CHAPTER 12

The CI/CD Pipeline

Chapter Summary

In this chapter we bring together what we've done so far: build activity, source control, and unit testing and frame it within the context of Continuous Integration/Continuous Delivery (CI/CD).

When Done, You Will

- Understand what CI/CD is.

- Understand what a CI/CD Pipelinc is.

- Setup Azure DevOps with GitHub to act as our CI/CD pipeline.

- Automatically Build, Test, and Package our API solution using Azure DevOps.

- Prepare for Deployment to Azure.

What Is CI/CD?

To talk about CI/CD is to talk about a pipeline of work" or, if you prefer another analogy: a production line, where a product (in this instance working software) is taken from is raw form (code[1]) and gradually transformed into working software that's usable by the end users.

---

[1]You could argue (and in fact I would!) that the business requirements are the starting point of the software "build" process. For the purposes of this book though, we'll use code as the start point of the journey.

© Les Jackson 2020

L. Jackson, *The Complete ASP.NET Core 3 API Tutorial*, https://doi.org/10.1007/978-1-4842-6255-9_12

Clearly, this process will include a number of steps, most (if not all) we will want to automate.

It's essentially about the faster realization of business value and is a central foundational idea of agile software development. (Fret not, I'm not going to bang *that* drum too much.)

CI/CD or CI/CD?

Don't worry, the heading is not a typo (we'll come on to that in a minute).

CI is easy; that stands for *Continuous Integration*. CI is the process of taking any code changes from one or more developers working on the same piece of software and merging those changes back into the main code "branch" by building and testing that code. As the name would suggest, this process is continuous, triggered usually when developers "check-in" code changes to the code repository (as you have already been doing with Git/GitHub).

The whole point of CI is to ensure that the main (or master) code branch remains healthy throughout the build activity and that any new changes introduced by the multiple developers working on the code don't conflict and break the build.

CD can be a little bit more confusing. Why? We'll you'll hear people using both the following terms in reference to CD: Continuous *Delivery* and Continuous *Deployment*.

What's the Difference?

Well, if you think of Continuous Delivery as an extension of Continuous Integration, it's the process of automating the release process. It ensures that you can deploy software changes frequently and at the press of a button. Continuous Delivery stops just short of automatically pushing changes into production though; that's where Continuous Deployment comes in.

Continuous Deployment goes further than Continuous Delivery, in that code changes will make their way through to production without any *human intervention* (assuming there are no failures in the CI/CD pipeline, e.g., failing tests).

Figure 12-1. *Continuous: integration, delivery, and deployment*

So Which Is It?

Typically, when we talk about CI/CD, we talk about Continuous Integration and Continuous Delivery, although it can be dependent on the organization. Ultimately, the decision to deploy software into production is a business decision, so the idea of Continuous Deployment is still overwhelming for most organizations.

In this book though, we're going to go all out and practice full-on Continuous Deployment!

The Pipeline

Google "CI/CD pipeline," and you will come up with a multitude of examples; I, however, like this one.

Figure 12-2. *The DevOps Pipeline*

You may also see it depicted as a "loop," which kind of breaks the pipeline concept but is nonetheless useful when it comes to understanding the continuous cycle of DevOps activity.

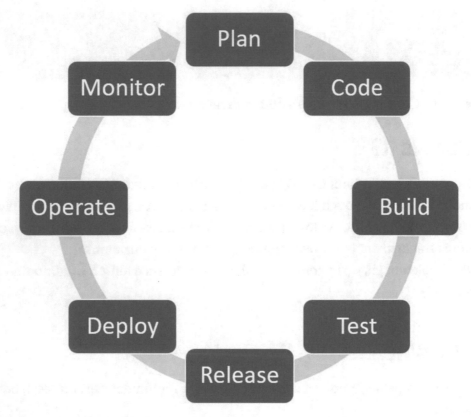

Figure 12-3. *The DevOps "loop"*

Coming back to the whole point of this chapter (which if you haven't forgotten is to detail how to use Azure DevOps), we are going to focus on the following elements of the pipeline.

Figure 12-4. *Our Focus*

What Is Azure DevOps?

Azure DevOps is a collection of tools that allow development teams to build and release software. It provides the following main features:

- **Dashboards**: For example, Red–Amber–Green (RAG) status of your pipeline, team members, etc.

- **Boards**: Allows you to capture and plan your work using methodologies like Scrum and Kanban.

- **Repos**: You can commit code (like we have done with GitHub) direct to Azure DevOps own repository.

- **Pipelines**: The automated CI/CD pipeline and our focus for Azure DevOps.

- **Test Plans**: End-to-end testing traceability for entire solutions.

- **Artifacts**: Package management, Artefact repo, etc.

In this chapter we are going to be focusing exclusively on the "Pipeline" feature and leave the other aspects untouched. As interesting as they are, to cover these would require a separate book and is outside our scope.

Alternatives

There are various on-premise and cloud-based alternatives to Azure DevOps: Jenkins is possibly the most "famous" of the on-premise solutions available, but you also have things like

- Bamboo

- Team City

- Werker

- Circle CI

That list is by no means exhaustive, but for now, we'll leave these behind and focus on Azure DevOps.

Technology in Context

Referring to our pipeline, in terms of our technology overlay, this is what we will be working with to build a CI/CD pipeline.

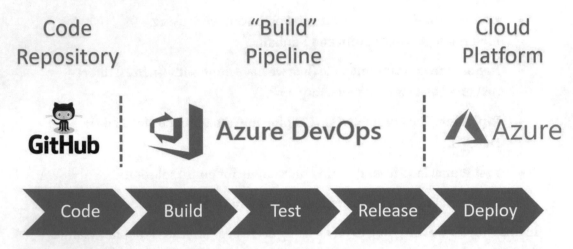

Figure 12-5. *The Technology mix we'll be using*

Indeed, Azure DevOps comes with its own "code repository" feature (as mentioned in Figure 12-5), which means we could do away with GitHub.

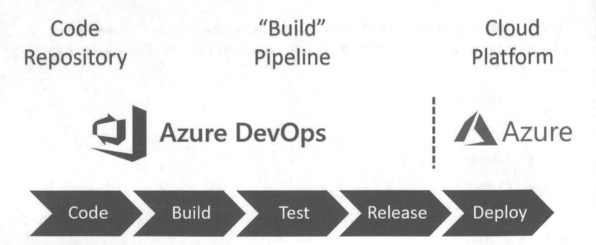

Figure 12-6. *Alternate technology mix*

So, our mix could look like the following.

Or if you wanted to take Microsoft technologies out of the picture, see Figure 12-7.

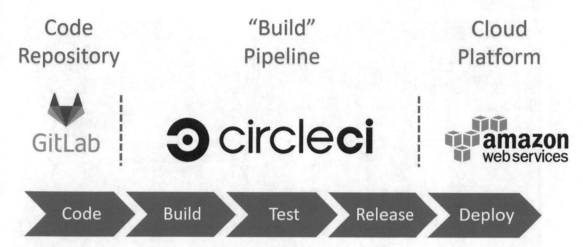

Figure 12-7. *Non-Microsoft mix*

Going further, you can even break down the Build ➤ Test ➤ Release ➤ Deploy, etc. components into specific technologies. I'm not going to do that here.

The takeaway points I wanted to make were

1. The relevant sequencing of technologies in our example.

2. Make sure you understand the importance of the code repository (GitHub) as the start point.

3. Be aware of the almost limitless choice of technology.

OK, enough theory; let's build our pipeline!

Create a Build Pipeline

If you've not done so already, go to the Azure DevOPs site, `https://dev.azure.com`, and sign up for a free account (be careful that you actually login to *Azure DevOps* and not Azure). The landing screen should look something like this (minus the projects I have).

311

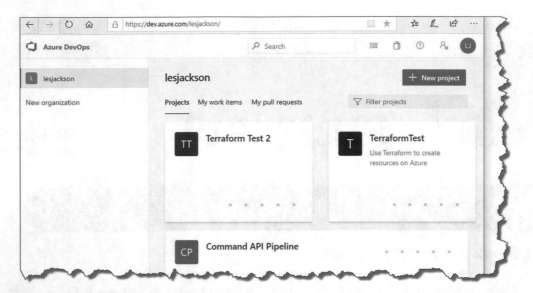

Figure 12-8. *Azure DevOps landing page*

⚠ **Warning!**   When working with both Azure and Azure DevOps, one thing I've noticed is that the user interfaces can change rapidly. At the time of writing this (May 2020), the screenshots are correct and current, but just be aware that given the nature of these products, they can change from time to time.

For the most part, these changes will be so small as to be inconsequential, for example, instead of "Create Project," it becomes "New Project." Other changes, while more significant, should still be easy enough to navigate through.

Once you have signed in/signed up, click "New Project."

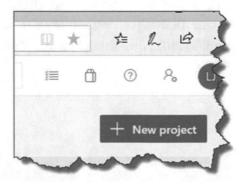

Figure 12-9. *Create New Project*

You can call it anything you like, so let's keep the theme going and call it *Command API Pipeline*.

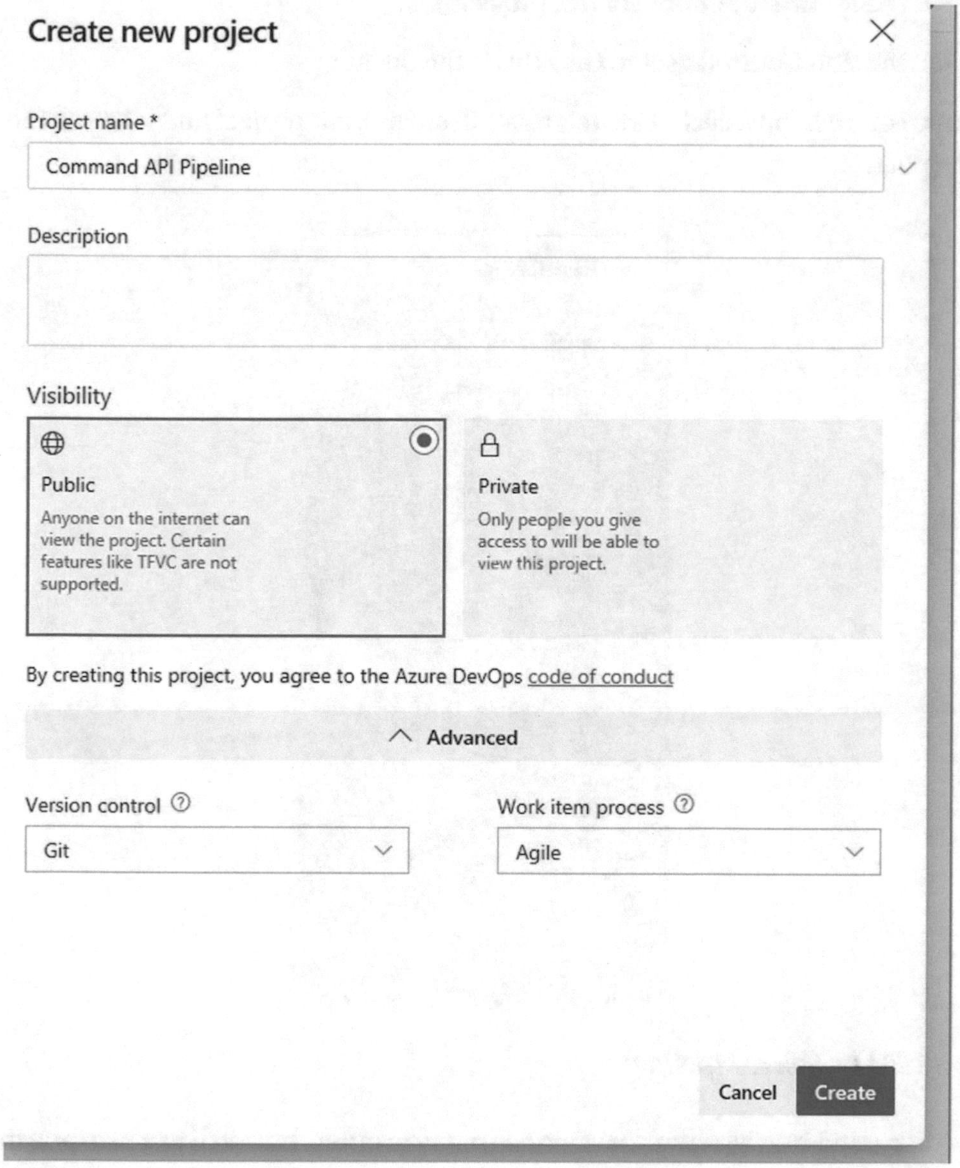

Create new project   ✕

Project name *

Command API Pipeline   ✓

Description

Visibility

🌐   ⦿   🔒

Public   Private

Anyone on the internet can   Only people you give
view the project. Certain   access to will be able to
features like TFVC are not   view this project.
supported.

By creating this project, you agree to the Azure DevOps code of conduct

⌃ Advanced

Version control ⑦   Work item process ⑦

Git   ⌄   Agile   ⌄

                                                     Cancel   Create

Figure 12-10. *Name the project and select Public Visibility*

313

Make sure

- You select the same "visibility" setting that your GitHub repo has (**recommend Public** for test projects).

- Version Control is set to Git – this is the default.

Once you're happy, click "Create"; this will create your project and take you into the landing page.

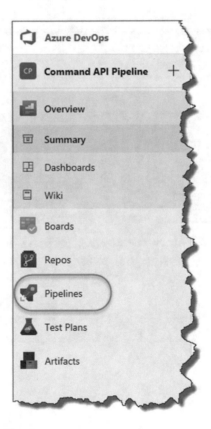

Figure 12-11. *Select Pipelines*

As discussed briefly, Azure DevOps has many features, but we'll just be using the "Pipelines" for now. Select Pipelines, then

1. Create pipeline.

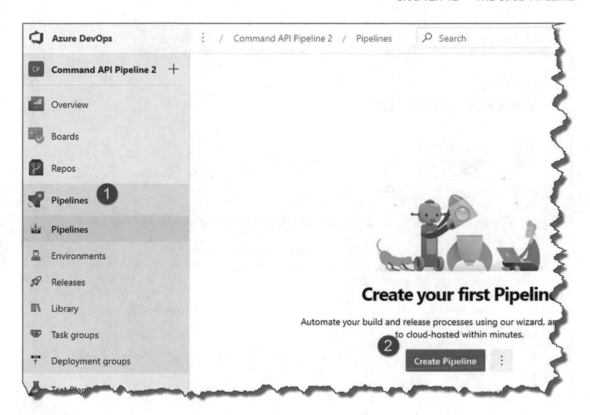

Figure 12-12. *Create a new Pipeline*

This first thing that it asks us is: "Where is your code?"

Well, where do you think?

Yeah – that's right – in GitHub!

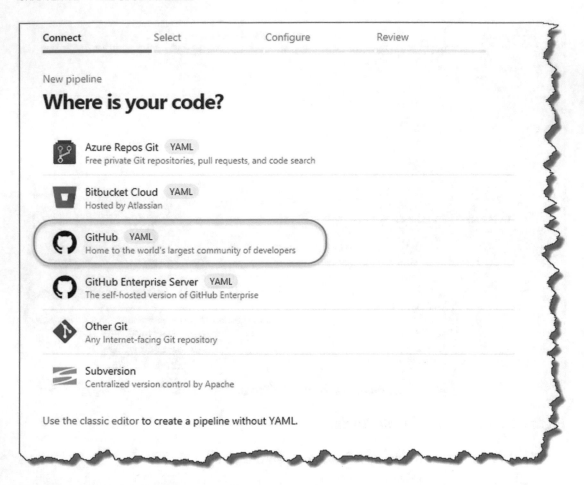

Figure 12-13. *GitHub is our code source*

Be careful to select GitHub, as opposed to GitHub Enterprise Server (which as the description states is the on-premise version of GitHub).

Important   If this is the first time you're doing this, you'll need to give Azure DevOps permission to view your GitHub account.

Figure 12-14. *You'll be asked to authenticate to GitHub*

Supply your GitHub account details and sign in. Once you've given Azure DevOps permission to connect to GitHub, you'll be presented with all your repositories.

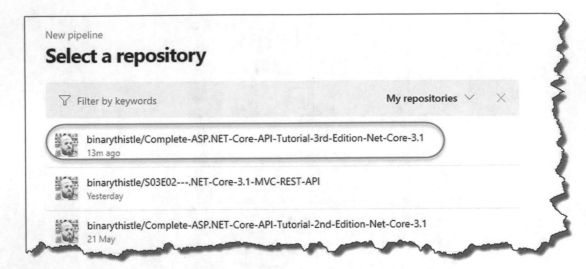

Figure 12-15.   *Select the relevant API Repository*

Pick your repository (my example repository is shown in Figure 12-15); once you click it, Azure DevOps will go off and analyze it to suggest some common pipeline templates; you'll see something like that in Figure 12-16.

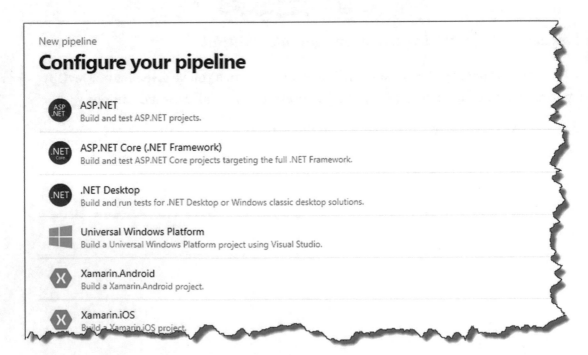

Figure 12-16.   *Pipeline Templates – we'll create our own*

ⓘ Note   Some readers have reported an additional step appearing here (that I cannot replicate) requesting that you approve and install Azure Pipelines. If you see this, I'd suggest you approve and proceed.

All this step will do is preconfigure the *azure-pipelines.yml* file for you (more on this next, but it's basically the instructions for our CI/CD pipeline). We are going to create our *azure-pipelines.yml* file from the ground up so it doesn't really matter which one you choose as we'll be overwriting it. Anyway, select an option and continue.

Les' Personal Anecdote   This is one of the areas of Azure DevOps that appears to change a lot! I have at times in my career suggested using one of the off-the-shelf configurations as shown in Figure 12-16, but they seem to change so much that I felt a safer, more stable bet would be to create our own from the ground up.

Irrespective of which template you pick you'll get a default *azure-pipelines.yml* file, take a quick look (chances are yours will look different).

```
azure-pipelines.yml

1    # ASP.NET Core
2    # Build and test ASP.NET Core projects targeting .NET Core.
3    # Add steps that run tests, create a NuGet package, deploy, and more:
4    # https://docs.microsoft.com/azure/devops/pipelines/languages/dotnet-core
5
6    trigger:
7    - master
8
9    pool:
10     vmImage: 'ubuntu-latest'
11
12   variables:
13     buildConfiguration: 'Release'
14
15   steps:
16   - script: dotnet build --configuration $(buildConfiguration)
17     displayName: 'dotnet build $(buildConfiguration)'
18
```

Figure 12-17.   Example Azure-pipelines.yml

Select the entire contents, and press delete; your file should now be completely empty.

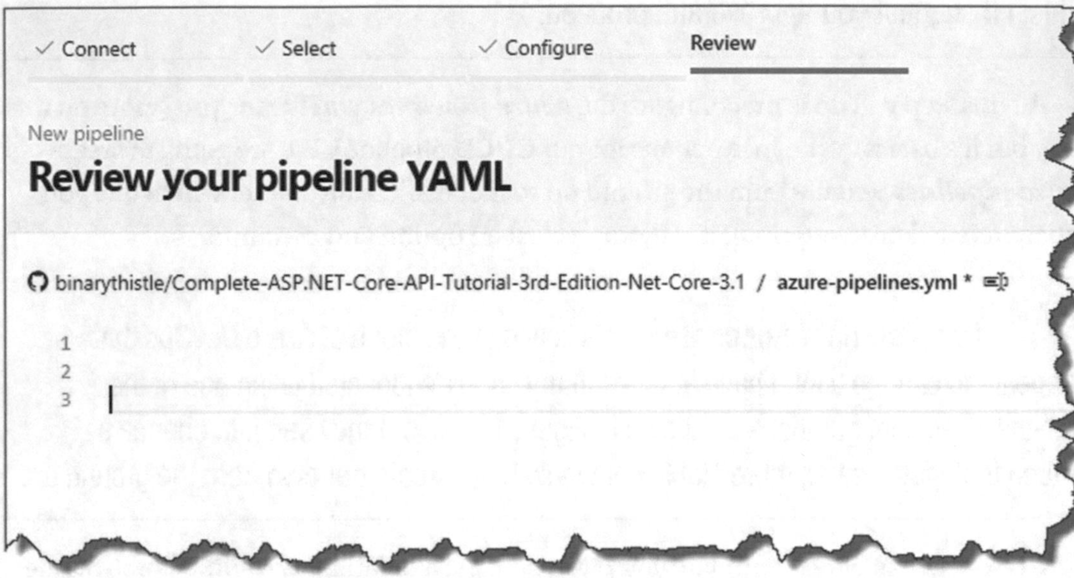

Figure 12-18. *Empty Azure-Pipelines .yml*

We are now going to add the first step to our file, which is simply to build our API Project. Before we do that, please read the warning below on formatting YAML files!

⚠ **Warning!**   YAML files are white case-sensitive, so you need to ensure the indentation is absolutely spot on! Thankfully the in-browser editor will complain if you've not indented correctly.

Add the following code you your **azure-pipeline.yml** file:

```
trigger:
- master

pool:
  vmImage: 'ubuntu-latest'

variables:
  buildConfiguration: 'Release'
```

```
steps:
- task: UseDotNet@2
- script: dotnet build --configuration $(buildConfiguration)
  displayName: 'dotnet build $(buildConfiguration)'
```

Your YAML file should look like this.

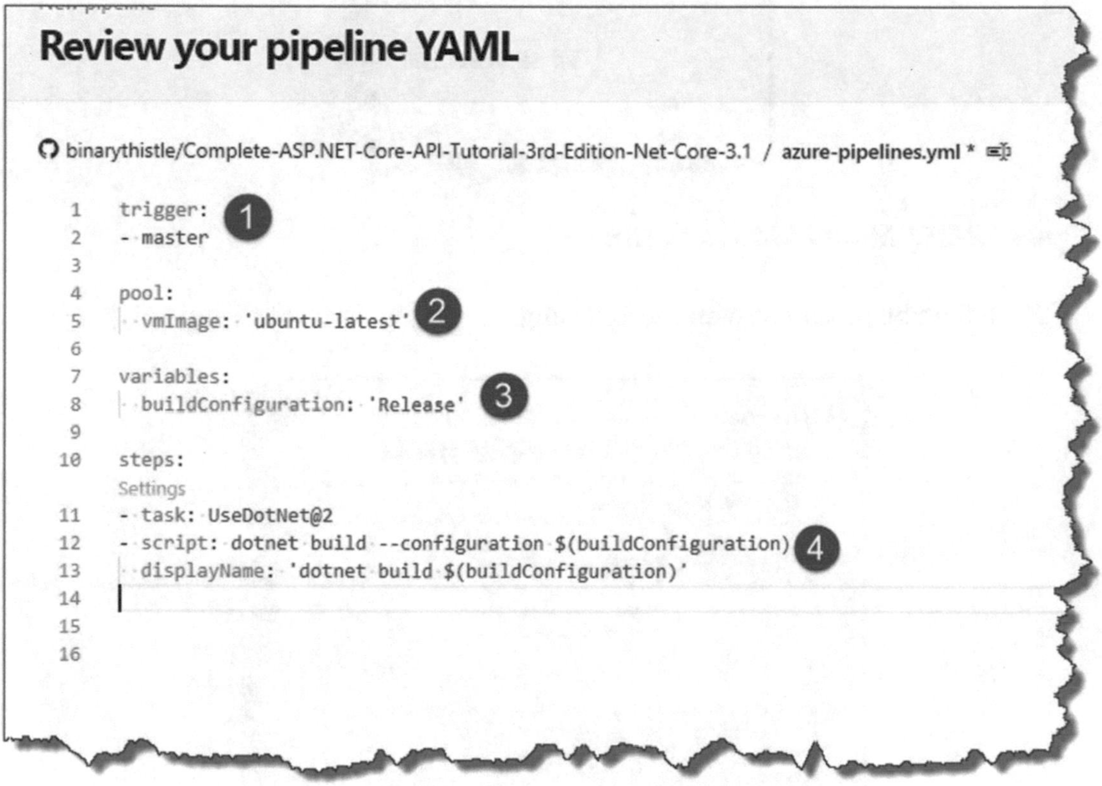

Figure 12-19. *Our Build Step*

1. The trigger point for the pipeline (GitHub).

2. The image we will be performing the pipeline activities with.

3. Setup a variable to specify the build configuration.

4. A script task that performs a dotnet build for "Release."

We're now ready to Click Save and run.

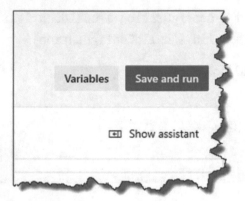

Figure 12-20. *Manual Save and run*

You'll then be presented with the following.

Figure 12-21. *Commit the Azure-pipelines.yml to our GitHub repo*

This is asking you where you want to store the ***azure-pipelines.yml*** file; in this case we want to add it directly to our GitHub repo (remember this selection though as it comes back later!), so select this option and click **Save and run.**

An "agent" is then assigned to execute the pipeline; you'll see various screens, such as in the next figures.

Figure 12-22. *Job Preparation on Azure DevOps*

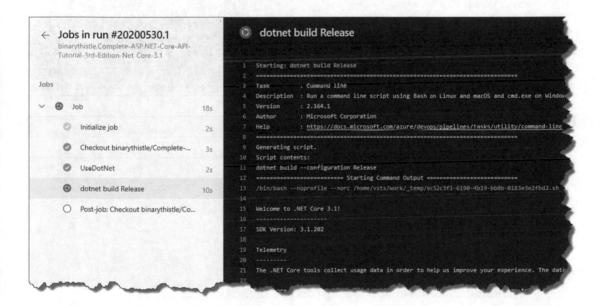

Figure 12-23. *In-progress Job*

And finally, you should see the completion screen.

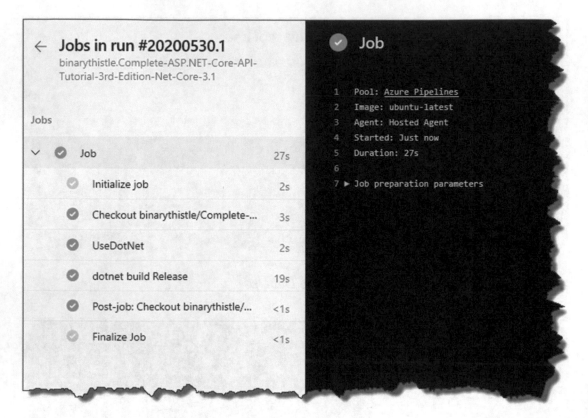

Figure 12-24. Successful completion

What Just Happened?

OK, to recap

- We connected Azure DevOps to GitHub.

- We selected a repository.

- We said that we wanted the pipeline configuration file (*azure-pipelines.yml*) to be placed in our repository.

- We manually ran the pipeline.

- Pipeline ran through the *azure-pipelines.yml* file and executed the steps.

- Our Solution was built.

Azure-Pipelines.yml File

Let's pop back over to our GitHub repository and refresh – you should see the following.

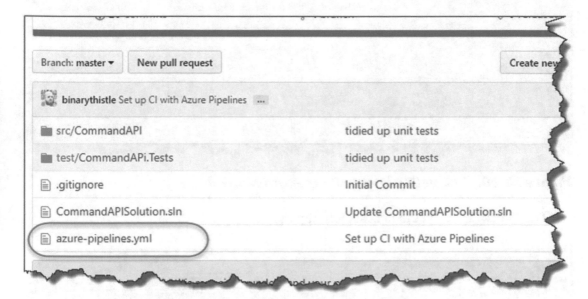

Figure 12-25. *azure-pipelines.yml is in our repo*

You'll see that the ***azure-pipelines.yml*** file has been added to our repo (this is important later).

I Thought We Wanted to Automate?

One of the benefits of a CI/CD pipeline is the automation opportunities it affords, so why did we manually execute the pipeline?

Great question!

We are asked to execute when we created the pipeline that is true, but we can also set up "triggers," meaning we can configure the pipeline to execute when it receives a particular event.

In your Azure DevOps project, click "Pipelines" under the Pipelines section, then select the pipeline.

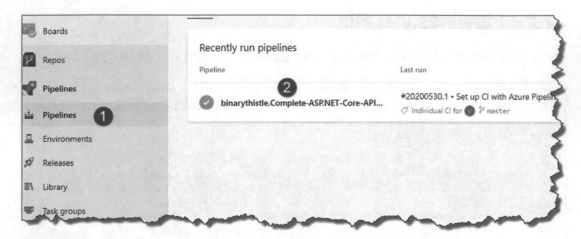

Figure 12-26. *Navigating back to Azure-pipelines.yml*

Then click "Edit" on the next screen (top right).

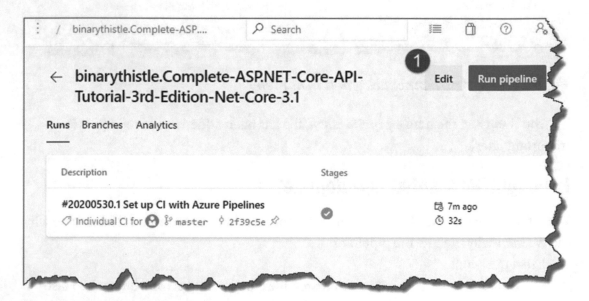

Figure 12-27. *Edit the pipeline*

After doing that you should be returned to the *azure-pipelines.yml* file (we will return here to edit it later):

1. Click the Ellipsis.

2. Select Triggers.

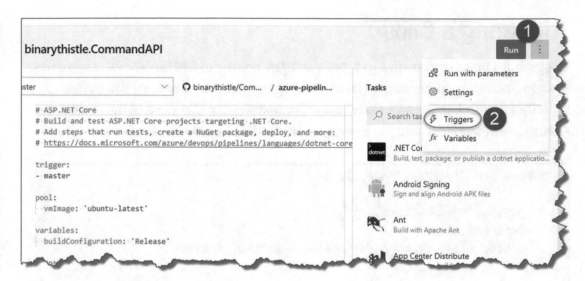

Figure 12-28. *Select our Triggers*

Here, you can see the Continuous Integration (CI) settings for our pipeline.

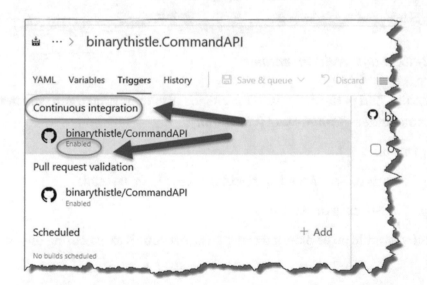

Figure 12-29. *Check if Pipeline triggers are enabled for GitHub commit*

You can see that the automation trigger is enabled by default (we have also configured this in the ***azure-pipeline.yml*** file), so now let's trigger a build! But how do we do that?

Triggering a Build

Triggering a build starts with a `git push origin master` to GitHub, so really any code change (including something trivial like adding or editing a comment) will suffice. With that in mind, back in VS Code, open `CommandsController` class in the "main" **CommandAPI** project, and put a comment in our `GetCommandItems` method.

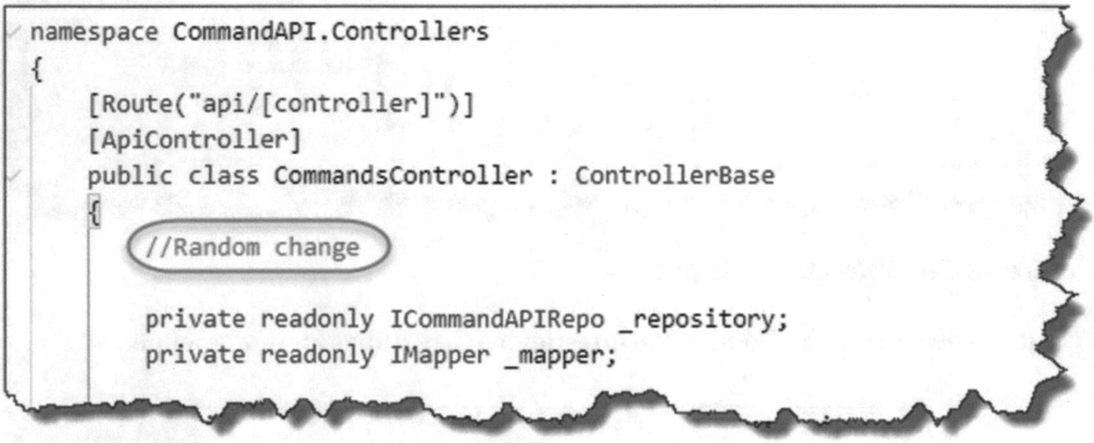

```
namespace CommandAPI.Controllers
{
    [Route("api/[controller]")]
    [ApiController]
    public class CommandsController : ControllerBase
    {
        //Random change

        private readonly ICommandAPIRepo _repository;
        private readonly IMapper _mapper;
```

Figure 12-30. *Some random change*

Save the file, and perform the usual sequence of actions (make sure you are in the main Solution Folder – **CommandAPISolution**):

- `git add .`

- `git commit -m "Added a reminder to clean up code"`

- `git push origin master`

Everything should go as planned except when it comes to executing the final push command.

```
PS D:\APITutorial\NET Core 3.1\CommandAPISolution> git push origin master
To https://github.com/binarythistle/Complete-ASP.NET-Core-API-Tutorial-2nd-Edition-Net-Core-3.1.git
 ! [rejected]        master -> master (fetch first)
error: failed to push some refs to 'https://github.com/binarythistle/Complete-ASP.NET-Core-API-Tutoria
hint: Updates were rejected because the remote contains work that you do
hint: not have locally. This is usually caused by another repository pushing
hint: to the same ref. You may want to first integrate the remote changes
hint: (e.g., 'git pull ...') before pushing again.
hint: See the 'Note about fast-forwards' in 'git push --help' for details.
PS D:\APITutorial\NET Core 3.1\CommandAPISolution> []
```

Figure 12-31. *Our Local and Remote Repos are out of sync*

What does this mean?

Well remember we added the ***azure-pipelines.yml*** file to the GitHub repo? Yes? Well that's the cause, essentially the local repository and the remote GitHub repository are out of sync (the central GitHub repo has some newer changes than our local repository). To remedy this, we simply type

```
git pull
```

Or if that doesn't work, use

```
git pull origin master
```

This pulls down the changes from the remote GitHub repository and merges them with our local one.

```
PROBLEMS    OUTPUT    DEBUG CONSOLE    TERMINAL

PS D:\APITutorial\NET Core 3.1\CommandAPISolution> git pull
remote: Enumerating objects: 12, done.
remote: Counting objects: 100% (12/12), done.
remote: Compressing objects: 100% (11/11), done.
remote: Total 11 (delta 7), reused 0 (delta 0), pack-reused 0
Unpacking objects: 100% (11/11), done.
From https://github.com/binarythistle/Complete-ASP.NET-Core-API-Tutorial-2nd
   259d1f5..c5d405f  master      -> origin/master
Merge made by the 'recursive' strategy.
 azure-pipelines.yml | 22 +++++++++++++++++++++++
 1 file changed, 22 insertions(+)
 create mode 100644 azure-pipelines.yml
PS D:\APITutorial\NET Core 3.1\CommandAPISolution> |
```

Figure 12-32. *Pull down the azure-pipelines.yml*

Indeed, if you look the VS Code file tree, you'll see our ***azure-pipelines.yml*** file has appeared!

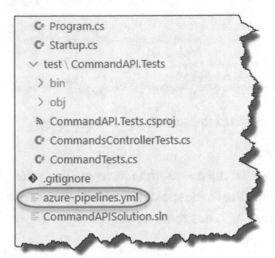

Figure 12-33. *We have azure-pipelines.yml locally now*

Now that we have synced our repositories, you can now attempt to push our combined local Git repo back up to GitHub (this includes the comment we inserted into our CommandsController class). Quickly jump over to Azure DevOps and click Pipelines ➤ Builds; you should see something like this.

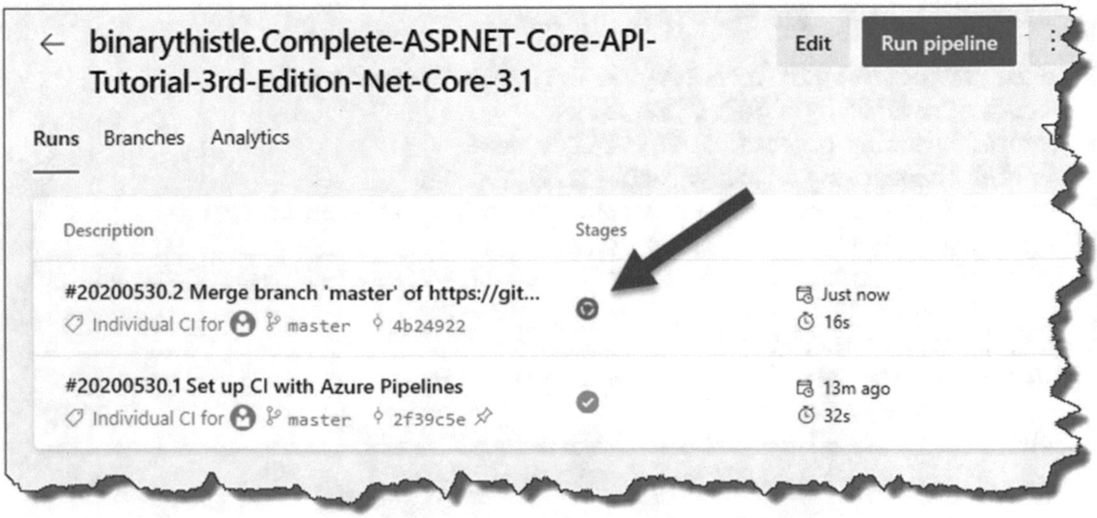

Figure 12-34. *Auto-triggered build*

A new build has been queued to start – this time triggered by a remote commit to GitHub!

Once it starts, all being well, this should succeed.

We are getting there, but there is still some work to do on our build pipeline before we move on to deploying – and that is ensuring that our unit tests are run – which currently they are not.

Revisit azure-pipelines.yml

Returning to our *azure-pipelines.yml* file in Azure DevOps (follow the steps earlier if you forgot how to get here), you should see the following.

```
master        ⌄      ☉ binarythistle/Complete-ASP.NET-Core-API-Tutorial-3rd-Edition-Net-Core-3.1  /

1    trigger:
2    - master
3
4    pool:
5      vmImage: 'ubuntu-latest'
6
7    variables:
8      buildConfiguration: 'Release'
9
10   steps:
     Settings
11   - task: UseDotNet@2
12   - script: dotnet build --configuration $(buildConfiguration)
13     displayName: 'dotnet build $(buildConfiguration)'
14
15
```

Figure 12-35. *Our azure-pipelines.yml*

This is of course the code we added before; you'll notice it doesn't perform any testing or packaging steps, yet.

Another VS Code Extension

As we are going to be doing a bit of editing of the *azure-pipelines.yml* file, there are two places you can do this:

1. Directly in the browser (we've already done this)

2. In VS Code

The advantage that editing in the browser *had* was that it gave you some Intellisense-like functionality where it suggested some code snippets, etc. However, Microsoft has now released a VS Code extension to provide similar functionality in VS Code, so we're going to install and use that (it means we do all our coding in the one place).

In VS Code, click the Extensions button, and search for "Azure Pipelines"; you should see the following.

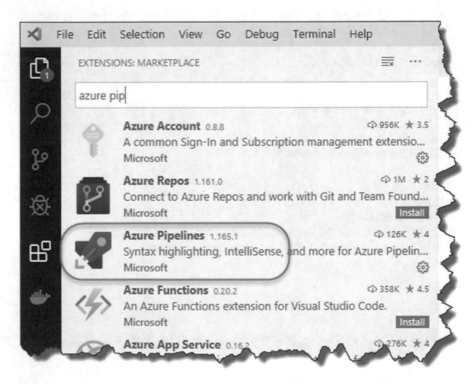

Figure 12-36. *Azure Pipelines Extension for VS Code*

Install it, and then open *azure-pipelines.yml* file that we just pulled down from GitHub.

Running Unit Tests

Returning to the steps in our pipeline view, see Figure 12-37.

Figure 12-37. *The pipeline we'll be building*

You'll see the suggested sequencing is Build ➤ **Test** ➤ Release, so let's add that task to our ***azure-pipelines.yml*** file now.

Move back to VS Code, open ***azure-pipelines.yml***, and *append* the following Task *after* the build Task:

```
- task: DotNetCoreCLI@2
  displayName: 'dotnet test'
  inputs:
    command: test
    projects: '**/*Tests/*.csproj'
    testRunTitle: 'xUNit Test Run'
```

So, overall, the file should like this, again with our new task step highlighted.

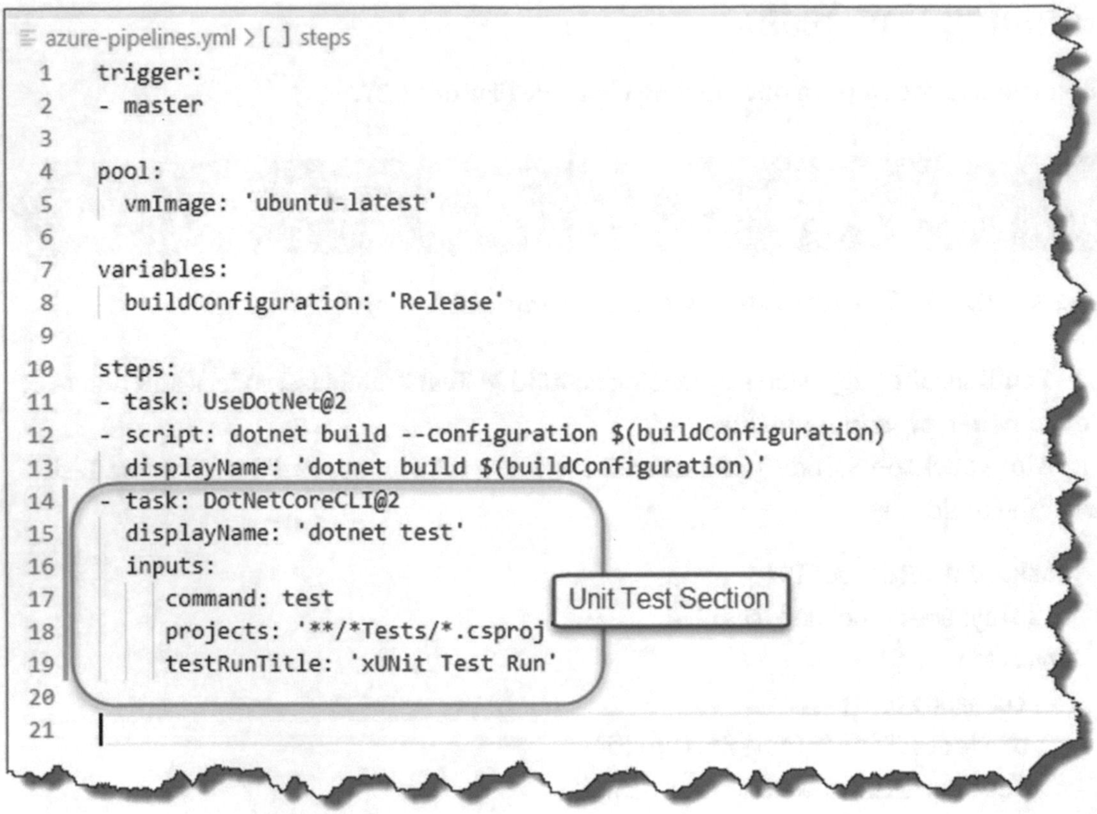

```
≡ azure-pipelines.yml > [ ] steps
1     trigger:
2     - master
3
4     pool:
5       vmImage: 'ubuntu-latest'
6
7     variables:
8       buildConfiguration: 'Release'
9
10    steps:
11    - task: UseDotNet@2
12    - script: dotnet build --configuration $(buildConfiguration)
13      displayName: 'dotnet build $(buildConfiguration)'
14    - task: DotNetCoreCLI@2
15      displayName: 'dotnet test'
16      inputs:
17        command: test                    Unit Test Section
18        projects: '**/*Tests/*.csproj
19        testRunTitle: 'xUNit Test Run'
20
21    |
```

Figure 12-38. *Testing step added*

The steps are quite self-explanatory, so save the file in VS Code, and perform the necessary Git command-line steps to commit your code and push to GitHub – this should trigger another build of our pipeline.

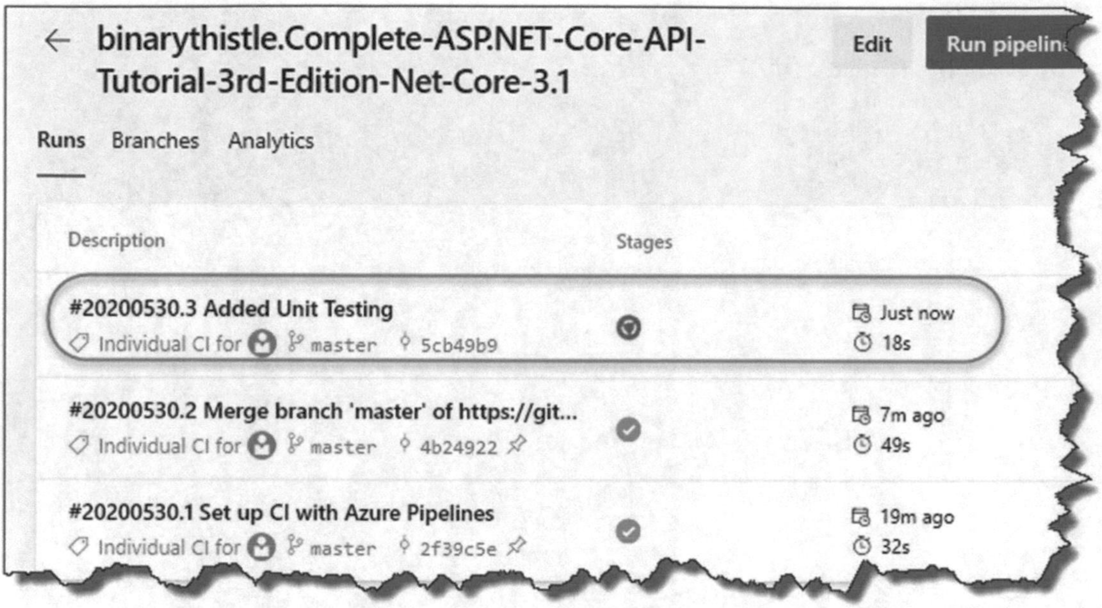

Figure 12-39. *Pipeline triggered again*

And this time the unit tests should execute too.

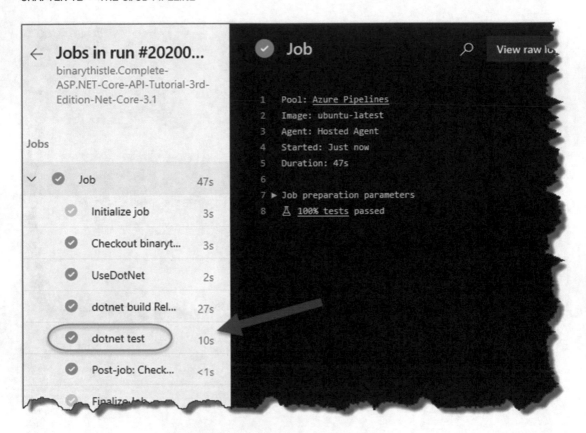

Figure 12-40. *Testing step has succeeded*

Click the dotnet test step as shown to drill down to see what's going on; you should see something like the following.

```
A total of 1 test files matched the specified pattern.
Results File: /home/vsts/work/_temp/_fv-az169_2020-05-30_06_50_35.trx

Test Run Successful.              Passing Tests
Total tests: 17  ⊘
      Passed: 17
 Total time: 5.2882 Seconds
Info: Azure Pipelines hosted agents have been updated to con       Link to Test Dashboard   3.1) SDK/Run
Some commonly encountered changes are:
If you're using `Publish` command with -o or --Output argument, you      l see that the output folder
Async Command Start: Publish test results
Publishing test results to test run '1000224'
Test results remaining: 17. Test run id: 1000224
Published Test Run : https://tfsprodeausu7.visualstudio.com/A0745f1de-d07c-480a-a09c-8a9b44640d70/Co
Async Command End: Publish test results
Finishing: dotnet test
```

Figure 12-41. *More detail on testing*

Clicking the link highlighted in Figure 12-41 takes you to the test result dashboard.

Figure 12-42. *Testing Dashboard*

Very nice! Indeed, this is the type of *Information Radiator* that you should make highly visible when working in a team environment, as it helps everyone understand the health of the build and, if necessary, take action to remediate any issues.

Breaking Our Unit Tests

Now just to labor the point of unit tests and CI/CD pipelines, let's deliberately break one of our tests.

Back in VS Code and back in our ***CommandAPI.Tests*** project, open our ***CommandsController*** tests, and edit one of your tests, and change the expected return type; I've chosen the test here and swapped NotFoundResult with OKResult:

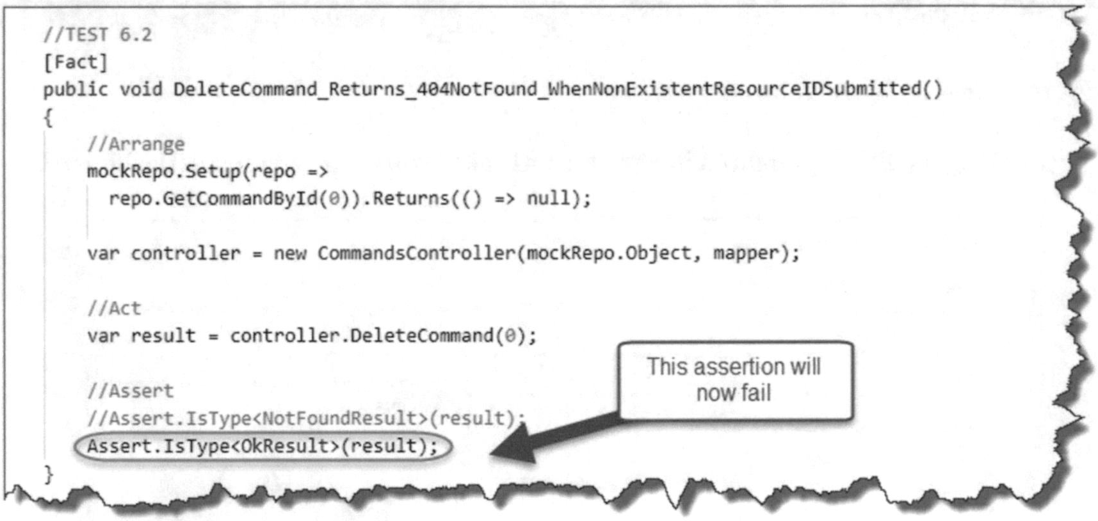

```
//TEST 6.2
[Fact]
public void DeleteCommand_Returns_404NotFound_WhenNonExistentResourceIDSubmitted()
{
    //Arrange
    mockRepo.Setup(repo =>
      repo.GetCommandById(0)).Returns(() => null);

    var controller = new CommandsController(mockRepo.Object, mapper);

    //Act
    var result = controller.DeleteCommand(0);

    //Assert
    //Assert.IsType<NotFoundResult>(result);
    Assert.IsType<OkResult>(result);
}
```

This assertion will now fail

Figure 12-43. *Break our unit test*

Save the file, and (ensuing you're "in" the ***CommandAPI.Tests*** project) run a build:

dotnet build

The *build of the project will succeed* as there is nothing here that would cause a compile-time error. However, if we try a

dotnet test

We'll of course get a failing result.

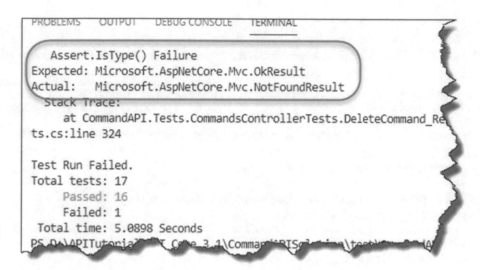

```
PROBLEMS    OUTPUT    DEBUG CONSOLE    TERMINAL

   Assert.IsType() Failure
Expected: Microsoft.AspNetCore.Mvc.OkResult
Actual:    Microsoft.AspNetCore.Mvc.NotFoundResult
   Stack Trace:
       at CommandAPI.Tests.CommandsControllerTests.DeleteCommand_Re
ts.cs:line 324

Test Run Failed.
Total tests: 17
     Passed: 16
     Failed: 1
 Total time: 5.0898 Seconds
PS D:\APITutoria
```

Figure 12-44. *Test has failed locally*

Now under normal circumstances, having just caused our unit test suite to fail locally, you **would not then commit** the changes and push them to GitHub! However, that is exactly what we are going to do just to prove the point that the tests will fail in the Azure DevOps build pipeline too.

Note   In this instance, we know that we have broken our tests locally, but there may be circumstances where the developer may be unaware that we have done so and commit their code; again this just highlights the value in a CI/CI build pipeline.

So, perform the three "Git" steps you should be familiar with now (ensure you do this at the solution level), and once you've pushed to GitHub, move back across to Azure DevOps, and observe what happens.

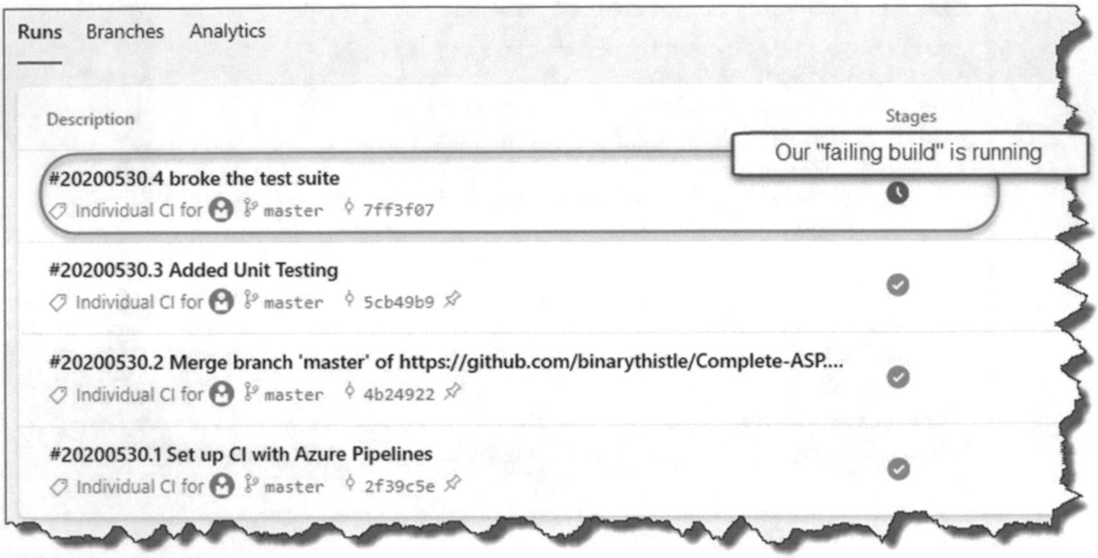

Figure 12-45. *In-progress Pipeline (it will error out)*

Then as expected, our test fails.

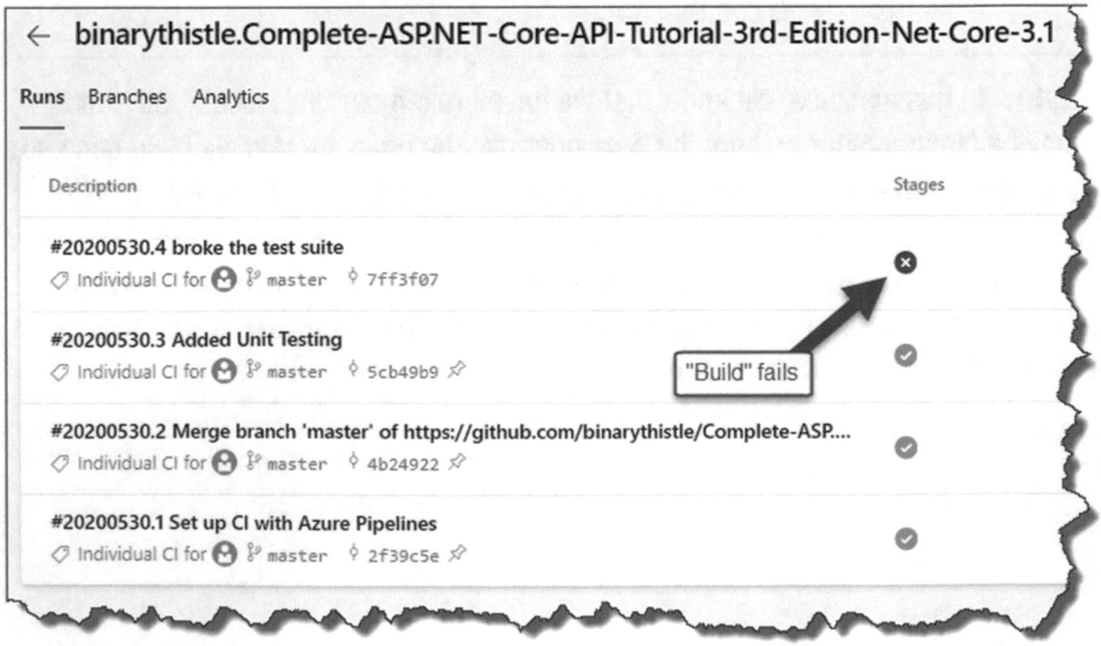

Figure 12-46. *Failed!*

Again, you can drill down to see what caused the error, and if, for example, you were displaying test results on a large LCD screen, it would be immediately apparent that there is something wrong with the build pipeline and that remedial action needs to be taken. Looking at the individual steps, see Figure 12-47.

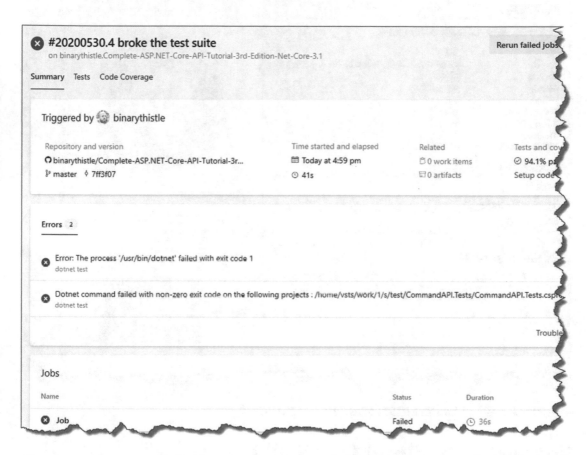

Figure 12-47.   *Detail of failures*

And then drilling further in to the dotnet test step and going to the test results dashboard (see Figure 12-48).

Figure 12-48. *Dashboard represents the failure*

Testing – The Great Catch All?

Now, this shows us the power of unit testing in that it will cause the build pipeline to fail and buggy software won't be released or even worse deployed to production! It also means we can take steps to remediate the failure.

So conversely, does this mean that if all tests pass, you won't have failed code in production? No, it doesn't for the simple reason that your tests are only as good as, well, your tests. The point that I'm making (maybe rather depressingly) is that even if all your tests pass, the confidence you have in your code will only be as good as your test coverage – ours is not bad at this stage though – so we can be quite confident in moving to the next step.

Before we do that though, revert the change we just made to *ensure that all our unit tests are passing* and that our pipeline returns to a green state.

⚠ **Warning!**   Do not progress to the next section without ensuring that all your tests are passing!

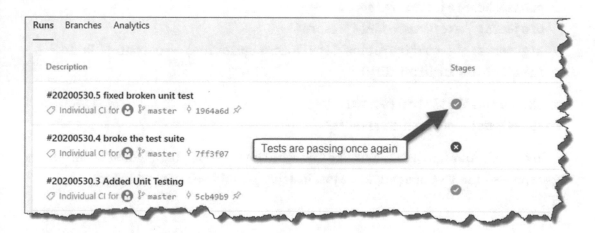

Figure 12-49. *Make sure you fix your pipeline before continuing*

Release/Packaging

Referring to our pipeline again, we're now at the Release stage; this is where we need to package our build ready to be deployed.

Figure 12-50. *Revisit our pipeline*

So once again, move back into VS Code, and open ***azure-pipelines.yml*** file, and append the following steps:

```
- task: DotNetCoreCLI@2
  displayName: 'dotnet publish'
  inputs:
    command: publish
    publishWebProjects: false
    projects: 'src/CommandAPI/*.csproj'
    arguments: '--configuration $(buildConfiguration) --output $(Build.
    ArtifactStagingDirectory)'

- task: PublishBuildArtifacts@1
  displayName: 'publish artifacts'
```

So overall, your file should look like this, with the new code highlighted (again watch those spaces – the VS Code plugin we just installed should help you with this).

```
≡ azure-pipelines.yml > [ ] steps > 🖭 task
 1    trigger:
 2    - master
 3
 4    pool:
 5      vmImage: 'ubuntu-latest'
 6
 7    variables:
 8      buildConfiguration: 'Release'
 9
10    steps:
11    - task: UseDotNet@2
12    - script: dotnet build --configuration $(buildConfiguration)
13      displayName: 'dotnet build $(buildConfiguration)'
14    - task: DotNetCoreCLI@2
15      displayName: 'dotnet test'
16      inputs:
17        command: test
18        projects: '**/*Tests/*.csproj'
19        testRunTitle: 'xUNit Test Run'
20
21    - task: DotNetCoreCLI@2
22      displayName: 'dotnet publish'
23      inputs:
24        command: publish
25        publishWebProjects: false
26        projects: 'src/CommandAPI/*.csproj'
27        arguments: '--configuration $(buildConfiguration) --output $(Build.ArtifactStagingDirectory)'
28
29    - task: PublishBuildArtifacts@1
30      displayName: 'publish artifacts'
31
32
```

Figure 12-51. *Package and publish steps*

The steps are explained in more detail in the Microsoft Documents,[2] but in short

- A dotnet publish command is issued for our **CommandAPI** project only.[3]

- The output of that is zipped.

- The zipped artifact is published.

---

[2]https://docs.microsoft.com/en-us/azure/devops/pipelines/ecosystems/
dotnet-core?view=azure-devops&tabs=yaml
[3]We don't want to publish our tests anywhere!

Les' Personal Anecdote   Ensure that you put in the following line:

`publishWebProjects: false`

When researching this, I spent about 2-3 hours trying to understand why the packaging step was not working – it was because of this! The default is `true`, so if you don't include that, the step fails. ARGHHHH!

Save the file, and again: add, commit, and push your code. The pipeline should succeed, and if you drill into the successful build, you'll see our two additional `task` steps.

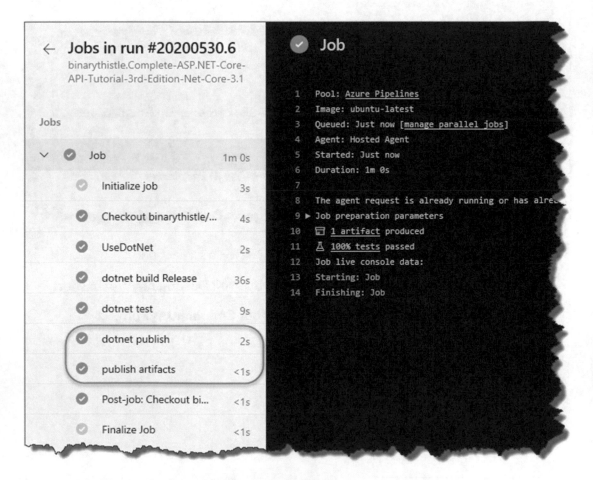

Figure 12-52.   *Steps shown in the running Job*

≝ Celebration Checkpoint   Excellent work! You have completed the: build, test, and release steps of our pipeline using Azure DevOps.

Wrap It Up

A lot of ground covered here, where we

- Setup a CI/CD pipeline on Azure DevOps

- Connected Azure DevOps to GitHub (and ensured CI triggers were enable)

- **Added**: Build, Test, and Packaging steps to our *azure-pipeline.yml* file

We are now almost ready to deploy to Azure!

## CHAPTER 13

Deploying to Azure

Chapter Summary

In this chapter we deploy our API onto Azure for use in the real world. On the way, we create the Azure resources we need and revisit the discussion on runtime environments and configuration.

When Done, You Will

- Know a bit more about Azure.

- Have created the Azure resources we need to deploy our API.

- Update our CI/CD pipeline to deploy our release to Azure.

- Provide the necessary configuration to get the API working in a Production Environment.

We have a lot to cover – so let's get going!

Creating Azure Resources

Azure is a huge subject area and could fill many books, many times over, so I'll be focusing only on the aspects we need to get our API and database up and running in a "production-like" environment – which should be more than enough.

© Les Jackson 2020
L. Jackson, *The Complete ASP.NET Core 3 API Tutorial*, https://doi.org/10.1007/978-1-4842-6255-9_13

In simple terms, everything in Azure is a "resource," for example, a database server, virtual machine, web app, etc. So, we need to create a few resources to house our app. There are different ways to create resources in Azure:

1. Create resources manually via the Azure Portal.

2. Create resources automatically via Azure Resource Manager Templates.

3. Create resources automatically using third-party tools, for example, Terraform.

In this chapter, we'll be manually creating the resources we need as

-   It's simpler (in our case anyway, see next point).

-   We only have a small number of resources.

-   I think it's the right approach to learning (our focus is still our API).

Create Our API App

The first resource we are going to create is an API App; this unsurprisingly is where our API code will run. To do so, log-in to Azure (or if you don't have an account, you'll need to create one), and click "Create a resource":

Figure 13-1. *Create an Azure Resource*

⚠   Again, I'll mention the point that the following screenshots were correct at the time of writing, but given the fast pace of change in Azure, they may be subject to change.

Fundamentally though, resource creation in Azure is not that difficult, so small UI changes should not stump someone as smart as yourself!

In the "search box" that appears in the new resource page, start to type "API App"; you will be presented with the API App resource type.

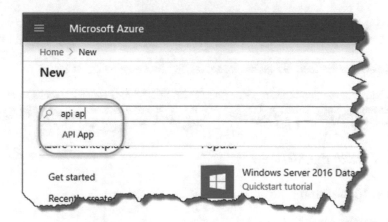

Figure 13-2. *Search for API App*

Select "API App," then click "Create."

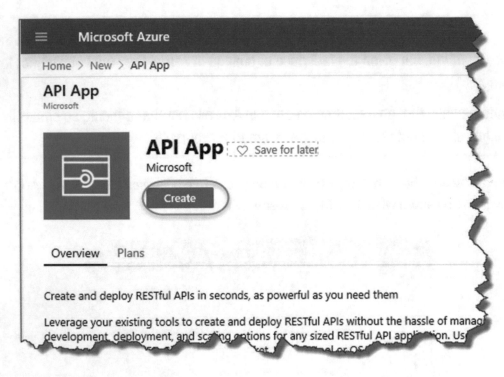

Figure 13-3. *Create the API App*

On the Next "page," enter

1. A name for your API App.[1]

2. Select your subscription (I just have a "pay as you go").

3. A name for your new "Resource Group" – these are just groupings of "resources"; if you don't have an existing resource group, you'll need to create one.

---

[1]This needs to be unique in Azure, so your name will be different to mine.

Figure 13-4. *Configure your API App – make sure you configure a free plan!*

WAIT! Before you click Create, click the App Service plan/location.

Les' Personal Anecdote   The *API App* resource describes what you are getting; the *App Service Plan and Location* tells you how that API App will be delivered to you.

For example, do you want your API App

- Hosted in the United States, Western Europe, Asia, etc.

- On shared or dedicated hardware

- Running on certain processor speed, etc.

By default, if you've not used Azure before, you'll be placed on a Standard plan **which can incur costs!** (This is a personal anecdote because I did that and was shocked when my test API started costing me money!)

So be careful of the Service Plan you set up; I detail the free plan next.

After clicking the Service Plan, click "Create new."

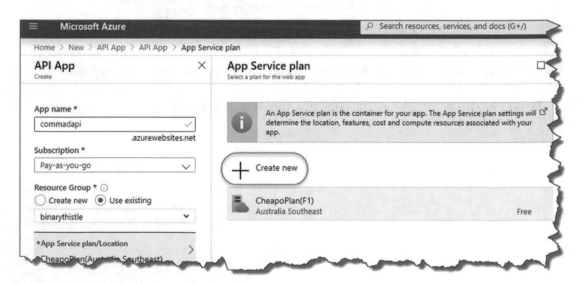

Figure 13-5. *Creating an App Service Plan*

On the "New App Service Plan" widget, enter an App Service Plan name, and pick your location, then click the Pricing Tier.

New App Service Plan   □ ✕
Create a plan for the web app

App Service plan *

| FreePlan | ✓ |

Location *

| Australia East | ∨ |

*Pricing tier   >
S1 Standard

Click here next...

Figure 13-6. *The Pricing Tier*

After, click the *Pricing Tier*.

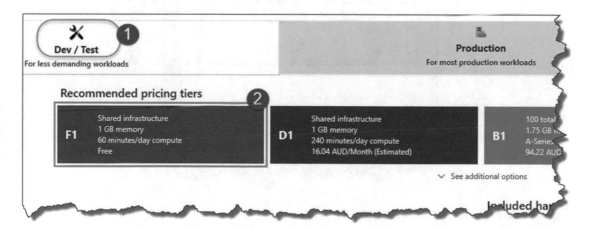

Figure 13-7. *Select the Free option*

355

1. Select the Dev/Test tab.

2. Select the "F1" Option (Shared infrastructure/60 minutes compute).

3. Click Apply.

We have selected the cheapest tier with "Free Compute Minutes," although please be aware that I cannot be held responsible for any charges on your Azure Account! (After I create and test a resource if I don't need it – I "stop it" or delete it).

Then click OK.

Figure 13-8. *You're ready to go*

Then click "Create" (ensure your new App Service Plan is selected).

Figure 13-9. *Free plan has been applied to the API APP*

After clicking Create, Azure will go off and create the resource ready for use.

Figure 13-10. *Deployment will take a few minutes...*

You will get notified when the resource is successfully created; if not, click the little "Alarm Bell" icon near the top right-hand side of the Azure portal.

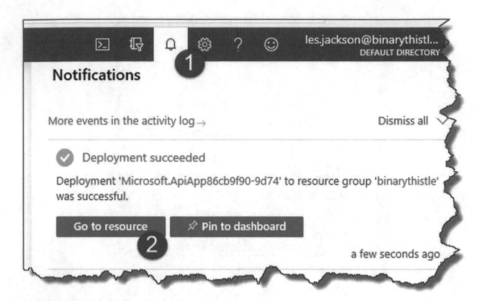

Figure 13-11. *Notification of Resource Creation*

Here you can see the resource was successfully created; now click "Go to resource."

Figure 13-12. *API App Overview including URI*

This just gives us an overview of the resource we created and gives us the ability to stop or even delete it. You can even click the location URL, and it will take you to where the API App resides.

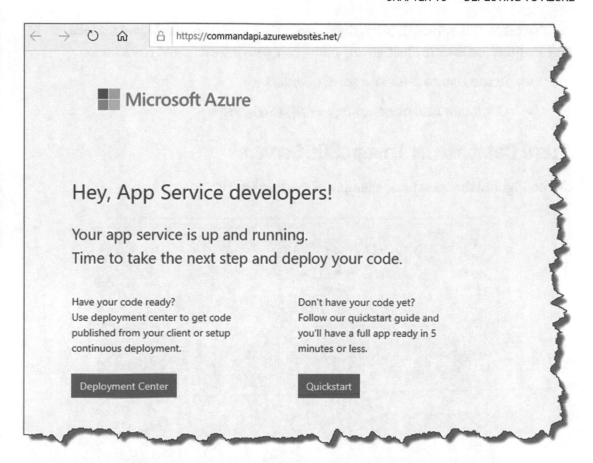

Figure 13-13. *Default public landing page*

As we have not deployed anything, you'll get a similar landing page as shown in Figure 13-13 (of course for reasons already mentioned, it may look a bit different, but that is of no consequence to us at this point).

Celebration Checkpoint   You've just created your first Azure resource, one of the primary components of our production solution architecture!

Create Our PostgreSQL Server

Now, there are a number of different ways that you can create a PostgreSQL database on Azure, but I'm going to take a slightly unorthodox route and spin up a PostgreSQL Server in a Container Instance in Azure (think Docker containers).

I've taken this approach primarily because the setup is so simple and the cost implications are low. To illustrate my point, compare the estimated costs for

- Azure Database for PostgreSQL Servers
- Container Instance running a PostgreSQL Image

Azure Database for PostgreSQL Servers

I've configured the most basic example of this that I could.

Figure 13-14.   *Cost estimate for Postgres Server*

Container Instance Pricing

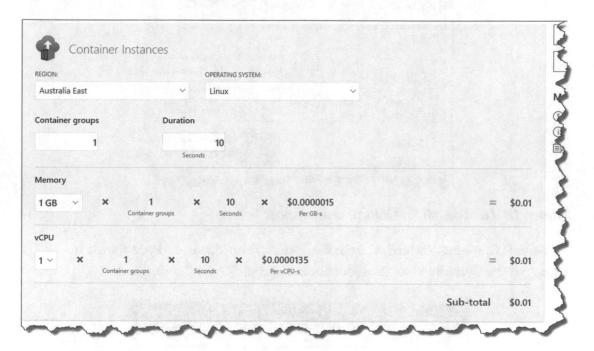

Figure 13-15. *Container instance pricing*

Now, I don't need to tell you that "you get what you pay for" in this life, so clearly the *Azure Database for PostgreSQL* option is a purpose-built resource that's designed to work as a database, whereas the container option I'm taking is in no way optimized for Production performance!

⚠ **Warning!**   If you restart the PostgreSQL container instance that we create in the next section, it essentially resets, and **you will lose your configuration and data** relating to it – just something to bear in mind.

From a learning (and cost!) perspective, I still think this option is acceptable. If, however, you are moving to a "real" Production environment, then you'll really need to look at something a little more fit for purpose.

So back in Azure, once again click "Create a Resource," and this time search for "Container Instances."

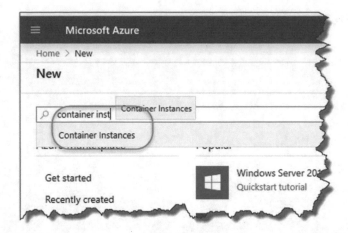

Figure 13-16. *Search for Container Instances*

Select "Container Instances" from the options drop-down, and you should be displayed the Container Instances detail screen; click "Create" to continue.

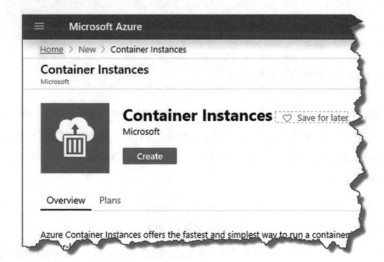

Figure 13-17. *Overview of Container Instances*

You'll get taken to the Basics tab on the creating wizard; fill out the details as relevant to you; however, the image name must be ***postgres***.

Create container instance

Basics   Networking   Advanced   Tags   Review + create

Azure Container Instances (ACI) allows you to quickly and easily run containers on Azure without managing servers or having to learn new tools. ACI offers per-second billing to minimize the cost of running containers on the cloud.
Learn more about Azure Container Instances

Project details

Select the subscription to manage deployed resources and costs. Use resource groups like folders to organize and manage all your resources.

Subscription * ⓘ   Pay-as-you-go ①

Resource group * ⓘ   binarythistle ②
                         Create new

Container details

Container name * ⓘ   cmdapidb ③

Region * ⓘ   (Asia Pacific) Australia East ④

Image source * ⓘ   ○ Quickstart images
                         ○ Azure Container Registry ⑤
                         ◉ Docker Hub or other registry

Image type * ⓘ   ◉ Public ○ Private ⑥

                                                        ⑦
Image * ⓘ   postgres
                         ❶ If not specified, Docker Hub will be used for the container registry and the
                            latest version of the image will be pulled.

OS type *   ◉ Linux ○ Windows ⑧
                         ❶ This selection must match the OS of the image chosen above.

Size * ⓘ   1 vcpu, 1.5 GiB memory, 0 gpus ⑨
                         Change size

Next : Networking >

Figure 13-18. *Configure your Container Instance*

1. Your subscription.

2. Resource group (I'd make this the same as the one you placed the API app into).

3. Container name can be anything, but I'd name it something that identified it as a PostgreSQL server.

4. Region (I'd make this the same as the one you placed the API app into).

5. **Image Source**: Select Docker Hub (this is where we'll get our postgres image).

6. **Image Type**: Select Public (the postgres image we use in the next step is publicly available on Docker Hub).

7. **Image Name**: As mentioned earlier, this needs to be the exact name of the image on Docker Hub, so in this case ***postgres***.

8. **OS Type**: Select Linux.

9. **Size**: Leave these as the defaults.

When you're happy click "Next: Networking >."

Figure 13-19. *Networking*

And supply the following details in the Networking Tab.

Figure 13-20. *Networking configuration*

1. Select "Public" for a public IP Address (note this can change if the container restarts).

2. Add a DNS name label as the IP Address can change if the container restarts.

3. Add the standard 5432 TCP port for PostgreSQL.

When you're happy, click "Next: Advanced >."

Figure 13-21. *Onto Advanced Settings*

And enter the following details on the Advanced tab.

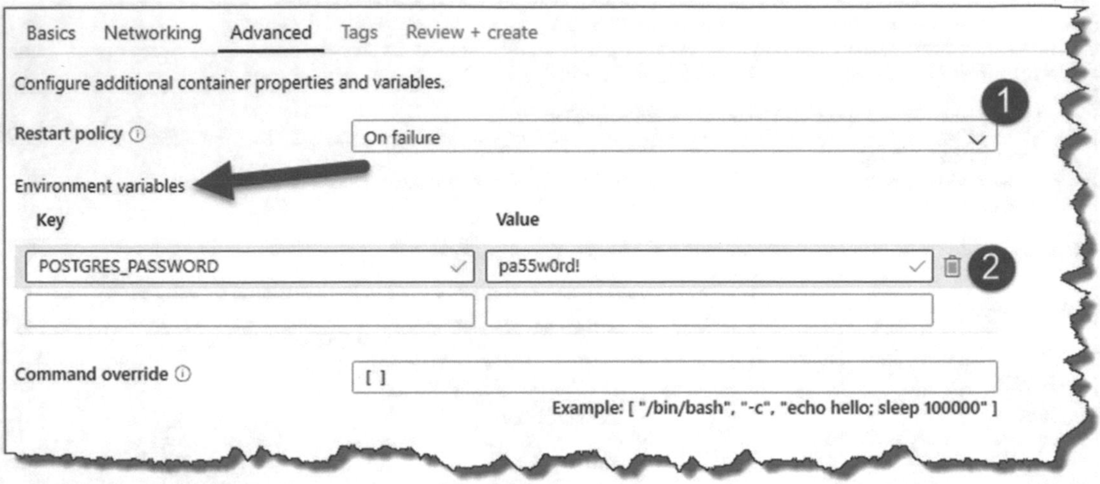

Figure 13-22. *Setup Environment variables*

1. Set the Restart Policy to "On Failure."

2. Create an "environment variable" for the Postgres password for the default database; the Key you should use for this is

POSTGRES_PASSWORD

The choice of password (the value) is up to you. In my case, I used

pa55w0rd!

⚠ **Warning!**   As you can see our PostgreSQL password is in plain text; again this is not a production-suitable solution. We are using it for (cheap!) testing purposes only.

If you pop back to Chapter 7 where we set up an instance of PostgreSQL locally using Docker Desktop, there is a bit more of a discussion on these settings – so we don't need to go over old ground here. Just a point of note, however, the environment variable for the PostgreSQL DB password (POSTGRES_PASSWORD) is exactly the same as the one we used when setting up our local Docker instance.

Click "Review and Create" (we can skip the "Tags" tab).

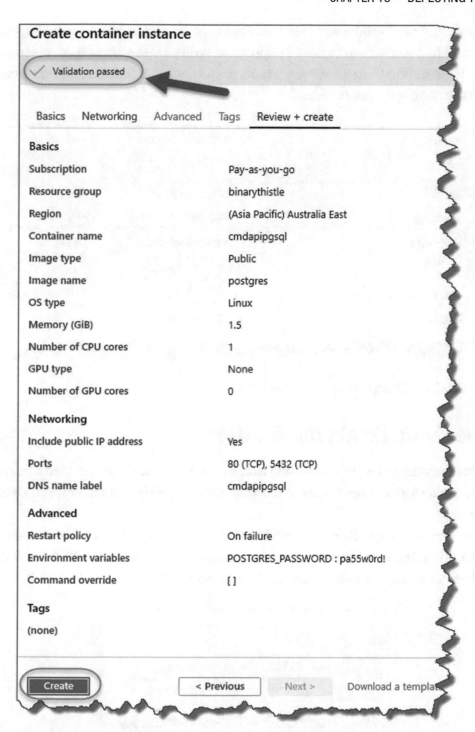

Figure 13-23. *Validation Passed*

You should see "Validation Passed" at the top of the screen; when you're happy, click Create, and in a similar way to the API App, Azure will go off and create your resource.

You'll get notified when both your resources are set up: by clicking All resources, you can see everything we have created.

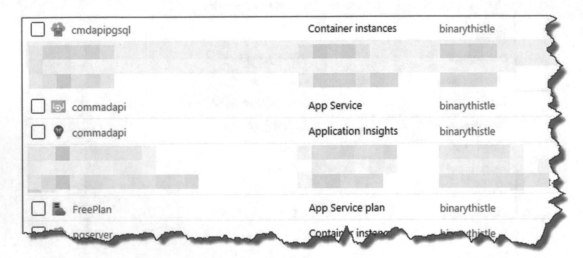

Figure 13-24. *Resources up and running*

Connect and Create Our DB User

As before we want to create a dedicated user to connect in and use our database, the exercise is also a great opportunity to test that our PostgreSQL container instance is up and running.

First, we need to get the Fully Qualified Domain Name (FDQN) of the container instance, so in Azure find your container instance resource, and select it; this will display a number of details, most important of which is our FDQN.

Figure 13-25. *Location of the API*

Make a note of the FDQN, and move over to DBeaver, and create a new connection to a PostgreSQL instance – this is exactly the same as when we connected into our local instance, the only differences being the host and possibly the password for the postgres user (depending on what you set in the container instance environment variables).

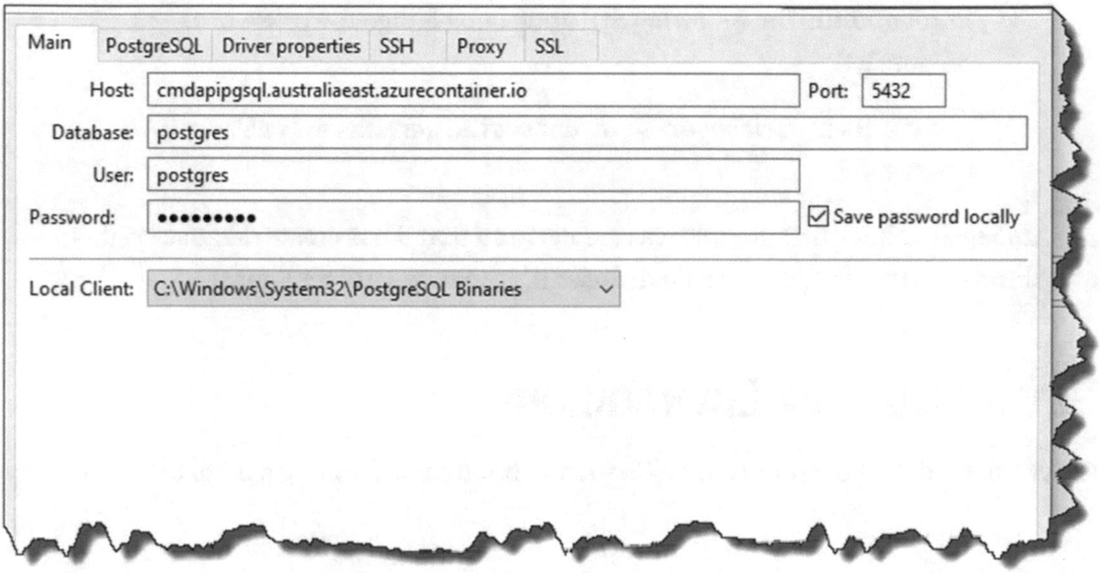

Figure 13-26. *Connect to the Azure instance*

Remember to tick "Show all databases" on the PostgreSQL tab.

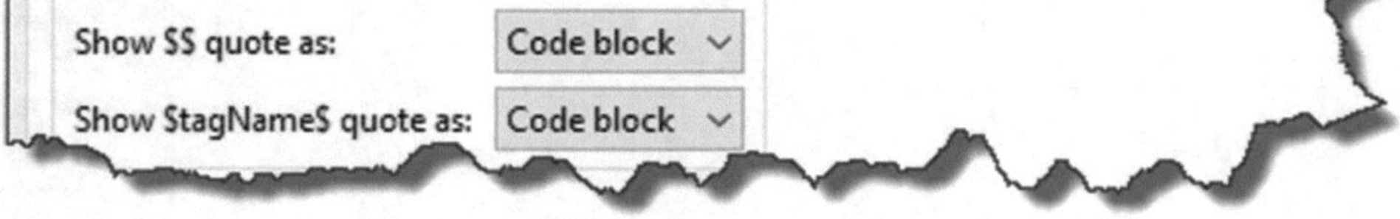

Figure 13-27. *Ensure Show all Databases is ticked*

You can test the connection or press Finish to setup our connection to our Azure-based instance.

Again, we'll just repeat the user creation steps in Chapter 7:

- Open a New SQL Editor Window.

- Enter and run the following SQL (you can change the password obviously!):

```
create user cmddbuser with encrypted password 'pa55w0rd!'
createdb;
```

And again, check that the role was created and that it has create database rights. Along with the FDQN, set aside the user ID and password for later.

Revisit Our Dev Environment

We've covered a lot of ground since Chapter 8, but it's worth doing a bit of a review.

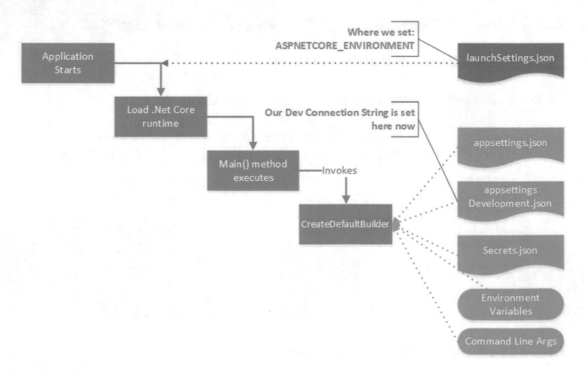

Figure 13-28. *Revisit configuration*

- We set our environment in *launchSettings.json* (in the ASPNETCORE_ENVIRONEMENT variable).

- Our Connection Strings can sit in *appsettings.json* or the environment specific variants of that file, for example, *appsettings.Development.json*. This is where our Development connection string sits.

- "Secret" information, such as Database log-in credentials, can be broken out into **Secrets.json** via The Secret Manager tool. Meaning, we don't check in sensitive data to our code repository.

Also, remember that we chose to build our full connection string in our `Startup` class using

- Non-sensitive Connection String stored in *appSettings. Development.json*).

- Our User ID, stored in a User Secret called `UserID`.

- Our Password, stored in a User Secret called `Password`.

Setting Up Config in Azure

When you deploy a .NET Core app as an Azure API App, it sits on top of a configuration layer that we access via the .NET Core Configuration API in *exactly the same way* as we have done to date with our local Development environment. In setting up our production environment, we will

- Require some simple config settings in our API App.

- Require *no code changes in our app*; there would be something very wrong if we needed to change our code to move into production – that should all be handled by configuration.

Configure Our Connection String

OK, so go back to your list of Azure resources, and select your *API App Service*. On the resulting screen, select *Configuration* in the *Settings* section as shown here.

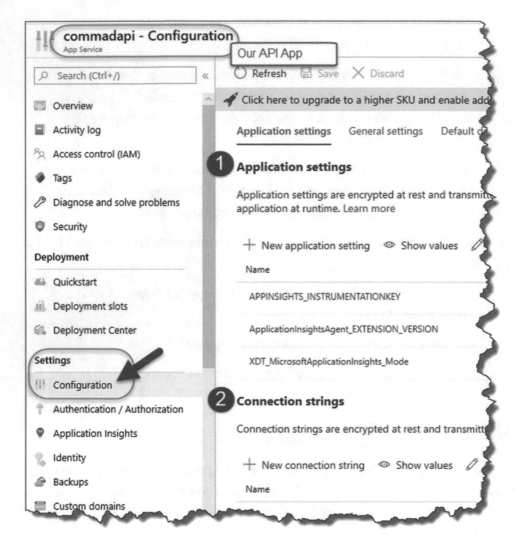

Figure 13-29. *Application settings and connection strings in the API app*

You'll see there are two sections here for use to play with:

1. Application Settings

2. Connection Strings

We are going to add our *Production Connection* string to the (surprise, surprise)
Connection Strings settings of our API App. Looking at the *Development* connection
string I have in ***appsettings.Development.json***

```
Host=localhost;Port=5432;Database=CmdAPI;Pooling=true;
```

Not that much needs to change, except the Host attribute. We simply substitute that for the PostgreSQL Container Instance FDQN that you should have set aside from the section earlier. So, I now have the following (yours will look different depending on your container instance name and location of course):

```
Host= pgserver.australiaeast.azurecontainer.io;
Port=5432;Database=CmdAPI;Pooling=true;
```

To add this string to our API App Connection String settings, click + *New connection string*. In the resulting form, enter

1. Connection String Name (**this should be the *same name* as our development connection string – I cannot stress that enough!**).

2. The connection string we generated earlier (note we'll be configuring our User ID and Password separately below).

3. Set the type to *Custom*.

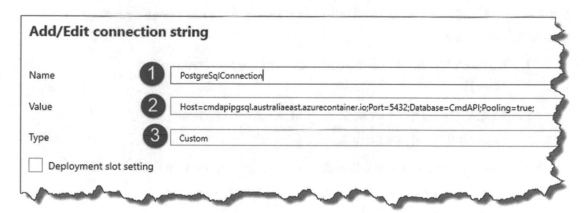

Figure 13-30. Add the connection string; be careful to name it correctly

---

⚠ **Warning!**   You do have the option of "PostgreSQL" for the connection string type – however, I've had significant issues trying to use this – so use it at your peril!

Click OK, and you'll see the connection string has been added to our collection.

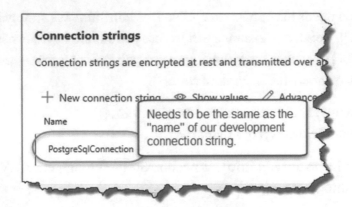

Figure 13-31. *Again, ensure it's named correctly*

Configure Our DB User Credentials

We're going to add our Production User ID and Password configuration items in a very similar way, except this time, we'll add these items to the *Application Settings* section of our API App Configuration. To add our User ID, click + *New application setting.* In the resulting form, enter

1. **Name**: This should be the same as our *User Secret* name for User ID.

2. **Value**: This is the user account you set up on the PostgreSQL Container Instance earlier.

For example, if you've been following the tutorial step by step these should be

- **Name**: UserID

- **Value**: cmddbuser

So, add them as an Application Setting as follows.

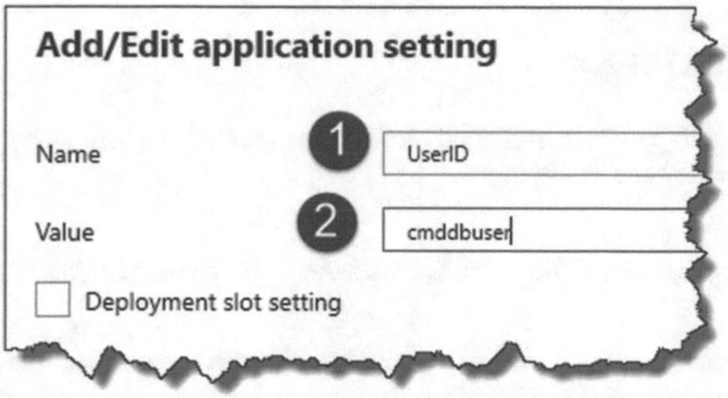

Figure 13-32. *Create User ID Application Setting*

Again, just be careful that the User ID attribute *name* is exactly the same as the local user secret *name* and what your app is expecting to ingest when it creates the connection string as shown next.

```
public void ConfigureServices(IServiceCollection services)
{
    var builder = new NpgsqlConnectionStringBuilder();
    builder.ConnectionString = Configuration.GetConnectionString("PostgreSqlConnection");
    builder.Username = Configuration["UserID"];
    builder.Password = Configuration["Password"];
    services.AddDbContext<CommandContext>(opt => opt.UseNpgsql(builder.ConnectionString));

    services.AddControllers();
```

Figure 13-33. *Make sure you name it correctly*

Click OK, and you'll see the new UserID application setting.

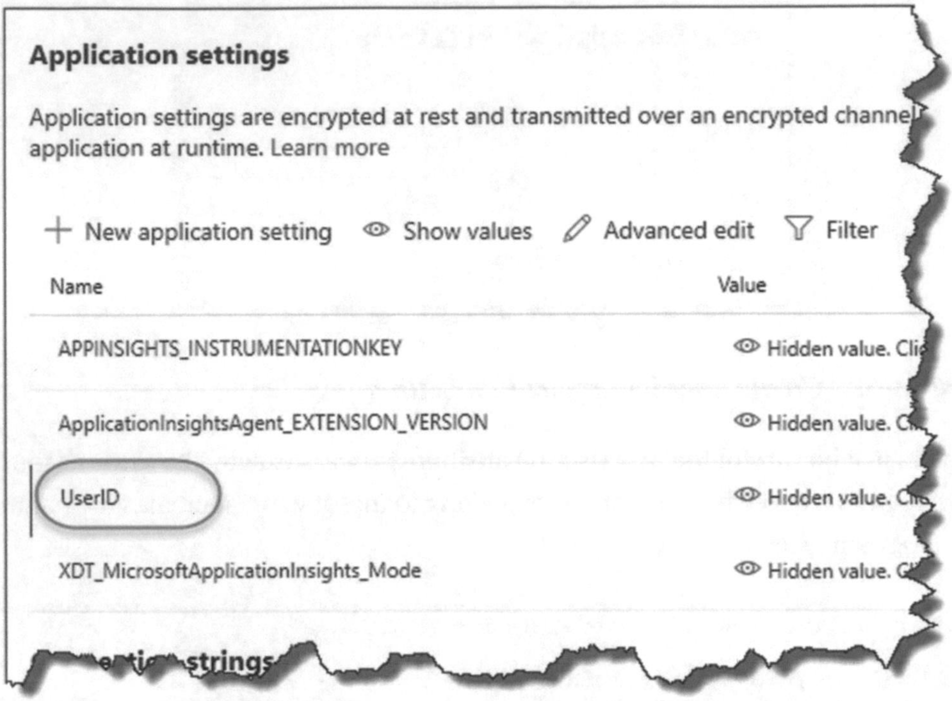

Figure 13-34.   *UserID added to Application Settings*

☞ **Learning Opportunity**   Add a second *Application setting* for our ***Password***. This should follow the same process as UserID.

⚠ **Warning!**   Storing passwords in Application Settings possibly isn't the best location for them, one reason being that you can see what they are in plain text. Even though Azure is "secured," that is, only authorized users will have access to it – plain text passwords are just generally not a great idea.

In a real production environment, you'd want to opt for something like Azure Key Vault or a third-party product such a Vault.[2] I feel that detailing that here would just be taking us too far out the way of what we want to achieve today.

---

[2]www.vaultproject.io/

Configure Our Environment

Finally, we want to set our runtime environment to "Production"; we do this simply by adding another Application setting as follows:

- **Name**: ASPNETCORE_ENVIRONMENT

- **Value**: Production

See Figure 13-35.

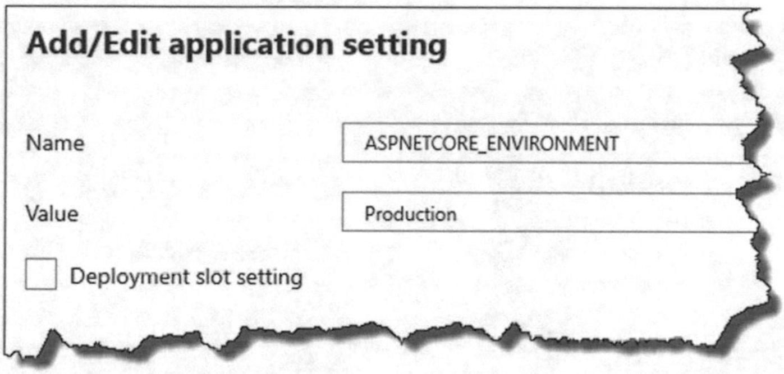

Figure 13-35. *Specifying our environment*

Click OK and you should now have added four production configuration settings:

1. **Application settings**: ASPNETCORE_ENVIRONMENT

2. **Application settings**: Password

3. **Application settings**: UserID

4. **Connection string**: PostgreSQLConnection

I've shown my setup as it appears in Azure in Figure 13-36.

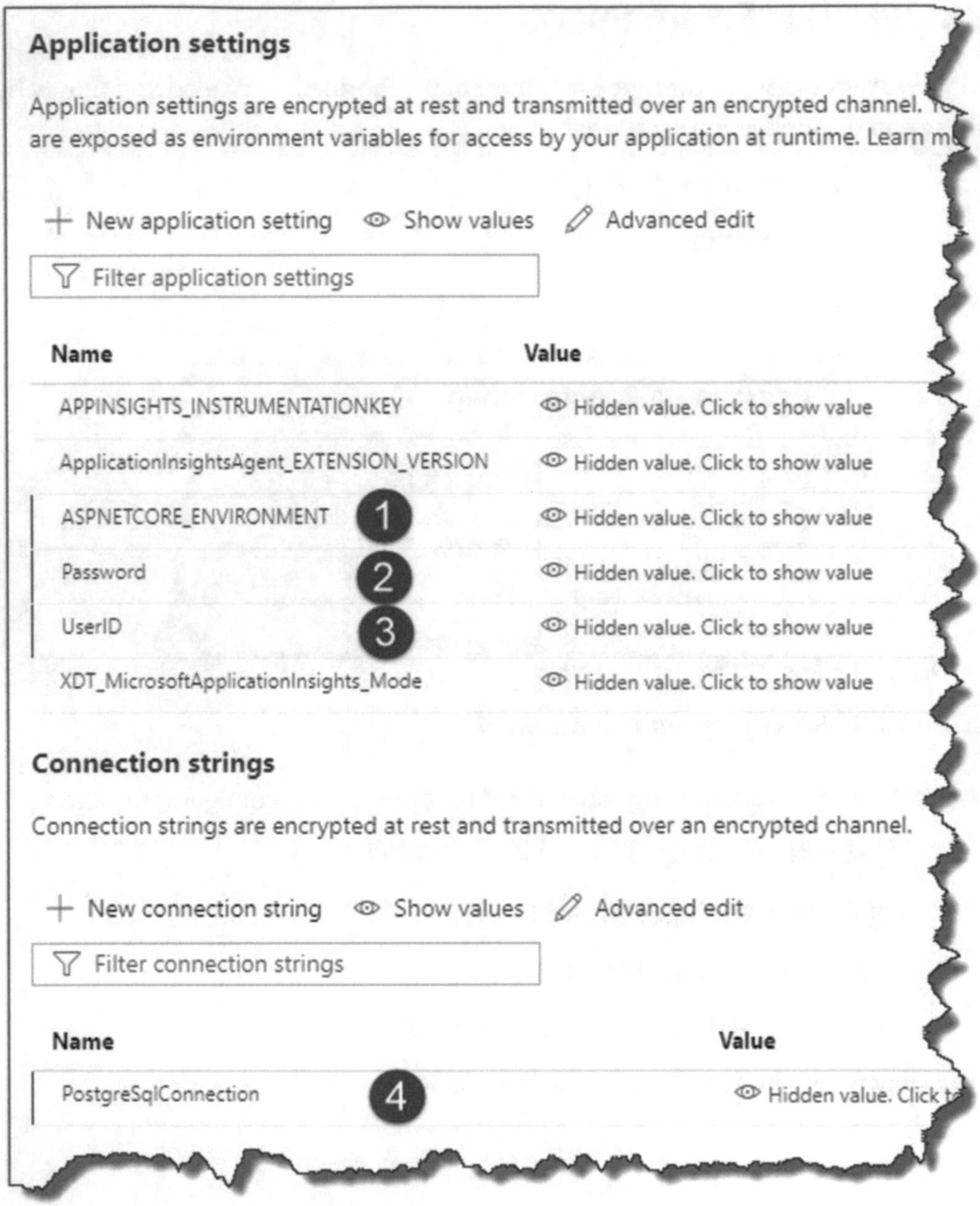

Application settings
Application settings are encrypted at rest and transmitted over an encrypted channel.
are exposed as environment variables for access by your application at runtime. Learn m
New application setting
Show values
Advanced edit
Filter application settings
Name
Value
APPINSIGHTS_INSTRUMENTATIONKEY
ApplicationInsightsAgent_EXTENSION_VERSION
ASPNETCORE_ENVIRONMENT
Password
UserID
XDT_MicrosoftApplicationInsights_Mode
Hidden value. Click to show value
1
2
3
Connection strings
Connection strings are encrypted at rest and transmitted over an encrypted channel.
New connection string
Show values
Advanced edit
Filter connection strings
Name
Value
PostgreSqlConnection
4

Figure 13-36. *Newly created Application Settings*

Again, I know I keep repeating myself, but you need to make sure the *Names* of these configuration items are the same as their Development counterparts, as that is what our application is expecting – please double-check these! The values of these items I have to leave up to you to get correct!

> ⚠ **Warning!**   Every time you make a configuration change, you need to save it - see Figure 13-37.

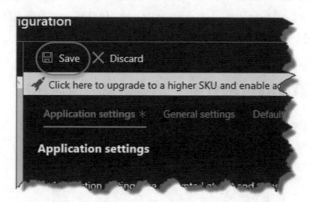

Figure 13-37. *Make sure you save!*

Make sure you click Save to apply your changes (when starting out with this stuff, I didn't and spent a lot time trying to understand what was wrong!).

🎂 **Celebration Checkpoint**   You have just set up all your Azure Resources and have configured them ready for our deployment!

Completing Our Pipeline

At last! We create the final piece of the puzzle in our CI/CD pipeline: Deploy.

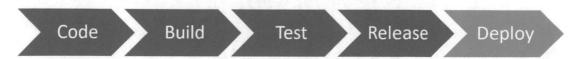

Figure 13-38. *The pipeline*

A quick recap on our CI/CD Pipeline so far

- We created what Azure DevOps calls a *Build Pipeline* that does the following:

    - Builds our projects

- Runs our unit tests

- Packages our release

What we now need to do in Azure DevOps is create a *Release Pipeline* that takes our package and releases and deploys it to Azure. So basically, our full CI/CD Pipeline = Azure DevOps **Build** Pipeline + Azure DevOps **Release** Pipeline.

Creating Our Azure DevOps Release Pipeline

Back in Azure DevOps, click Pipelines ➤ Releases.

Figure 13-39. *Release Pipeline*

The click New Pipeline.

Figure 13-40. *Create a new Release Pipeline*

On the next screen, select and *Apply* the *Azure App Service deployment* template.

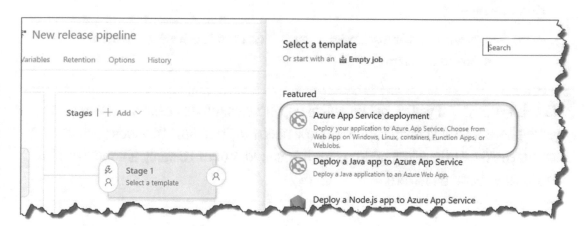

Figure 13-41. *Select Azure App Service deployment*

In the "Stage" widget

1. Change the stage name to "Deploy API to Prod Azure" (or whatever you like so long as it's meaningful).

2. Click the Job/Task link in the designer.

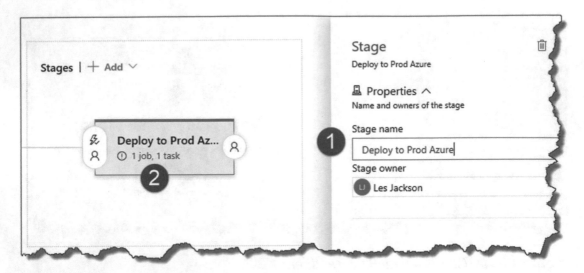

Figure 13-42. *Name the stage and fix up the task errors*

Here, we need to

1. Select our Azure subscription (you will need to **"authorize"** Azure DevOps to use Azure).

⚠ **Warning!**   If you've got an active pop-up blocker, this can cause you some issues here as the authentication window needs to "pop up." Depending on your setup, you'll need to allow pop-ups for this site in order to cleanly authenticate Azure DevOps to use Azure.

---

2. App Type (remember this is an API App)

3. App Service Name (all of your API Apps will be retrieved from Azure – select the one you created earlier)

Figure 13-43. *Fix up the errors and remember to save!*

Don't forget to *Save*. When you do, you'll be presented with the following.

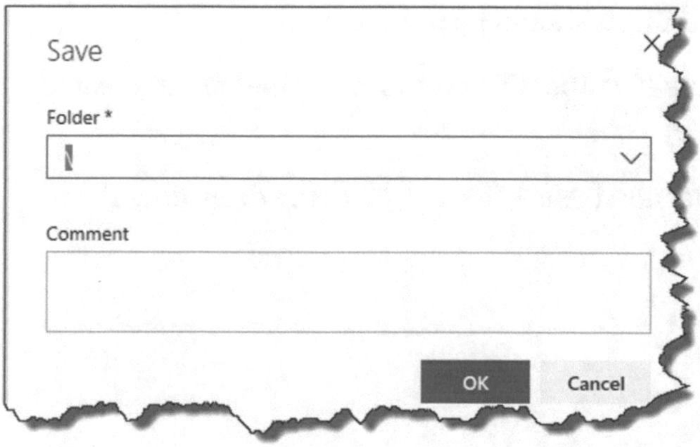

Figure 13-44. *Add a comment if you need to*

Just click OK.

Click back on the "Pipeline" tab, then on Add (to add an artifact).

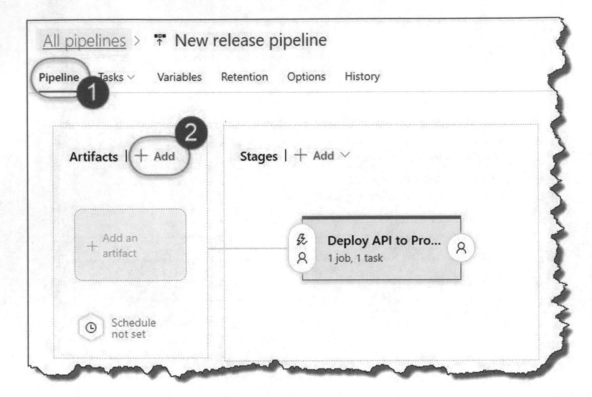

Figure 13-45. *Adding an artifact for deployment*

Here, you will need to provide

1. The Project (this should be preselected)

2. The Source Pipeline (this is our *Build* pipeline we created
   previously)

3. Default version (select "Latest" from the drop-down)

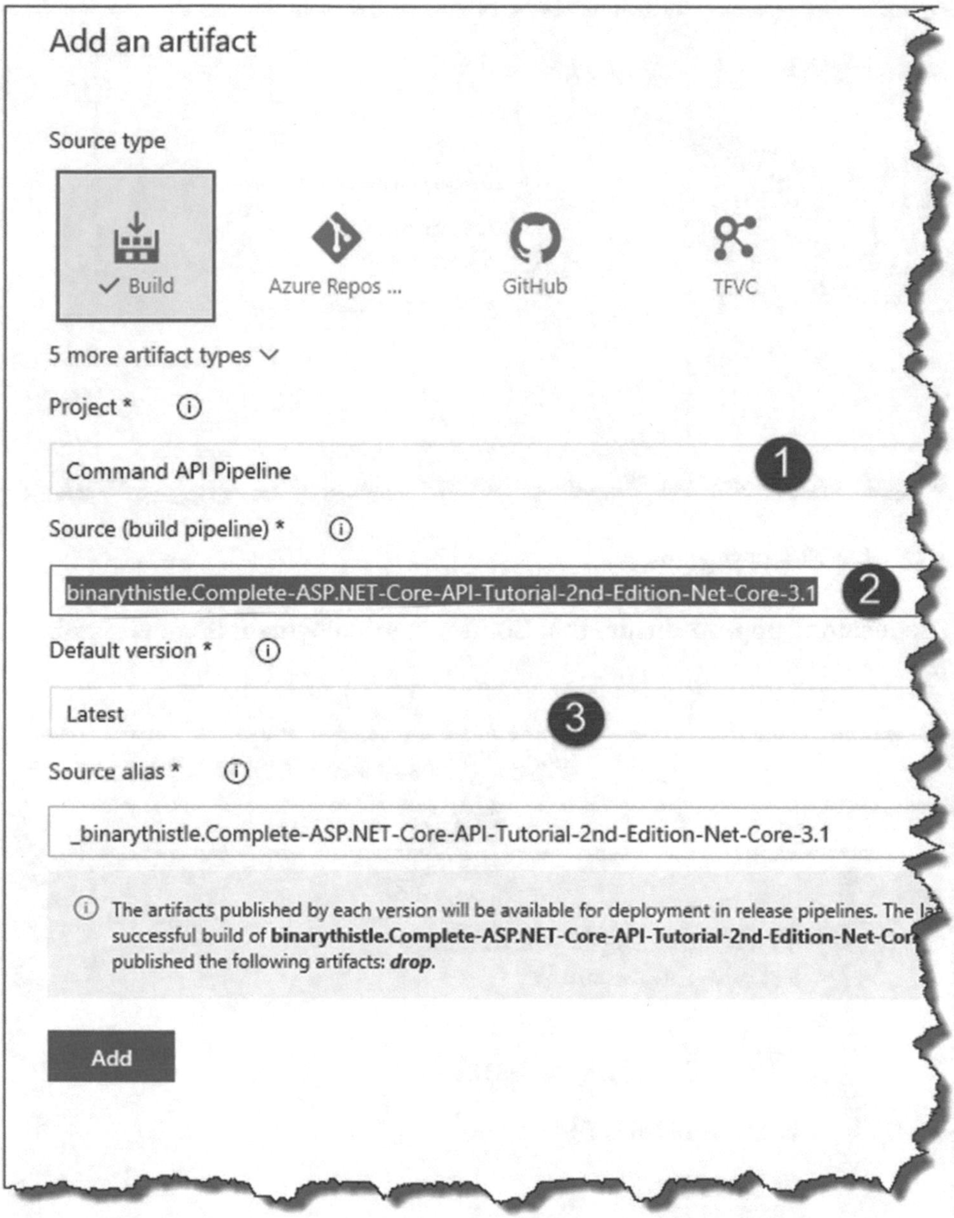

Figure 13-46. *Configure the artifact*

Click Add. Then click the lightning bolt on the newly created Artifact node.

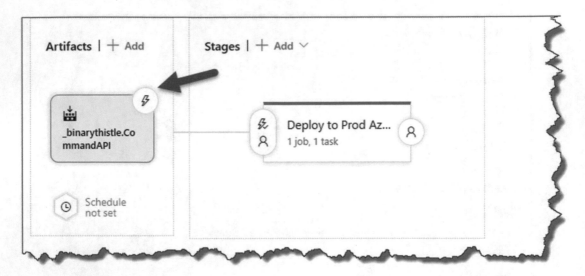

Figure 13-47. *Select triggers*

In the resulting pop-up, ensure that Continuous deployment trigger is **enabled**, then click *Save*.

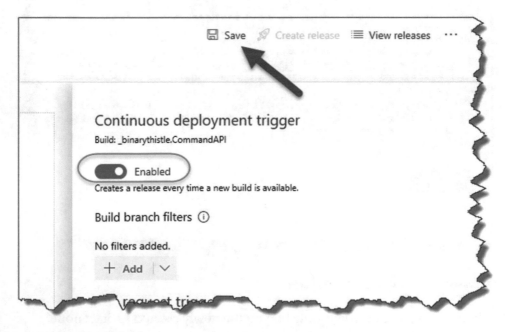

Figure 13-48. *Enable the Continuous deployment trigger*

Note   It is this setting that switches us from Continuous Delivery to Continuous Deployment.

You'll get asked to supply a comment when turning this on; do so if you like.

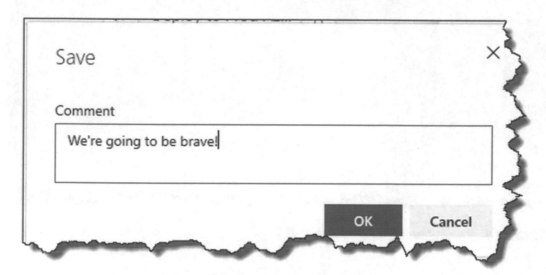

Figure 13-49. *Again, add a comment if you want to*

Click Releases; you'll see that we have a new pipeline but no release; this is because the pipeline has not yet been executed.

Figure 13-50. *Release Pipeline created*

Pull the Trigger – Continuously Deploy

OK, the moment of truth. If we have set everything up correctly, all we need to do now to test our entire CI/CD pipeline end to end is to perform another code commit to GitHub, which will trigger the *Build Pipeline*. Then, as we've just configured, the *Release Pipeline* will be triggered by the Build Pipeline, which will deploy our API App to Azure.

Wait! What About EF Migrations?

Just before you do that – cast your mind back to Chapter 7 where we set up our DB Context and performed a database migration at the command line:

```
dotnet ef database update
```

Nowhere in our CI/CD pipeline have we accounted for this step, where we tell Azure it has to create the necessary schema in our PostgreSQL DB. There are a few ways we can do this, but the simplest is to update the `Configure` method in the `Startup` class.

This approach means that migrations will be applied when the app is started for the first time.

In VS Code, open the `Startup` class, and make the following alterations to the `Configure` method:

```
public void Configure(IApplicationBuilder app, IHostingEnvironment env,
CommandContext context)
{
  context.Database.Migrate();
  if (env.IsDevelopment())
  {
    app.UseDeveloperExceptionPage();
  }
  app.UseMvc();
}
```

For clarity, the `Configure` method changes are highlighted in Figure 13-51.

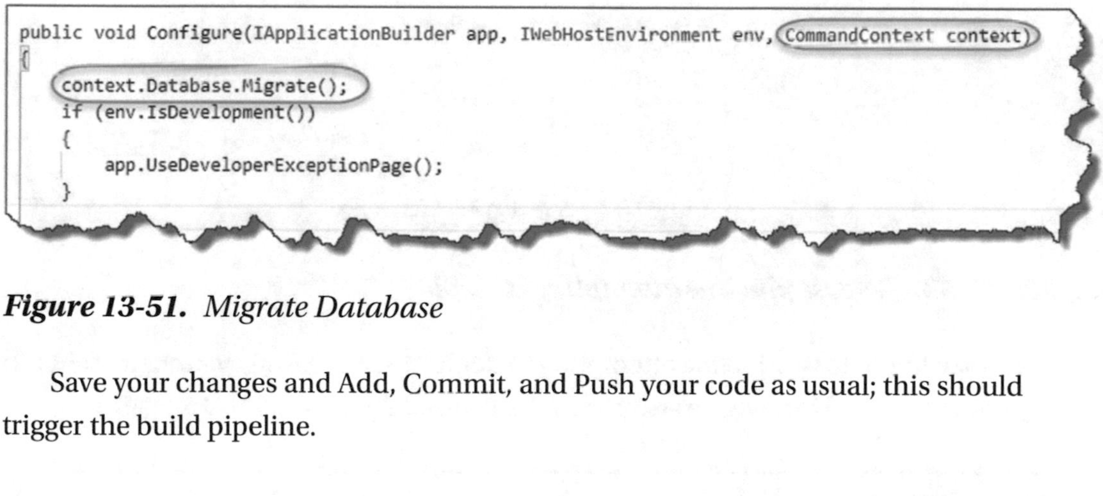

```
public void Configure(IApplicationBuilder app, IWebHostEnvironment env, CommandContext context)
{
    context.Database.Migrate();
    if (env.IsDevelopment())
    {
        app.UseDeveloperExceptionPage();
    }
```

***Figure 13-51.** Migrate Database*

Save your changes and Add, Commit, and Push your code as usual; this should trigger the build pipeline.

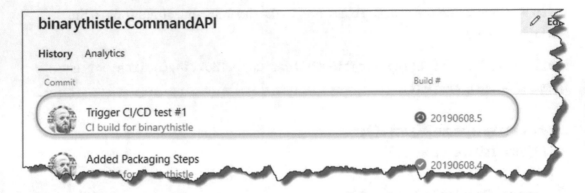

Figure 13-52. *Pipeline triggered again*

When the Build Pipeline finished executing (successfully), click "Releases."

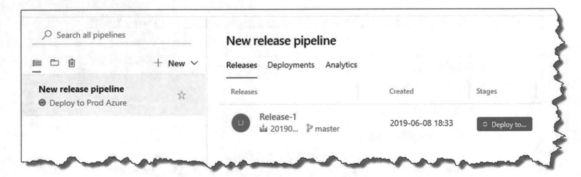

Figure 13-53. *Release pipeline attempting to deploy*

You'll see the Release Pipeline attempting to deploy to Azure And eventually it should deploy (you may need to navigate away from the Release Pipeline and back again).

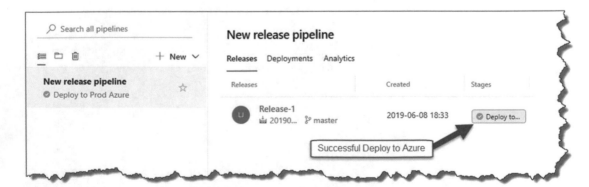

Figure 13-54. *Deployed!*

And now the moment of truth; let's see if our API is working; first obtain the base app URL from Azure:

- Click All resources.

- Select you API App (App Service type).

Figure 13-55. *Get the URI for your API App*

Note: Yours will be named differently.

Now fire up Postman, and prepare to make a GET request to retrieve all our commands (we won't have any yet).

Figure 13-56. *Call the API on Azure from Postman*

Remember to append: `/api/commands` to the base URL

Then click Send.

If the deployment and Azure configuration were successful, you'll get an empty payload response and an OK 200 Status.

Figure 13-57. *Success – but we have no data*

🎂 **Celebration Checkpoint**   Rad![3] Our API is deployed and working in our Production Azure environment; moreover, it's there via process of Continuous Integration/Continuous Deployment!

Double-Check

Just to double-check everything, let's make a POST request to create some data.

Using the following JSON string:

```
{
    "howTo": "Create an EF migration",
    "platform": "Entity Framework Core Command Line",
    "commandLine": "dotnet ef migrations add"
}
```

---

[3]Children of the 1990s will get this superlative.

Create a new Postman request and set

1. Request Verb to POST.

2. The request URL is correct (e.g., `https://commadapi.azurewebsites.net/api/commands`).

3. Click Body.

4. Select Raw and JSON for the request body format.

5. Paste the JSON into the body payload window.

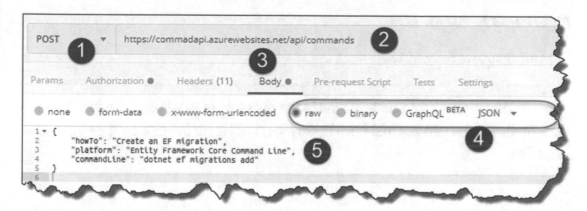

Figure 13-58. *POSTing Data to out Azure hosted API*

Finally, if you're brave enough, click "Send" to make the request.

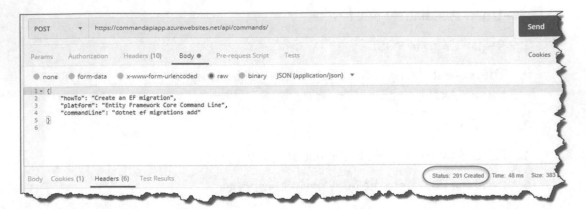

Figure 13-59. *201 Success!*

And again, we have success!

🎂 **Celebration Checkpoint**   Revel in the enormity of what you have just done! Not many people can say that have deployed an API on to the cloud via a CI/CD pipeline.

CHAPTER 14

Securing Our API

Chapter Summary

In this chapter we discuss how we can secure our API; specifically, we'll add the "Bearer" authentication scheme into the mix that will allow only authorized clients to access our API resource through the use of Tokens.

When Done, You Will

- Understand the Bearer authentication scheme.
- Use Azure Active Dircctory to secure our API.
- Create a simple client that is authorized to use the API.
- Deploy to Azure.

We have a lot to cover – so let's get going!

What We're Building

Our Authentication Use Case

Before delving into the technicalities of our chosen authentication scheme, I just wanted to cover our authentication *use case*. For this example, we are going to "secure" our API by using Azure Active Directory (AAD), and then create and configure a client (or daemon) app with the necessary privileges to authenticate through and use the API. We are *not* going to leverage "interactive" user-entered User Ids and passwords. This use case is depicted in Figure 14-1.

© Les Jackson 2020

L. Jackson, *The Complete ASP.NET Core 3 API Tutorial*, https://doi.org/10.1007/978-1-4842-6255-9_14

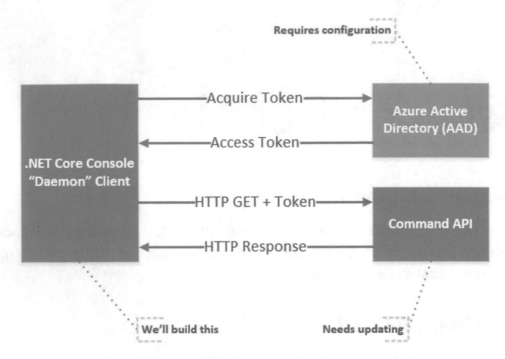

Figure 14-1. Authentication use case

Overview of Bearer Authentication

There are a number of authentication schemes that we could have used, a non-exhaustive list is provided in the table.

Scheme	Description
Basic	A common, relatively simple authentication scheme. Requires the supply of a user name and password that's then encoded as a Base64 string; this is then added to the authorization header of a http request. Natively, this is not encrypted, so it's not that secure, unless you opt so make requests over https, in which case the transport is encrypted
Digest	Follows on from Basic Authentication but is more secure as it applies a hash function to any sensitive data (e.g. username and password) before sending
Bearer	Token-based authentication scheme where anyone in possession of a valid "token" can gain access to the associated secured resources, in this case our API. Considered secure, it is widely adopted in industry and is the scheme (specified in RFC 6750); we'll use to secure our API

(continued)

Scheme	Description
NTLM	Microsoft-specific authentication scheme, using Windows credentials to authenticate. Perfectly decent, secure scheme but as it's somewhat "proprietary" (and I'm trying to avoid that), we'll leave our discussion there for now

Bearer Token vs. JWT

The use of "tokens" in Bearer authentication is a central concept. A token is issued to a requestor (in this case a daemon client) and the client (or "bearer of the token") then presents it to a secure resource in order to gain access.

So, what's JWT?

JWT (or JSON Web Tokens) is an encoding standard (specified in RFC 7519) for tokens that contain a JSON payload. JWTs can be used across a number of applications; however, in this instance, we're going to use JWT as our encoded token through our use of Bearer authentication.

In short

- Bearer authentication is the authentication scheme that makes use of (bearer) "tokens."

- JWT is a specific implementation of bearer tokens, in particular those with a JSON payload.

Again, rather than dwelling on copious amounts of theory, the concepts will make more sense as we build them below.

Build Steps

As I've mentioned before, I like a bit of 50,000ft view of what we're going to build before we start building it as it helps contextualize what we need to do, and it also allows us to understand the progress we're making. Therefore, in terms of the configuration and coding we need to perform, I've detailed the steps we'll follow here.

Steps for Our API Project

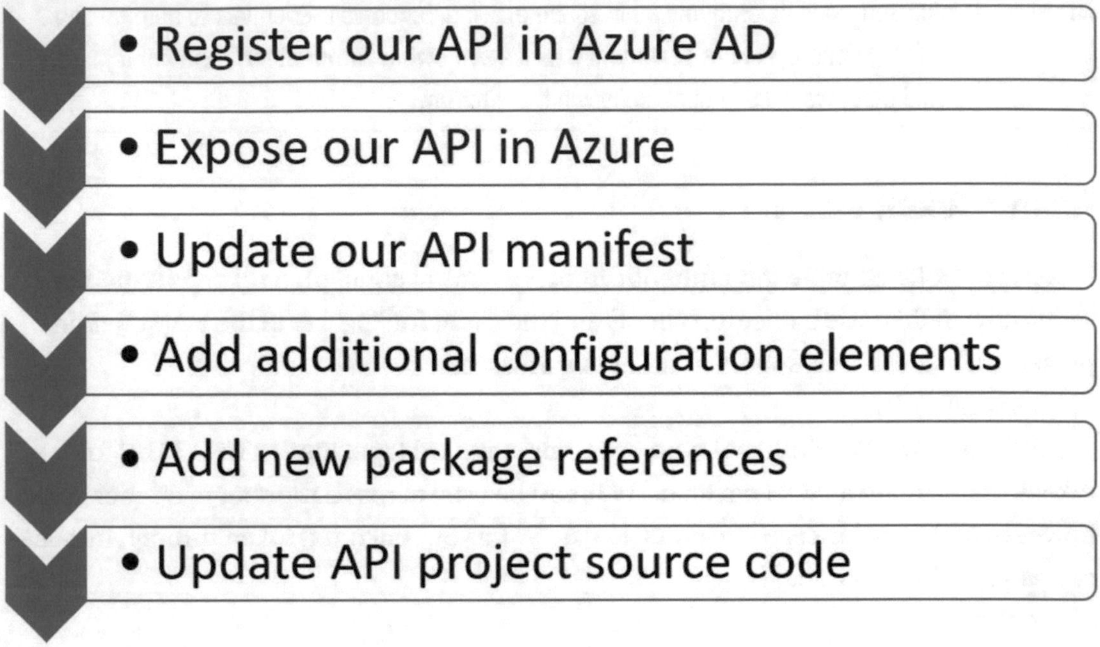

- Register our API in Azure AD
- Expose our API in Azure
- Update our API manifest
- Add additional configuration elements
- Add new package references
- Update API project source code

Figure 14-2. *API build steps*

Steps for Our Daemon Client

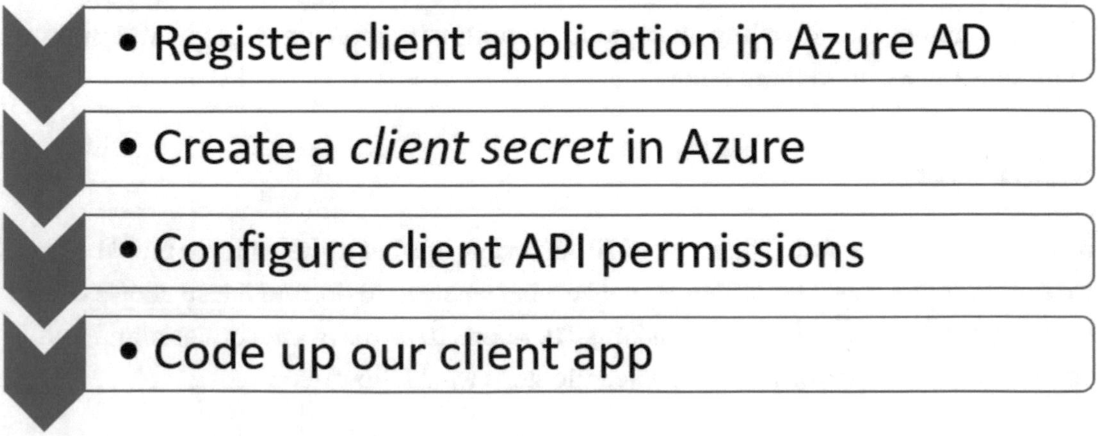

- Register client application in Azure AD
- Create a *client secret* in Azure
- Configure client API permissions
- Code up our client app

Figure 14-3. *Client build steps*

You can see there is actually a lot to do – so let's get on it!

Registering Our API in Azure AD

The first thing we need to do is register our API with Azure Active Directory (AAD), as we're using AAD as our Identity and Access Management *directory service*.

Les' Personal Anecdote   One of my first jobs out of university was as part of a team supporting a large (I believe at the time the second largest in the world) deployment of Novell NetWare Directory Services (NDS), which was weird as I had neither the background nor inclination to learn NDS.

Anyhow, this product was considered relatively leading-edge at the time as it took the approach of storing user accounts (as well as other "organizational objects") in a hierarchical directory tree structure that was both distributed and replicated (in this case) nationwide. In short it was hugely scalable and could cater for 10,000s (we had well over 100,000) of user accounts.

At the time Microsoft only used Windows NT Domains which were arguably more basic (they were "flat"), less scalable, distributable, and reliable than their NetWare counterparts. Blue screen of death anyone?

Microsoft was obviously, cough, "inspired," cough again, by NDS (and Banyan Vines – see next section) to such an extent that they brought out a rival product, Active Directory, which bore a remarkable resemblance to, drum roll, NDS. You could argue this was poetic justice as Novell had been "inspired" by an earlier product called Banyan VINES.[1] Interestingly, Jim Allchin, engineering supremo at Banyan, joined Microsoft due to creative and strategic differences with the Banyan leadership.

The rest is history.

Banyan and Novell's products withered and died due to a number of different strategic missteps, as well as the fact that Microsoft had a compelling value proposition.

---

[1] https://en.wikipedia.org/wiki/Banyan_VINES

So, if you use a Windows PC at work and have to "log-in," then you're most likely logging into an Active Directory. Now with the emergence of Azure, you don't even need to host your AD on premise and can opt to use Azure Active Directory, which is what we'll be using for this chapter.

Create a New AD?

Now this step is optional, but I have created a "test" AAD in addition to the AAD that gets created when you sign up for Azure. This is really just to ring-fence what is in essence my "production AAD" (the one that holds my login for Azure) from any development activities I undertake.

You can create a new AAD in exactly the same way as you create any other resources in Azure, so I won't detail the steps here. If you do opt for this approach though (remember it is optional), the only thing you need to be aware of is that when you want to create objects in your "Development AAD," you'll need to switch to it in the Azure Portal.

Switching Between AADs

To switch between your AADs, click the person icon at the top right hand of the Azure Portal.

Figure 14-4. *Switching Active Directory*

On the resulting pop-up, you can then click Switch Directory (see circled section on Figure 14-4); you should then get the option to select and switch between the AADs you have (I have two as you can see in Figure 14-5).

Figure 14-5. *I created a second AD for test purposes*

Register Our API

Select the AAD you're using for this exercise; the click Azure Active Directory from your portal landing page.

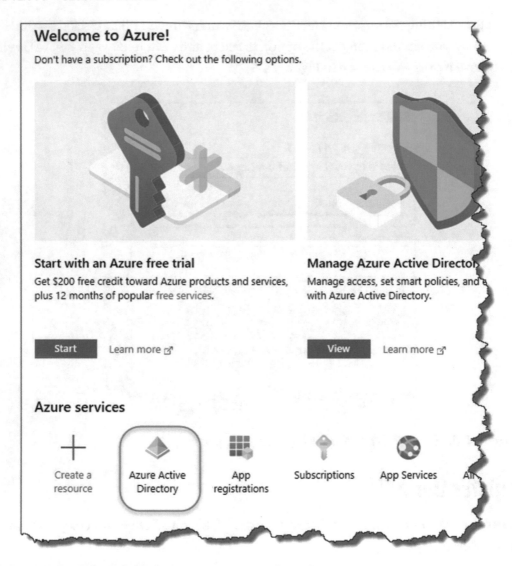

Figure 14-6. *Select the AD you want to work with*

This should then take you into the Azure Active Directory overview screen.

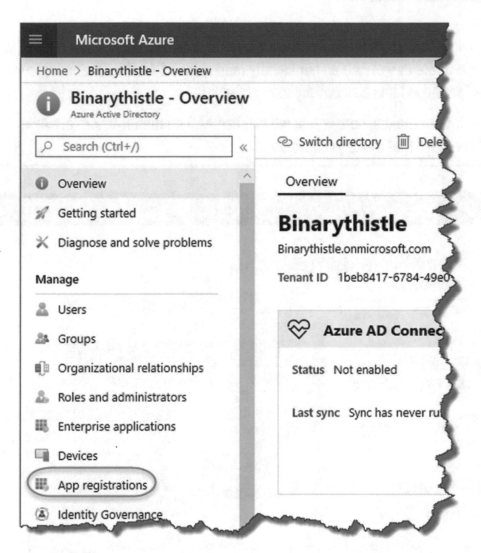

Figure 14-7. *Select App registrations*

Select "App registrations" as shown in Figure 14-7. You can see from the next example that I already have an existing app registered on my AAD, but we're going to create a new one for our CommandAPI running on our "development" environment (i.e., the one running locally on our PC). We'll come on to our Azure-deployed API later.

ℹ   Even though we are running our development API on our local machine, we can still make use of AAD as our Identity management service (assuming our development PC has connectivity to the Internet!).

The point I'm making here is that we can use AAD no matter where our APIs (and client for that matter) are located.

Figure 14-8.   *Create a new registration*

Select "New registration," and you'll see the following.

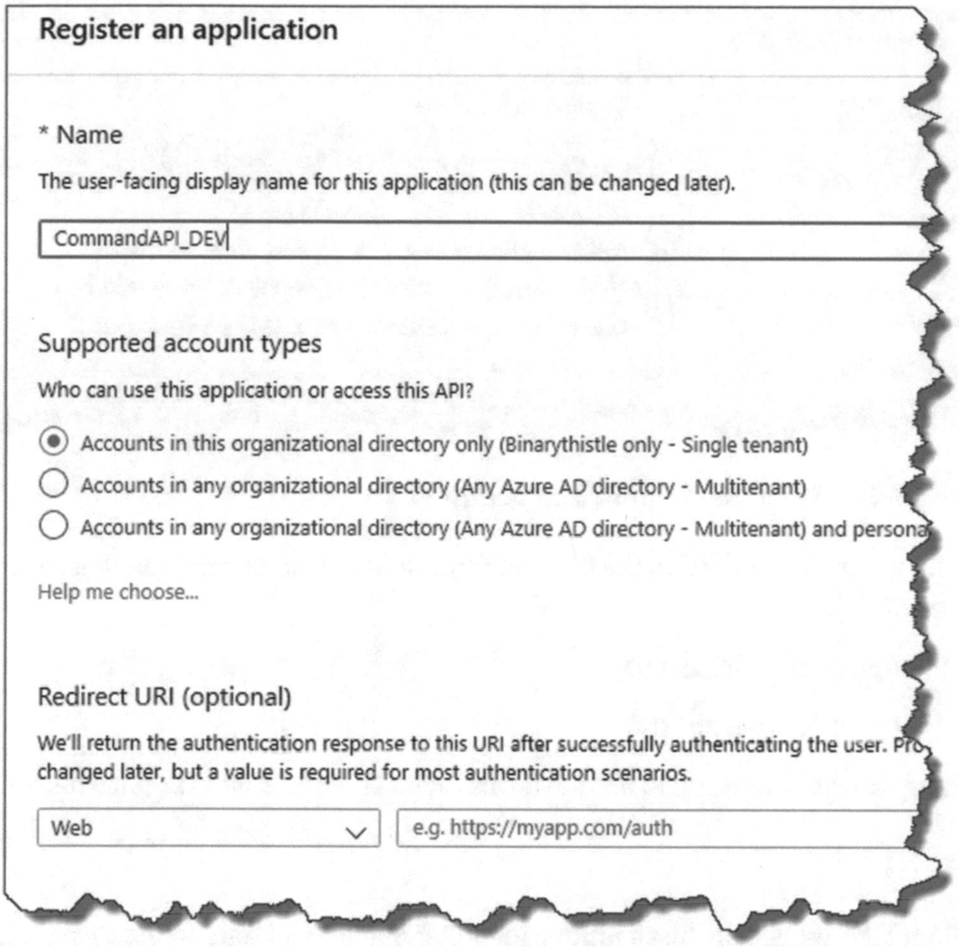

Figure 14-9. *Configure the registration*

Enter a name for the app registration; it can be anything, but make it meaningful, (I've appended "_DEV" to this registration to differentiate it from any Production Registrations we subsequently create). Also, ensure that "Accounts in this organization directory only" ([*Your AAD Name*] only – Single tenant) is selected.

We don't need a Redirect URI, so click "Register" to complete the initial registration, after which you'll be taken to the overview screen.

Figure 14-10. *We'll use client Id and tenant id*

Here, we are introduced to the first two important bits of information that we need to be aware of:

1.   Application (client) ID

2.   Directory (tenant) ID

Going forward I'm going to use the terms Client ID and Tenant ID, but what are they?

Client ID

The client ID is essentially just a unique identifier that we can refer to the *Command API* in reference to our AAD.

Tenant ID

A unique id relating to the AAD we're using, remembering that we can have multiple (i.e. multi-tenant) AADs at our disposal.

We'll come back to these items later when we come to configuring things at the application end; for now we need to move on as we're not quite finished.

Expose Our API

So far, we've merely *registered* our API; we now need to *expose* it for use, so click "Expose an API" from our left-hand menu options on our Registrations page.

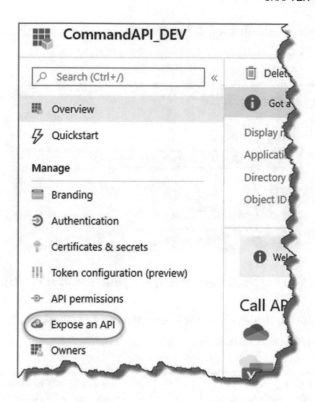

Figure 14-11. *Exposing our API*

What we need to do here is create an "Application ID URI" (sometimes referred to as a "Resource ID"), so click "Set" as shown in Figure 14-12.

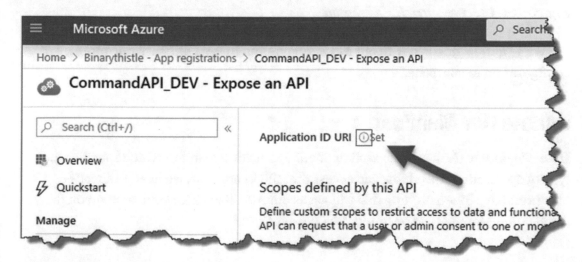

Figure 14-12. *Set the Resource ID*

Azure will provide a default suggestion for this; go with it (it's the Client ID with
"api://" prepended).

Figure 14-13. *Auto-generated Resource ID (Application ID URI)*

Click Save and you're done. Clicking back into the overview of the app registration,
you should see this reflected here too.

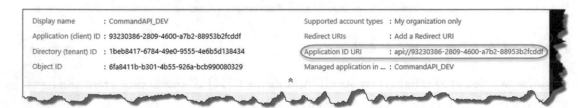

Figure 14-14. *Resource ID is created*

We're almost finished with our API configuration in AAD but have one more bit of
configuration to complete.

Update Our Manifest

Here, we update the appRoles section of our application manifest which specifies the
type of application role(s) that can access the API. In our case, we need to specify a
noninteractive "daemon" app that will act as our API client. More information on the
Application Manifest can be found in Microsoft Docs.[2]

---

[2]https://docs.microsoft.com/en-au/azure/active-directory/develop/
reference-app-manifest

Anyway, back to the task at hand, we need to insert the following JSON snippet at the appRoles section of our manifest:

```
.
.
.
"appRoles": [
  {
    "allowedMemberTypes": [
      "Application"
    ],
    "description": "Daemon apps in this role can consume the web api.",
    "displayName": "DaemonAppRole",
    "id": "6543b78e-0f43-4fe9-bf84-0ce8b74c06a3",
    "isEnabled": true,
    "lang": null,
    "origin": "Application",
    "value": "DaemonAppRole"
  }
],
.
.
.
```

So, click "Manifest" in the left-hand window of our App Registration config page.

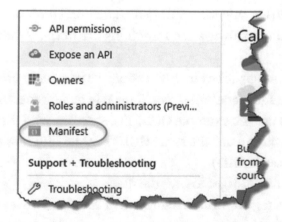

Figure 14-15. *Update the manifest*

And insert the json given earlier into the correct spot (essentially updating the existing empty `appRoles` section).

Figure 14-16. *Ensure you update the manifest correctly*

Make sure you keep the integrity of the json, and don't omit or introduce any additional commas. You can always use something like `https://jsoneditoronline.org/` to check.

You can add multiple `appRoles` to this section; we need only one, although if you do decide to add some additional roles, you'll need to ensure that the "id" attribute is a unique GUID. You can use the example GUID I've supplied with the JSON here, or you can create your own (you can use the same GUID's across different AADs – you just can't duplicate them in the same AAD).

When completed, don't forget to save the file.

That's it for our API registration in Azure; we need to move over to our API now and make some config and code changes so it can make use of AAD for authorization.

Add Configuration Elements

We need to make our API "aware" of the AAD settings we've just set up so that it can use AAD for authenticating clients. We need to configure

- The log-in "Instance"

- Our AAD Domain

- The Tenant ID

- The Client ID

- The Application ID URL (or Resource ID)

ℹ️   Remember we're currently working with our API in our *Development* Environment, before we move on to configuring our API on Azure.

As we've already discussed, you can store your application config in a number of places (e.g., ***appsettings.json, appsettings.Development.json,*** etc.); in this section, I'm going to make use of User Secrets once again (refer to Chapter 8 for a refresher).

The primary reason I'm taking this approach is that I'll be pushing my code up to a public GitHub repository and I don't want those items visible in something like ***appsettings.json***.

The table details the name of the user secret variables I'm going to use for each of the config elements.

Config element	User secret variable
The log-in "instance"	Instance
Our AAD Domain	Domain
The Tenant ID	TenantId
The Client ID	ClientId
The Application UD URL (Or Resource ID)	ResourceId

As a quick refresher to add the "Instance" User Secret, at a command prompt "inside" the API Project root folder (**CommandAPI**), type:

```
dotnet user-secrets set "Instance" "https://login.microsoftonline.com/"
```

This will add a value for our Login Instance (you should use the same value I've used here). The other User Secrets I'll leave for you to add yourself, as the values you need to supply will be unique to your own App Registration (refer to these values on the App Registration overview screen for your API).

After adding all my User Secrets, the contents of my ***secrets.json*** file now looks like this.

```
{} secrets.json  ×

{} secrets.json > ...
  1   {
  2       "UserID": "cmddbuser",
  3       "TenantId": "1beb8417-6784-49e0-9555-4e6b5d138434",
  4       "Password": "pa55w0rd!",
  5       "Instance": "https://login.microsoftonline.com/",
  6       "Domain": "Binarythistle.onmicrosoft.com",
  7       "ClientId": "93230386-2809-4600-a7b2-88953b2fcddf",
  8       "ResourceId": "api://93230386-2809-4600-a7b2-88953b2fcddf"
  9   }
```

Figure 14-17. *Example contents of my secrets.json file*

Some points to note

- The value you have for Instance should be exactly the same as I've used earlier.

- The values you have for UserID and Password *may* be the same as what I've just shown if you've been following the tutorial *exactly* as I've described (they may of course be different if you've chosen your own values!).

- The values you have for TenantId, Domain, ClientId, and ResourceId will be different to mine.[3]

---

[3]The chances of the same GUID being generated for us both is quite slim.

Update Our Project Packages

Before we start coding, we need to add a new package that will be required to support the code we're going to introduce, so at a command prompt "inside" the API project, type

```
dotnet add package Microsoft.AspNetCore.Authentication.JwtBearer
```

This should successfully add the following package reference to the .csproj file.

```
<ItemGroup>
  <PackageReference Include="AutoMapper.Extensions.Microsoft.DependencyInjection" Version="7.0.0" />
  <PackageReference Include="Microsoft.AspNetCore.Authentication.JwtBearer" Version="3.1.4" />
  <PackageReference Include="Microsoft.AspNetCore.JsonPatch" Version="3.1.4" />
  <PackageReference Include="Microsoft.AspNetCore.Mvc.NewtonsoftJson" Version="3.1.4" />
  <PackageReference Include="Microsoft.EntityFrameworkCore" Version="3.1.4" />
  <PackageReference Include="Microsoft.EntityFrameworkCore.Design" Version="3.1.4">
    <IncludeAssets>runtime; build; native; contentfiles; analyzers; buildtransitive</IncludeAssets>
    <PrivateAssets>all</PrivateAssets>
  </PackageReference>
  <PackageReference Include="Npgsql.EntityFrameworkCore.PostgreSQL" Version="3.1.3" />
</ItemGroup>

</Project>
```

Figure 14-18. *Add Reference to allow JWT Bearer Authentication*

Updating our Startup Class

Over in the startup class of our API project, we need to update both our ConfigureServices and Configure methods. First though, add the following using directive to the top of the startup class file:

```
using Microsoft.AspNetCore.Authentication.JwtBearer;
```

Update Configure Services

We need to set up bearer authentication in the ConfigureServices method; to do so, add the following code (new code is highlighted):

413

.
.
.

```
services.AddDbContext<CommandContext>(opt => opt.UseNpgsql(builder.
ConnectionString));
```

services.AddAuthentication(JwtBearerDefaults.AuthenticationScheme)
  .AddJwtBearer(opt =>
  {
    opt.Audience = Configuration["ResourceId"];
    opt.Authority = $"{Configuration["Instance"]}{Configuration["TenantId"]}";
  });

```
services.AddControllers();
```

.
.
.

To put the changes in context, it should look like this.

```
public void ConfigureServices(IServiceCollection services)
{
    var builder = new NpgsqlConnectionStringBuilder();
    builder.ConnectionString =
        Configuration.GetConnectionString("PostgreSqlConnection");
        builder.Username = Configuration["UserID"];
        builder.Password = Configuration["Password"];

    services.AddDbContext<CommandContext>(opt => opt.UseNpgsql(builder.ConnectionString));

    services.AddAuthentication(JwtBearerDefaults.AuthenticationScheme).AddJwtBearer(opt =>
    {
        opt.Audience = Configuration["ResourceID"];
        opt.Authority = $"{Configuration["Instance"]}{Configuration["TenantId"]}";
    });

    services.AddControllers().AddNewtonsoftJson(s => {
        s.SerializerSettings.ContractResolver = new CamelCasePropertyNamesContractResolver();
    });
```

Figure 14-19. *register Authentication service in Startup*

The preceding code adds authentication to our API, specifically Bearer authentication using JWT Tokens. We then configure two options:

- **Audience**: We set this to the ResourceID of our App Registration in Azure.

- **Authority**: Our AAD Instance that is the token issuing authority (a combination of Instance and TenantId).

Update Configure

All we need to do now is add authentication and authorization to our request pipeline via the Configure method:

```
app.UseAuthentication();
app.UseAuthorization();
```

as shown in Figure 14-20.

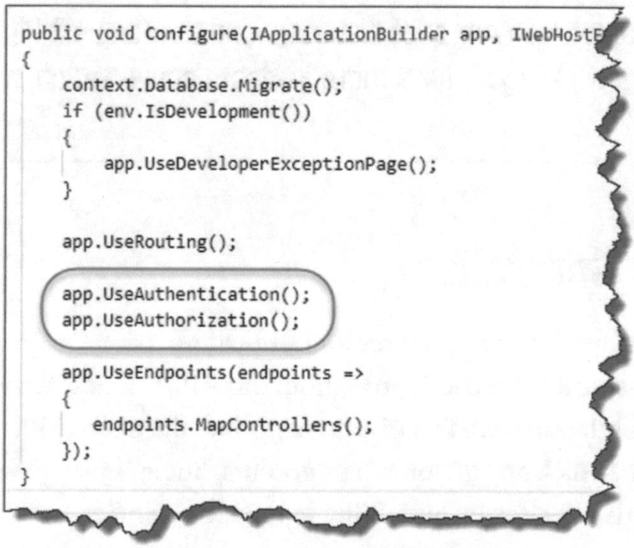

```
public void Configure(IApplicationBuilder app, IWebHostE
{
    context.Database.Migrate();
    if (env.IsDevelopment())
    {
        app.UseDeveloperExceptionPage();
    }

    app.UseRouting();

    app.UseAuthentication();
    app.UseAuthorization();

    app.UseEndpoints(endpoints =>
    {
        endpoints.MapControllers();
    });
}
```

Figure 14-20. *Update the configure method in Startup*

Authentication vs. Authorization

As we've added both Authentication and Authorization to our request pipeline, I just want to quickly outline the difference between these two concepts before we move on:

- **Authentication (The "Who")**: Verifies who you are, essentially it checks your identity is valid.

- **Authorization (The "What")**: Grants the permissions/level of access that you have.

So in our example, our client app will be authenticated via AAD; once it has, we can then determine *what* endpoints it can call on our API (authorization).

⚠ **Warning!**   As authentication happens first (we need to identify you before we can authorize you to do anything), the order in which you add these components to the Request Pipeline (via the `Configure` method) is critically important. So please make sure you add them in the order specified earlier.

Refer back to Chapter 4 on our brief discussion on the Request Pipeline if you've forgotten (it was a while ago!); for a more in-depth conversation, refer to the Microsoft Docs.[4]

Update Our Controller

We have added the foundations of Bearer authentication using JWT tokens to our `Startup` class to enable it to be used throughout our API, but now we want to use it to protect one of our endpoints. We can of course protect the entire API, but let's just start small for now. We can pick any of our API endpoints, but let's just go with one of our simple GET methods, specifically our ability to retrieve a single Command.

Before we update our controller action, just make sure you add the following using directive at the top of our `CommandsController` class:

```
using Microsoft.AspNetCore.Authorization;
```

---

[4]https://docs.microsoft.com/en-us/aspnet/core/fundamentals/middleware/

The new code for our controller action is simple; we just decorate it with the [Authorize]attribute as shown here:

```
[Authorize]
[HttpGet("{id}", Name = "GetCommandById")]
public ActionResult<CommandReadDto> GetCommandById(int id)
{
  var commandItem = _repository.GetCommandById(id);
  if (commandItem == null)
  {
    return NotFound();
  }
    return Ok(_mapper.Map<CommandReadDto>(commandItem));
}
```

Save all the new code, build, then run the API locally. Once running, make a call to our newly protected endpoint in Postman.

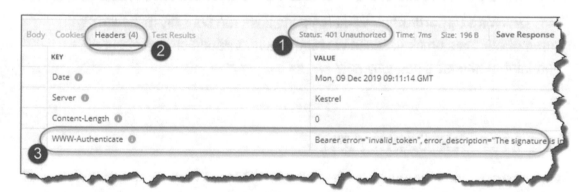

Figure 14-21. *Our endpoint is secured*

Here, you will see

1. We get a 401 Unauthorized response

2. Selecting the return headers, we see

3. That the authentication type is "Bearer" (and we have a token error back from AAD)

To double-check we have only protected this endpoint, make a call to our other GET action, and you'll see we still get a list of commands back.

Figure 14-22. *This endpoint is not secured and can still be accessed*

🎓 **Learning Opportunity**   What happens if we run our Unit Test suite? Will some of our tests break because we require authorization on one of our API endpoint methods? If not, why not?

Register Our Client App

In the next section, we're going to write a simple .NET Core Console application that will act as an authorized "client" of the API. As this is a "daemon app," it needs to run without user authentication interaction, so we need to configure it as such.

ⓘ   There are a number of different authentication use cases we could explore when it comes to consuming an API, for example, a user authenticating against AAD (username/password combo), to grant access to the API.

The use case I've decided to go with in this example (a "daemon app") resonated with me more in terms of a real-world use case.

Back over in Azure, select the same AAD that you registered the API in, and select App Registrations once again.

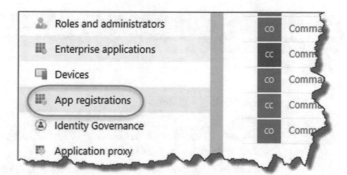

Figure 14-23. *Create an App Registration for our client app*

Then select "+ New registration," and on the resulting screen enter a suitable name for our client app as shown next.

Register an application

Home > Binarythistle - App registrations > Register an application

Register an application

* Name

The user-facing display name for this application (this can be changed later).

```
CommandAPI_Client_DEV
```

Supported account types

Who can use this application or access this API?

○ Accounts in this organizational directory only (Binarythistle only - Single tenant)

○ Accounts in any organizational directory (Any Azure AD directory - Multitenant)

○ Accounts in any organizational directory (Any Azure AD directory - Multitenant) and personal Microsoft accounts (e.g. Skype,

Help me choose...

Figure 14-24. *Name the registration*

Again, select the *Single tenant* supported account type option, and click "Register"; this will take you to the overview screen of your new app registration.

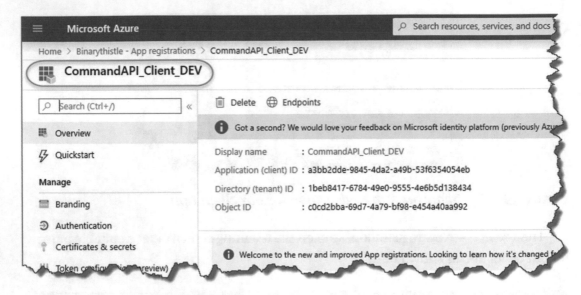

Figure 14-25. *Client registration overview*

As before it will prepopulate some of the config elements for you, for example, Client ID, Tenant ID, etc.

🎓 **Learning Opportunity**   What do you notice about the Tenant ID for our client registration when compared to the Tenant ID of API registration?

Create a Client Secret

Next click "Certificates & secrets" in the left-hand menu.

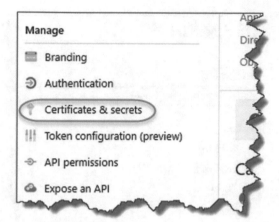

Figure 14-26. *Create a client secret*

Here we are going to configure a "Client Secret." This is a unique ID that we will use in combination with our other app registration attributes to identify and authenticate our client to our API. Click "+ New client secret."

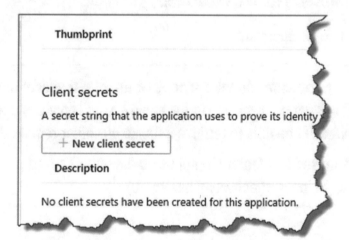

Figure 14-27. *Select New client Secret*

And on the resulting screen, give it

- A description (can be anything but make it meaningful)

- An expiry (you have a choice of 3 options)

Figure 14-28. *Name the secret and set expiry*

When you're happy, click "Add."

⚠ **Warning!**   Make sure you **take a copy of the client secret now;** shortly after creation it will not be displayed in full again – you'll only see a redacted version, and you won't be able to retrieve it unlike our other registration attributes.

This is a by design security feature to help stop the unauthorized propagation of the client secret (which is effectively a password).

Configure API Permissions

Now click "API Permissions"; here we are going to (drum roll please) configure access to our Command API.

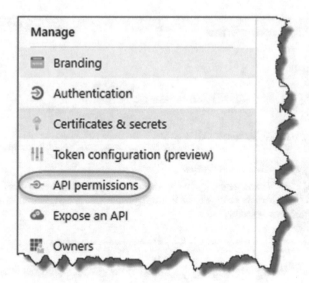

Figure 14-29. *Setup Permissions to our API*

Click "+ Add a permission."

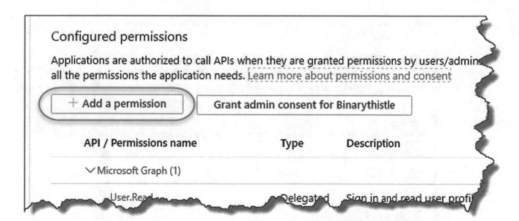

Figure 14-30. *Add a permission*

In the "Request API permissions" window that appears, select the "My APIs" tab.

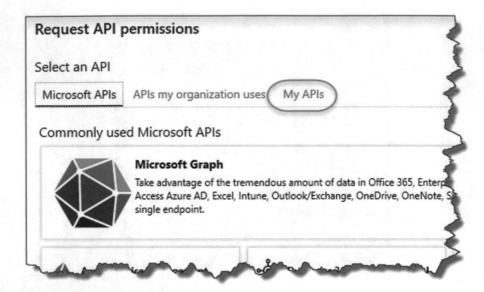

Figure 14-31. *select "My APIs"*

And find the Command API, and select it.

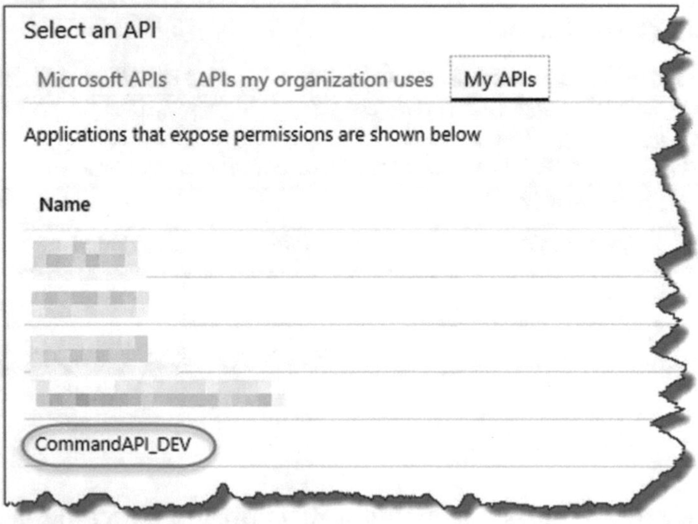

Figure 14-32. *Select the CommandAPI_DEV instance*

On the resulting screen, ensure that

1.   Application permissions is selected.

2.   You "check" the DaemonAppRole Permission.

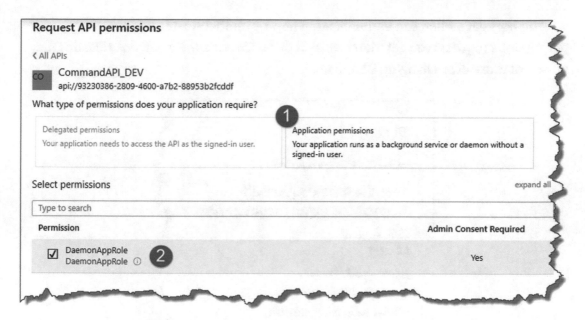

Figure 14-33. *Configure permissions accordingly*

When you're happy, click "Add permission," and your permission will be added to the list.

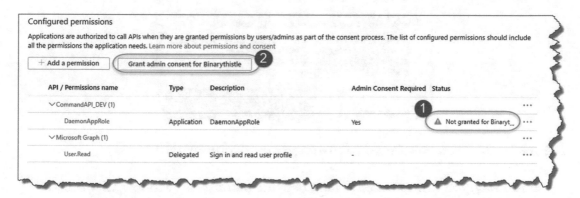

Figure 14-34. *Grant consent*

You'll notice

1. The permission has been "created" but not yet "granted."

2. You'll need to click the "Grant admin consent for *<Name of Your AAD Here[5]>*" button – do so now.

---

[5]The button will be labeled differently to mine depending on the name of your AAD.

You *may* get a Microsoft authentication pop-up; authenticate and accept any permissions requests you get (don't worry if this does not appear – it looks like this may be one of those ever-changing UI updates).

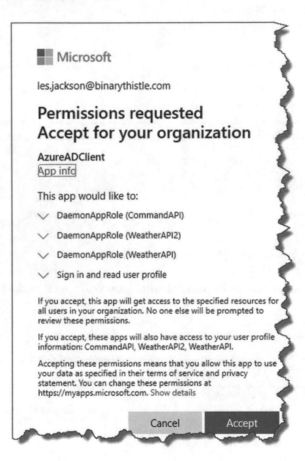

Figure 14-35.   *You may be asked to accept permission request*

Either way, you'll be returned to the Configure permissions window, where after a short time, your newly created API Permission will have been granted access.

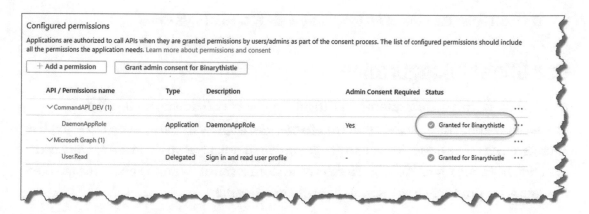

Figure 14-36. Permissions fully granted

And with that, the registration of our (yet to be created) client app is complete.

Create Our Client App

The final part of this chapter is to create a simple client that we can use to call our protected API, so we're going to create new console project to do just that.

ℹ   I don't consider this app part of our "solution" (containing our API and Test Projects), so I'm going to create it in a totally separate working project directory outside of *CommandAPISolution* folder.

Note   As we'll only be creating 1 project, I'm *not* going to make use of a "solution" structure.

You can find the code to this project here on GitHub:

`https://github.com/binarythistle/Secure-Daemon-Client/`

At a command prompt in a new working directory "outside" of our *CommandAPISolution* folder, type

```
dotnet new console -n CommandAPIClient
```

Once the project has been created, open the project folder *CommandAPIClient* in your development environment, so if you're using VS Code, you could type

```
code -r CommandAPIClient
```

This will open the project folder ***CommandAPIClient*** in VS Code.

Our Client Configuration

As I'm making this code available on GitHub for you to pull down and use, I'm deliberately going to store the config in an ***appsettings.json*** file as opposed to using User Secrets, as it will be easier for you to get going with it quickly if you choose to work with the code from the repo.[6] We will, therefore, be storing sensitive config elements in here; therefore, for production systems **you would not do this!**

☞ **Learning Opportunity**   Following the approach we took for our API; "convert" the Client App example here to use user secrets.

Create an ***appsettings.json*** file in the root of your project folder; once done it should look like this if you're using VS Code.

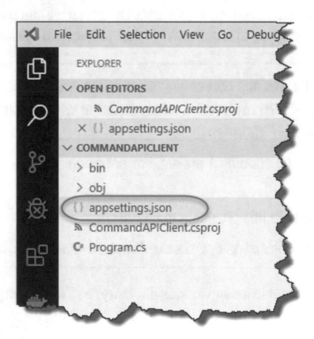

Figure 14-37. *Create an Appsettings.json file*

---

[6]I appreciate it's totally counter to the point I made before in regard to our API but feel this is a slightly different use case.

Into that file, add the following JSON; making sure to populate the correct values for **your client** application registration (TenantId, ClientId, and ClientSecret), and in the case of the ResourceId, make sure it's the ResourceId for the **API**:

```
{
  "Instance": "https://login.microsoftonline.com/{0}",
  "TenantId": "[YOUR TENANT ID]",
  "ClientId": "[YOUR CLIENT ID]",
  "ClientSecret": "[YOUR CLIENT SECRET]",
  "BaseAddress": "https://localhost:5001/api/Commands/1",
  "ResourceId": "api://[YOUR API CLIENT ID]/.default"
}
```

So, for example, my file looks like this.

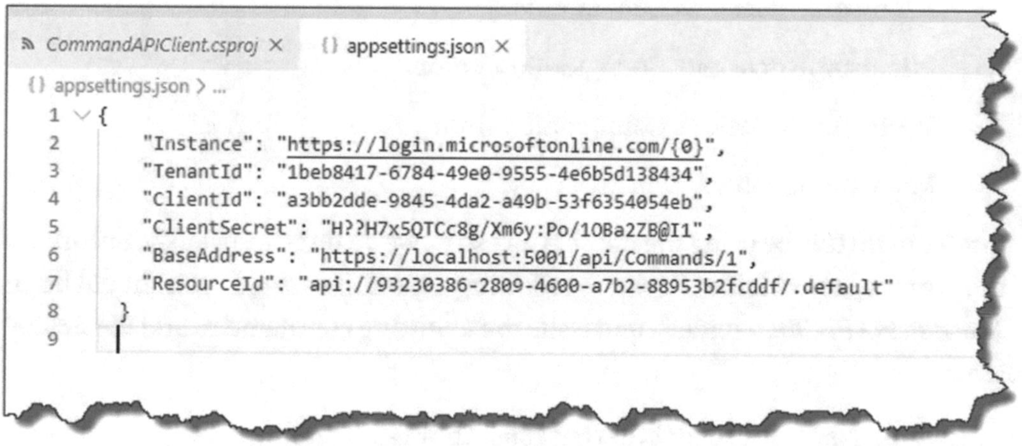

Figure 14-38. Client configuration

A couple of points to just double-check on:

- **BaseAddress**: This is just the local address of the command API (we'll update to our production URL later). Note that I'm deliberately specifying the API Controller Action that requires authorization.

- **ResourceId**: This is the ResourceId of our **API App** Registration.

The other attributes are straightforward and can be retrieved from Azure, except the ClientSecret which you should have made a copy of when you created it.

> ⚠ **Warning!**   All the attributes given are enough to get access to our restricted API without the need for any additional passwords, etc. So, you **should not** store it like this in production; you should make use of user secrets or something similar.
>
> Again, I've chose to provide it in an ***appsettings.json*** file to allow you to get up and running quickly with the code and have left it as a learning exercise for you to implement the *user secrets* approach.

Add Our Package References

Before we start coding, we need to add some package references to our project to support some of the features we're going to use, so we'll add

- Microsoft.Extensions.Configuration

- Microsoft.Extensions.Configuration.Binder

- Microsoft.Extensions.Configuration.Json

- Microsoft.Identity.Client

I prefer to do this by using the dotnet CLI , so as we've done previously, ensure your "in" the correct project folder (if you're following the tutorial exactly you should be "in" the ***CommandAPIClient*** folder), and issue the following command to add the first of our packages:

```
dotnet add package Microsoft.Extensions.Configuration
```

Repeat so you add all four packages; your project .csproj file should look like this when done.

```
CommandAPIClient.csproj
1   <Project Sdk="Microsoft.NET.Sdk">
2
3     <PropertyGroup>
4       <OutputType>Exe</OutputType>
5       <TargetFramework>netcoreapp3.1</TargetFramework>
6     </PropertyGroup>
7
8     <ItemGroup>
9       <PackageReference Include="Microsoft.Extensions.Configuration" Version="3.1.1" />
0       <PackageReference Include="Microsoft.Extensions.Configuration.Binder" Version="3.1.1" />
1       <PackageReference Include="Microsoft.Extensions.Configuration.Json" Version="3.1.1" />
2       <PackageReference Include="Microsoft.Identity.Client" Version="4.8.1" />
3     </ItemGroup>
4
5   </Project>
6
```

Figure 14-39. *Package References for our client*

Client Configuration Class

For ease of use, we're going to create a custom class that will allow us to read in our ***appsettings.json*** file and then access those config elements as class attributes. In the client project, create a new class file in the root of the project, and call it ***AuthConfig.cs*** as shown in Figure 14-40.

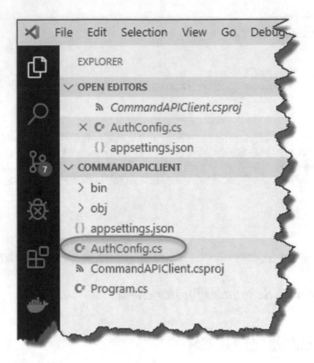

Figure 14-40. *AuthConfig class to read in and manage client configuration*

Then enter the following code:

```
using System;
using System.IO;
using System.Globalization;
using Microsoft.Extensions.Configuration;

namespace CommandAPIClient
{
  public class AuthConfig
  {
    public string Instance {get; set;} =
      "https://login.microsoftonline.com/{0}";
    public string TenantId {get; set;}
    public string ClientId {get; set;}
    public string Authority
    {
```

```
    get
    {
      return String.Format(CultureInfo.InvariantCulture,
                           Instance, TenantId);
    }
  }
  public string ClientSecret {get; set;}
  public string BaseAddress {get; set;}
  public string ResourceID {get; set;}

  public static AuthConfig ReadFromJsonFile(string path)
  {
    IConfiguration Configuration;

    var builder = new ConfigurationBuilder()
      .SetBasePath(Directory.GetCurrentDirectory())
      .AddJsonFile(path);

    Configuration = builder.Build();

    return Configuration.Get<AuthConfig>();
  }
 }
}
```

When complete your AuthConfig class should look like this.

```
namespace CommandAPIClient
{
  public class AuthConfig
  {
    public string Instance {get; set;} =
      "https://login.microsoftonline.com/{0}";
    public string TenantId {get; set;}
    public string ClientId {get; set;}                                    1
    public string Authority
    {
      get
      {
        return String.Format(CultureInfo.InvariantCulture, Instance, TenantId);
      }
    }
    public string ClientSecret {get; set;}
    public string BaseAddress {get; set;}
    public string ResourceID {get; set;}

    public static AuthConfig ReadFromJsonFile(string path)    2
    {
      IConfiguration Configuration;    3

      var builder = new ConfigurationBuilder()
        .SetBasePath(Directory.GetCurrentDirectory())    4
        .AddJsonFile(path);

      Configuration = builder.Build();

      return Configuration.Get<AuthConfig>();    5
    }
  }
}
```

Figure 14-41.   *Walk-through of Authconfig class*

Notable code listed here

1. We combine the Instance and our AAD Tenant to create
    something called the "Authority"; this is required when we come
    to attempting to connect our client later.

2. Our class has one static method that allows us to specify the name
    of our JSON config file.

3. We create an instance of the .NET Core Configuration subsystem.

4. Using `ConfigurationBuilder`, we read the contents of our json config file.

5. We pass back our read-in config bound to our AuthConfig class.

To quickly test that this all works, perform a build, and assuming we have no errors, move over to our Program class, and edit the Main method so it looks like this:

```
static void Main(string[] args)
{
  AuthConfig config = AuthConfig.ReadFromJsonFile("appsettings.json");

  Console.WriteLine($"Authority: {config.Authority}");
}
```

Build your code again then run it; assuming all is well, you should get output similar to this.

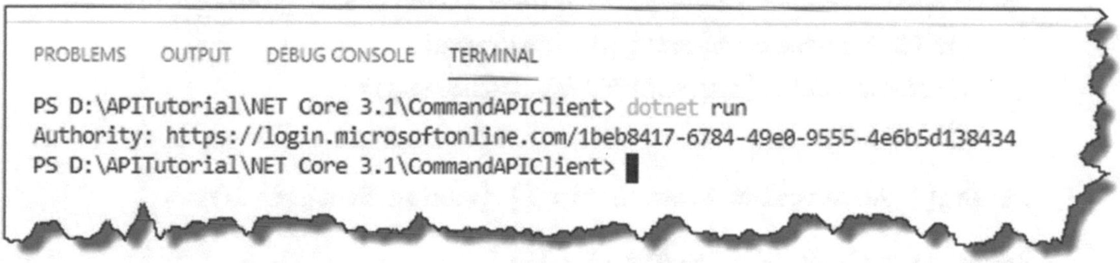

Figure 14-42. *Run the client*

Finalize Our Program Class

As mentioned previously, the first thing our client will have to do is obtain a JWT token that it will then attach to all subsequent requests in order to get access to the resources it needs, so let's focus in on that.

Still in our Program class, we're going to create a new static asynchronous method called `RunAsync`; the code for our reworked `Program` class is shown next (noting new or changed code is bold and highlighted):

```
using System;
using System.Threading.Tasks;
using Microsoft.Identity.Client;
```

```csharp
namespace CommandAPIClient
{
  class Program
  {
    static void Main(string[] args)
    {
        Console.WriteLine("Making the call...");
        RunAsync().GetAwaiter().GetResult();
    }

    private static async Task RunAsync()
    {
      AuthConfig config = AuthConfig.ReadFromJsonFile("appsettings.json");

      IConfidentialClientApplication app;

      app = ConfidentialClientApplicationBuilder.Create(config.ClientId)
          .WithClientSecret(config.ClientSecret)
          .WithAuthority(new Uri(config.Authority))
          .Build();

      string[] ResourceIds = new string[] {config.ResourceID};

      AuthenticationResult result = null;
      try
      {
        result = await app.AcquireTokenForClient(ResourceIds).
        ExecuteAsync();
        Console.ForegroundColor = ConsoleColor.Green;
        Console.WriteLine("Token acquired \n");
        Console.WriteLine(result.AccessToken);
        Console.ResetColor();
      }
      catch (MsalClientException ex)
      {
        Console.ForegroundColor = ConsoleColor.Red;
        Console.WriteLine(ex.Message);
```

```
        Console.ResetColor();
    }
  }
}
}
```

I've tagged the points of interest here.

```
static void Main(string[] args)
{
    Console.WriteLine("Making the call...");
    RunAsync().GetAwaiter().GetResult();  1
}

private static async Task RunAsync()
{
    AuthConfig config = AuthConfig.ReadFromJsonFile("appsettings.json");

    IConfidentialClientApplication app;  2

    app = ConfidentialClientApplicationBuilder.Create(config.ClientId)   3
        .WithClientSecret(config.ClientSecret)
        .WithAuthority(new Uri(config.Authority))
        .Build();

    string[] ResourceIds = new string[] { config.ResourceID };  4

    AuthenticationResult result = null;  5
    try
    {
        result = await app.AcquireTokenForClient(ResourceIds).ExecuteAsync();
        Console.ForegroundColor = ConsoleColor.Green;
        Console.WriteLine("Token acquired \n");                            6
        Console.WriteLine(result.AccessToken);
        Console.ResetColor();
    }
    catch (MsalClientException ex)
    {
        Console.ForegroundColor = ConsoleColor.Red;
        Console.WriteLine(ex.Message);
        Console.ResetColor();
    }
}
```

Figure 14-43. *Progressing the client*

1. Our RunAsync method is asynchronous and returns a result we're interested in, so we chain the GetAwaiter and GetResult methods to ensure the console app does not quit before a result is processed and returned.

2. ConfidentialClientApplication is a specific class type for our use case; we use this in conjunction with the ConfidentialClientApplicationBuilder to construct a "client" with our config attributes.

3. We set up our app with the values derived from our AuthConfig class.

4. We can have more than one ResourceId (or scope) that we want to call; hence, we create a string array to cater for this.

5. The AuthenticationResult contains (drum roll) the result of a token acquisition.

6. Finally, we make an asynchronous AcquireTokenForClient call to (hopefully!) return a JWT Bearer token from AAD using our authentication config.

Save the file, build your code, and assuming all's well, run it too; you should see the following.

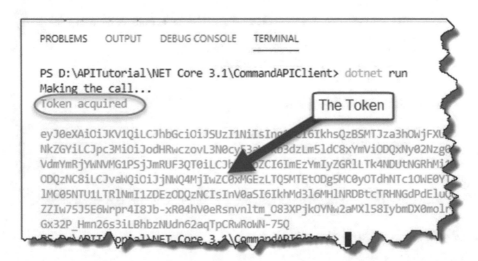

Figure 14-44. *Successful token acquisition*

> 🎂 **Celebration Checkpoint**   Good job! There was a lot of config and coding to
> get us to this point, obtaining a JWT token, so the rest of this chapter is all too easy!
> So well done!

We move onto the second and final part of our RunAsync method, and that is to call
our protected API endpoint with the token we just obtained in the previous step, so
directly after the catch statement in our RunAsync method, add the following code (take
note of the three additional using statements too):

```
using System.Net.Http;
using System.Net.Http.Headers;
using System.Linq;
.

.

.
if (!string.IsNullOrEmpty(result.AccessToken))
{
  var httpClient = new HttpClient();
  var defaultRequestHeaders = httpClient.DefaultRequestHeaders;

  if(defaultRequestHeaders.Accept ==null ||
    !defaultRequestHeaders.Accept.Any(m => m.MediaType == "application/
    json"))
  {
    httpClient.DefaultRequestHeaders.Accept.Add(new
      MediaTypeWithQualityHeaderValue("application/json"));
  }
  defaultRequestHeaders.Authorization =
    new AuthenticationHeaderValue("bearer", result.AccessToken);
```

```
HttpResponseMessage response = await httpClient.GetAsync(config.
BaseAddress);
if (response.IsSuccessStatusCode)
{
  Console.ForegroundColor = ConsoleColor.Green;
  string json = await response.Content.ReadAsStringAsync();
  Console.WriteLine(json);
}
else
{
  Console.ForegroundColor = ConsoleColor.Red;
  Console.WriteLine($"Failed to call the Web Api: {response.
  StatusCode}");
  string content = await response.Content.ReadAsStringAsync();
  Console.WriteLine($"Content: {content}");
}
Console.ResetColor();
}
```

I've highlighted some interesting code sections here.

```
catch (MsalClientException ex)
{
    Console.ForegroundColor = ConsoleColor.Red;
    Console.WriteLine(ex.Message);
    Console.ResetColor();
}
if (!string.IsNullOrEmpty(result.AccessToken))
{
    var httpClient = new HttpClient();       (1)
    var defaultRequestHeaders = httpClient.DefaultRequestHeaders;

    if (defaultRequestHeaders.Accept == null ||         (2)
        !defaultRequestHeaders.Accept.Any(m => m.MediaType == "application/json"))
    {
        httpClient.DefaultRequestHeaders.Accept.Add(new
          MediaTypeWithQualityHeaderValue("application/json"));
    }

    defaultRequestHeaders.Authorization =
      new AuthenticationHeaderValue("bearer", result.AccessToken);   (3)
                                                                  (4)
    HttpResponseMessage response = await httpClient.GetAsync(config.BaseAddress);
    if (response.IsSuccessStatusCode)   (5)
    {
        Console.ForegroundColor = ConsoleColor.Green;
        string json = await response.Content.ReadAsStringAsync();
        Console.WriteLine(json);
    }
    else
    {
        Console.ForegroundColor = ConsoleColor.Red;
        Console.WriteLine($"Failed to call the Web Api: {response.StatusCode}");
        string content = await response.Content.ReadAsStringAsync();
        Console.WriteLine($"Content: {content}");
    }
    Console.ResetColor();
}
```

Figure 14-45. *Calling the API*

1. We use a `HttpClient` object as the primary vehicle to make the request.

2. We ensure that we set the media type in our request headers appropriately.

3. We set out authorization header to "bearer" as well as attaching our token received in the last step.

4. Make an asynchronous request to our protected API address.

5. Check for success and display.

Save your code, build it, and run it (also ensure the Command API is running); you should see something like the following.

```
Time Elapsed 00:00:01.95
PS D:\APITutorial\NET Core 3.1\CommandAPIClient> dotnet run
Making the call...
Token acquired

eyJ0eXAiOiJKV1QiLCJhbGci0iJSUzI1NiIsImg1dCI6IkhsQzBSMTJza3hOWjFXUXdtak9GXzZ
NkZGYiLCJpc3Mi0iJodHRwczovL3N0cy53aW5kb3dzLm5ldC8xYmViODQxNy02Nzg0LTQ5ZTAtO
3FGbmhuUFU2ZFFE3R3RheUFBPT0iLCJhcHBpZCI6ImEzYmIyZGRlLTk4NDUtNGRhMi1hNDliLTUzZ
ODQzNC8iLCJvaWQiOiJjNWQ4MjIwZC0xMGEzLTQ5MTEtODg5MC0yOTdhNTc1OWE0YTIiLCJyb2x
lMC05NTU1LTRlNmI1ZDEzODQzNCIsInV0aSI6I1lZT0xfTVk3WFUyZ1pubmtUdFFFtQUEiLCJ2ZXX
hmnoVs4tTf00ZPHE3DF-wD6Rw99H-KTnYbSF2a95ylG_r1AZUnogf1vjtRraEPPQsQAtlTv5SK2j
-oGhCtBWl-NP6cEpjgWPN9IBxdbAfPFoX7HYkhuO
("id":1,"howTo":"Create an EF migration","platform":"Entity Framework Core
PS D:\APITutorial\NET Core 3.1\CommandAPIClient>
```

Figure 14-46.   *Secure API Called*

where we have the JSON for our protected API endpoint returned.

Note: If you get at error similar to the following:

System.Security.AuthenticationException, the remote certificate is invalid.

Just check that you took the steps in Chapter 2 to "trust" local SSL Certificates. If you're too lazy to pop back, just type the following at a command line and rerun the client:

dotnet dev-certs https --trust

Updating for Azure

In order for our API code to continue to work when we deploy to Azure, we're going to have to add the following Application Settings to our Command API on Azure (remember we currently have these stored as *user secrets* in our local development instance).

Config element	Application setting name
The log-in "instance"	Instance
Our AAD Domain	Domain
The Tenant ID	TenantId
The Client ID	ClientId
The Application UD URL (Or Resource ID)	ResourceId

Before we do that though, while we could reuse the existing API App Registration (CommandAPI_DEV) that we created for our "local" Command API, I think its good practice to set up a new "production" registration for our Command API.

☞ **Learning Opportunity**   Rather than step through the exact same instructions to create a new "production" Command API registration, I'm going to leave you to do that now. As a suggestion, call this new app registration: CommandAPI_PROD.

Come back here when you're done!

How did you go? Easy right? You should now have something similar to the following in your app registrations list.

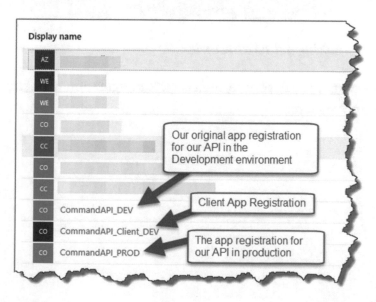

Figure 14-47. Production App Registrations

If like me you created your App Registrations in a different Azure Directory to your main one (i.e., where all your resources are), I'd take a note of all of the values for things like TenantId, ClientId, and ResourceId in the Production App Registration you just created before you switch back to your main AAD to add the new Application Settings for our API.

So, if needed, switch back to the AAD where you created the actual API App and Container instances.

Figure 14-48.   *Switching active directories*

Select your Command API service, then click "Configuration" to take you to the Application Settings screen.

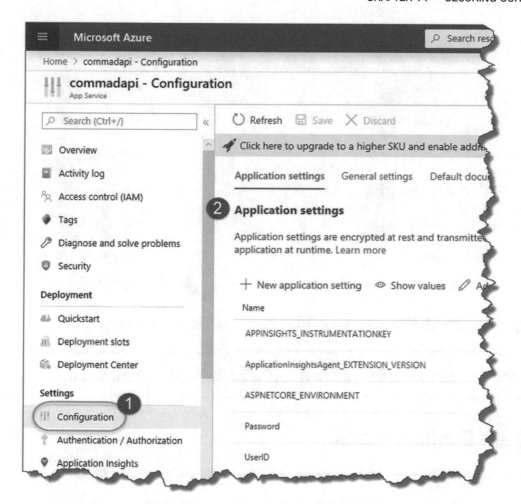

Figure 14-49. *API app settings*

Again, we've already added application settings before, so I'm going to leave it to you to add all the necessary application settings to allow our API to be correctly configured from an authentication perspective.

⚠ **Warning!** Make sure you give your application settings the exact same name as the User Secrets you set up before, with the relevant values from the Production API App registration (CommandAPI_PROD).

Here, you can see the new Application Settings I've added.

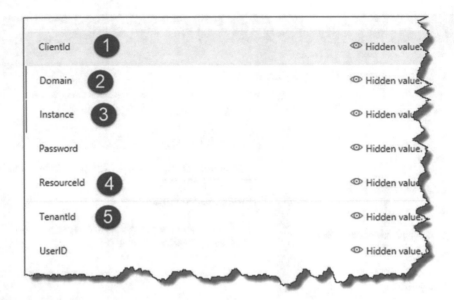

Figure 14-50. *Additional app settings to support authentication*

Note   Remember to Save the new Application Settings you've just added.

Client Configurations

To ensure our client can authenticate to our Production API, we should:

1. Create a Production Client App Registration on Azure.

2. Update the necessary local settings in our Client App's
   applicationsettings.json file.

☞ **Learning Opportunity**   You have learned everything you need to know in order to complete this work, so again I'm going to leave it to you complete the two steps mentioned.

Take your time, and remember to copy down the new values that are generated as part of the new production client app registration.

When done, come back here.

Deploy Our API to Azure

Back in our Command API Solution, we just want to kick off a deploy to Azure, so if you don't have any pending commits, make an arbitrary change to your code (insert a comment somewhere), and add/commit and push.

As before, our Build Pipeline should succeed as should our deployment. Using something like Postman to call an unsecured endpoint should still work as before.

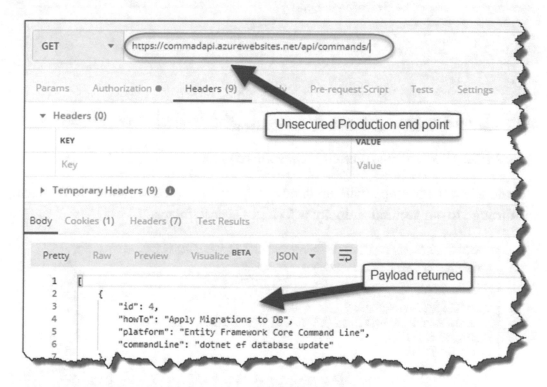

Figure 14-51. *Unsecured endpoint continues to work*

However, as expected when we attempt to call the secured endpoint (without a token), we should get a 401 Unauthorised response.

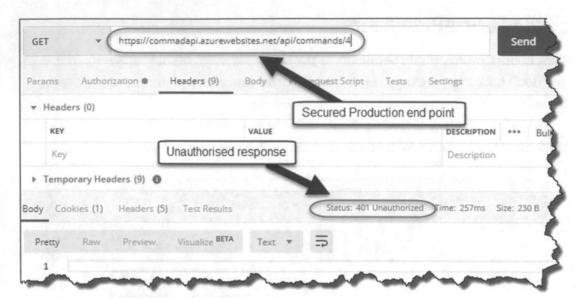

Figure 14-52. *Secured endpoint declines the request*

Turning to our client app (with updated configuration to access Production), making a call-through to our secured endpoint will yield a successful result.

Figure 14-53. *Successful call of our secure endpoint on Azure*

Epilogue

Firstly, if you've made it all the way through, and followed all the steps, then well done! I hope you found it a useful and entertaining exercise.

For me, although writing has always formed a large part of my career, I've never written a book before, so here are some of my thoughts on that:

- I thought taking my blog posts and other random works and tying them together in a book would take about two weeks. In reality it took well over four months.

- I am so grateful that I'm in a position where I could write a book, primarily because I was born into privilege, for which I am thankful and ashamed in equal measure. And by privilege, I don't mean that I or my family are rich (although I guess that's totally subjective depending on who you'd ask) but that I was born healthy, to lovely parents, in a country at peace, and with the very rare privilege of a free university education.

- There are so many clever, creative people out there sharing their knowledge that without them I'd not be able to complete such a book.

© Les Jackson 2020
L. Jackson, *The Complete ASP.NET Core 3 API Tutorial*, https://doi.org/10.1007/978-1-4842-6255-9

Index

A

Active Directory (AD)
    switching option, 400
    test purposes, 401

Application programming interface (API)
    command-line repository, 24, 25
    CRUD operations, 25
    JSON, 26–30
    meaning, 23
    payloads, 26

ASP.NET Core project
    files and folders, 41, 42
    Nuget, 42
    program class, 43, 44
    startup class
        ConfigureServices, 45
        dependency injection, 45
        execution sequence, 44
        method, 44
        middleware components, 45
        configure, 45
        request pipeline, 46

Asynchronous operations, 69

Authentication scheme
    API project/Daemon client, 398
    bearer authentication, 397, 398
    non-exhaustive list, 396
    registering API, 399, 400
    secure, 395
    user ids and passwords, 395

AutoMapper package
    API project folder, 197–199
    architecture check, 206
    CommandReadDTO, 204
    constructor dependency injection, 201
    context, 201
    controller, 202
    DTO representation, 202
    GET controller actions, 203
    mapping, 200
    multiple instances, 202
    postman query, 205
    profiles folder/CommandsProfile.cs
        file, 199, 200
    reference, 197
    service registration, 198
    startup class and register, 198

Azure Active Directory (AAD)
    AD (*see* Active Directory (AD))
    API exposes
        app registration, 408
        auto-generated
          resource ID, 408
        registrations page, 406
        resource ID, 407
    app registrations, 403
    authentication (*see* Authentication
        scheme)
    authentication *vs.*
        authorization, 416

© Les Jackson 2020
L. Jackson, *The Complete ASP.NET Core 3 API Tutorial*, https://doi.org/10.1007/978-1-4842-6255-9

U